TheWordPerfect® Expert 5.0

The WordPerfect® Expert 5.0

Neil J. Salkind

DOW JONES-IRWIN
Homewood, Illinois 60430

WordPerfect® is a trademark of WordPerfect Corporation.

© Neil J. Salkind, Ph.D., 1989

Dow Jones-Irwin is a trademark of Dow Jones & Company, Inc.

All rights reserved. No part of this publication may be reproduced, stored in a retrieval system, or transmitted, in any form or by any means, electronic, mechanical, photocopying, recording, or otherwise, without the prior written permission of the copyright holder.

This publication is designed to provide accurate and authoritative information in regard to the subject matter covered. It is sold with the understanding that neither the author nor the publisher is engaged in rendering legal, accounting, or other professional service. If legal advice or other expert assistance is required, the services of a competent professional person should be sought.

From a Declaration of Principles jointly adopted by a Committee of the American Bar Association and a Committee of Publishers.

Sponsoring editor: Susan Glinert Stevens, Ph.D.
Project editor: Carol G. Schoen
Production manager: Carma W. Fazio
Printer: Malloy Lithographing, Inc.

Library of Congress Cataloging in Publication Data

Salkind, Neil J.
  The WordPerfect expert 5.0

  Includes index.
  1. WordPerfect (Computer program) 2. Word processing.
I. Title.
Z52.5.W65S24 1989   652'.5   88–33497
ISBN 1-55623-081-8

Printed in the United States of America

1 2 3 4 5 6 7 8 9 0 ML 5 4 3 2 1 0 9 8

Acknowledgments

Susan Glinert, Dow-Jones Senior Editor has been terrific throughout this and other projects and I am in her debt for her support and advice. Bill Gladstone, my agent, deserves thanks for providing me the opportunity to complete this book. Thanks to Mark Bryne, Peggy Billings, and Nam Yong Kim for invaluable assistance as well.

For Mohammed's Quick Recovery

Table of Contents

Introduction

Welcome to WordPerfect! *1*
    If You Are New to Computers *1*
    If You Have Used WordPerfect Before *2*
How the Book Is Organized *2*
Keyboard Instructions *4*
Function Keys *4*
Tips and Macros *4*
Hardware and Software Requirements *6*
    The Computer *6*
    The Disk Drives *7*
    The Printer *7*
    The Monitor *8*
What's New about WordPerfect 5.0 *8*
When You Need Help *9*

Part 1 - Getting Started

Chapter 1 - Getting Started

Starting WordPerfect *11*
    Starting WordPerfect with Options *12*
    Retrieving a File Upon Start Up *12*
    Setting the Timed Backup Option - WordPerfect/b *12*
    Changing the Overflow Drive - WordPerfect/d [drive] *13*
    Starting a Macro - WordPerfect/m *13*
    Getting Rid of the Flash! - WordPerfect/nf *13*
    Loading WordPerfect into Memory - WordPerfect/r *14*
    Temporarily Returning to the Original Default Settings -
        WordPerfect/x *14*
    Defining the Screen Size - WordPerfect/ss *14*
The WordPerfect Screen *15*
    What's on the Screen *15*

Chapter 2 - Creating and Editing Text

Entering Text *17*
    Correcting Simple Errors *18*
Saving Text and Retrieving Text *18*
    Saving New Text *18*
    Using a Password *19*
    A Brief Visit with Macros *19*
    Retrieving Text *20*
    Saving "Old" Text *21*
    Saving a Document and Clearing the WordPerfect Screen *21*
    Saving and Exiting WordPerfect *22*
Editing Text *23*
    Moving by Characters, Words, Lines, and Pages *23*
    Deleting Characters, Words, and Paragraphs *24*
Undeleting Text *25*
    Searching for Text *25*
    Search and Replacing Text *25*
    Doing a "Wildcard" Search *26*
Moving Sentences, Paragraphs and Pages *27*
Using Blocks *28*
WordPerfect Reveal Codes *29*
    Deleting a Reveal Code *30*
    Searching and Replacing Reveal Codes *30*
Using WordPerfect Help *31*

Chapter 3 - Formatting with WordPerfect

Formatting WordPerfect Lines *34*
    Underlining with WordPerfect *34*
    Double Underlining *35*
    Boldfacing Text *36*
    Setting Margins *37*
    Working with WordPerfect Tabs *38*
    Clearing Tabs *38*
    Resetting Tabs *38*
    Aligning Tabs *39*
    Using Different Tab Styles *39*
    Setting Line Spacing *40*
    Using Subscripts and Superscripts *41*
    Justifying Lines *41*
    Converting Characters *41*
Formatting WordPerfect Pages *42*
    Centering a Page Vertically *43*

Doing Headers and Footers *43*
    Editing a Header or Footer *44*
    Including the Page Number in a Header *44*
    Setting Top and Bottom Page Margins *45*
Assigning Page Numbers *45*
    Assigning New Page Numbers *45*
Choosing a Paper Size *46*
No Page Formatting at All *47*
Formatting WordPerfect Documents *47*
    Changing the Pitch *48*
    Changing the Initial Settings *48*
    Creating a Document Summary *49*
    Changing the Font *49*

Chapter 4 - Printing with WordPerfect

The Print Menu *51*
    Selecting a Printer *51*
    Printing the Document *54*
        Printing from a Disk *54*
        What Can Your Printer Do? *55*
    Controlling What the Printer Does *55*
    Using WordPerfect Like a Typewriter *56*
    Previewing a WordPerfect Document *57*
    Changing the Quality of Graphics and Text *58*

Chapter 5 - Managing WordPerfect Files

The File Management Screen *60*
The File Management Options *61*
    Retrieving a File *61*
    Deleting a File *61*
    Moving and Renaming a File *62*
    Printing a File *62*
    Working with ASCII Files (the Text In item) *63*
    "Looking" at a File *63*
    Changing a Directory *63*
    Copying a File *64*
    Searching for Words *64*
    The Conditions Option *65*
    Wild Card Searches *66*
    Finding a File *66*

Working with Multiple Files   67

Part 2 - Advanced WordPerfect

Chapter 6 - Using WordPerfect Macros

What is a Macro?   69
When to Use Macros   70
    Converting 4.2 Macros   70
The Four Basic Steps in Creating a Macro   71
Starting the Definition   71
    Naming the Macro   72
    Describing the Macro   72
    Entering the Macro   72
        Ending the Macro   73
What to Name Your Macros   73
Alt Key versus Full Name Macros   74
    The Alt Key Method   74
    The Full Name Method   74
Where to Put Your Macros   75
Invoking a Macro   75
Stopping a Macro   76
Different Types of Macros   77
    Temporary and Permanent Macros   77
    Using a Temporary Macro   77
    Temporary Macros and Boilerplates   78
    The Repeating Macro   79
    Chaining or Combining Macros   79
Renaming and Copying Macros   81
Repeating a Macro   81
    A Macro that Repeats Itself or Repeat a Macro?   82
Macro Commands   82
    The Pause Option: Macros with User Input   83
    Seeing Your Macros Work   84
    Assigning a Value to a Variable   84
    Inserting Comments   84
The Macro Editor   85
    Starting the Macro Editor   85
Editing a Macro   87
Using the Macro Programming Language   88

Chapter 7 - WordPerfect Merge

Merge - What It Is and How It Works *91*
    The Secondary File *92*
    The Primary File *93*
    Defining Fields *95*
Merging the Primary and Secondary Files *96*
Using Special Merge Codes *97*
    Pausing for Keyboard Entries (^C) *97*
    Inserting the Date (^D) *98*
    Using a Dummy Record (^N) *99*
    Including a Macro in the Merge (^G^G) *99*
    Including a Message or a Prompt(^O^O) *100*
    Retrieving Primary and Secondary Files (^P^P) *101*
    Watching the Merge Happen (^U) *102*
    Printing Your Merged Documents Directly ^T *102*
Completing Special Forms *103*
Using Merge to Create a Report *105*
Printing Envelopes *106*

Chapter 8 - Using columns

Column Basics: Making Them Work *110*
    Defining a Column *111*
    Defining Newspaper Style Columns *111*
    Defining Parallel Columns *112*
    Turning Columns On *112*
    Producing Columns *113*
Editing Columns Definitions *113*
Creating Parallel Columns *114*
Editing Columns *11*
A Note about Footnotes and Columns *115*
Columns and Fonts *116*

Chapter 9 - Creating Tables, Lists, and Indexes

How WordPerfect Does Tables, Lists, and Indexes *117*
    Marking Text *117*
    Defining a Table, List, or Index *118*
    Generating a Table, List, or Index
Creating a Table of Contents *118*
    Planning Ahead *118*
    Marking Text for a Table of Contents *119*

Defining a Table of Contents   *121*
         Generating a Table of Contents   *123*
Creating a List   *124*
         Marking Text   *124*
         Defining a List   *125*
         Working with Multiple Lists   *126*
Creating an Index   *127*
         Marking Text   *127*
         Using a Concordance File   *128*
         Defining an Index   *128*
         Generating an Index   *129*

Chapter 10 - Using the Speller and Thesaurus

How the Spelling Checker Works   *131*
Checking a Document   *132*
The Spell Check Options   *133*
         Skip Once - Option #1   *133*
         Skip - Option #2   *134*
         Add Word - Option #3   *134*
         Edit - Option #4   *134*
         Look Up - Option #5   *135*
         Ignore Numbers - Option #6   *135*
         Word Count - Option #6   *135*
Using Wild Cards   *136*
When WordPerfect Isn't Perfect!   *136*
Other Menu Options   *137*
         Options #1 and #2   *137*
         Delete 2nd - Option #3   *137*
         Edit - Option #4   *138*
         Disable Double Word Checking - Option #5   *138*
The WordPerfect Thesaurus   *138*
         Using the WordPerfect Thesaurus   *138*
         The Thesaurus Screen   *139*
         Replace Word - Option #1   *140*
         View Document - Option #2   *140*
         Look Up Word - Option #3   *141*
         Clear Column - Option #4   *141*

Chapter 11 - Creating an Outline

Why Outlines Are Important   *143*
         What an Outline Looks Like   *144*

Doing a Simple Outline   *144*
Working with an Outline   *146*
    Editing an Outline   *146*
    Deleting a Section   *146*
    Inserting a New Section   *147*
    Moving Sections   *148*
    Promoting an Outline Section   *148*
    Demoting an Outline Section   *149*
More Than One Outline?   *150*
Outline Styles   *150*
    Choosing a New Outline Style   *151*
Numbering Paragraphs   *151*
    Inserting a New Paragraph   *152*
    Numbering Styles   *152*
Numbering Other Things; Figures and Lists   *153*

Chapter 12 - Sorting

Basic Sorting   *155*
    The Sort Screen   *157*
    Perform Action - Option #1   *158*
    View - Option #2   *158*
    Keys - Option #3   *158*
    Select - Option #4   *161*
        Words and Fields   *162*
    Action - Option #5   *162*
    Order - Option #6   *162*
    Type - Option #7   *163*
Sorting and Blocks   *164*

Chapter 13 - WordPerfect Math

Math Basics   *165*
    Setting Columns   *166*
    Defining the Math Columns   *167*
    Types of Columns   *167*
    Turning Math On   *169*
Entering Information   *169*
    Using Operators   *169*
    Calculating Values   *169*
Working with Calculation Formulas   *171*

Chapter 14 - The Master Document

What is a Master Document?   *176*
Creating a Master Document   *176*
Working with Subdocuments   *177*
    Editing within a Master Document   *178*
    Expanding a Document   *178*
    Saving an Expanded Document   *179*
    Condensing a Document   *180*
    More Subdocuments   *181*
Printing a Master Document   *181*
Generating Tables, Indexes and Lists   *181*

Chapter 15 - WordPerfect Graphics

Let's Get Right To It!   *183*
How WordPerfect Graphics Works   *184*
Using Different Types of Boxes   *186*
Creating a Graphics Box   *186*
    Filename - Option #1   *186*
    Caption - Option #2   *187*
    Type - Option #3   *187*
    Vertical Position - Option #4   *188*
    Horizontal Position - Option #5   *188*
    Size - Option #6   *189*
    Wrap Text - Option #7   *190*
    Edit - Option #8   *190*
Graphics Options   *190*
    Border Style - Option #1   *190*
    Outside Border Space - Option #2   *192*
    Inside Border Space - Option #3   *192*
    Numbering Methods - Options #4 and #5   *192*
    Number Style - Option #6   *192*
    Position of the Caption - Option #7   *193*
    Offset from Paragraph - Option #8   *194*
    Gray Shading - Option #9   *194*
Using Lines   *195*
    Drawing Horizontal Lines   *195*
    Drawing Vertical Lines   *196*
    Vertical Position   *197*
Editing a Graphic   *198*
    Editing a Graphic Image   *199*
    The Edit Options   *200*

Move *200*
Scaling a Graphic *201*
Rotating a Graphic *202*
Switching or Inverting an Image *202*
Wrapping Text Around Graphics *203*

Chapter 16 - Advanced Printing

Selecting Fonts *205*
Selecting Fonts and Font Attributes *206*
    Base Font - Option #4 *207*
        Changing Base Fonts *207*
    Size - Option #1 *209*
        The Size of Fonts *210*
    Appearance - Option #2 *211*
    Normal - Option #3 *212*
    Printing in Color - Option #5 *212*
        Custom Colors *213*
Using a Laser Printer with WordPerfect *213*
Loading Soft Fonts *214*
An Example: BitStream Fontware *214*
    Setting Up Bitstream Fontware *215*
    Adding Fontware Typefaces *215*
    Creating a Font *216*
    Using Your New Fonts *216*
Printing Special Characters *216*
    Using the Compose Feature *217*
Using Digraphs and Diacriticals *217*
Keyboard Definitions *218*
Designing Your Own Layout *219*
Tracking, Kerning and Page Orientation *221*
    Tracking *221*
    Kerning *222*
    Page Orientation: Portrait versus Landscape Printing *222*

Chapter 17 - WordPerfect and Other Products

Other WordPerfect Corporation Products *225*
    WordPerfect Library *225*
    PlanPerfect *226*
    DataPerfect *227*
    Repeat Performance *227*

Graphics Programs   228
    Publisher's PicturePak   228
    Graph in the Box   228
Fonts and Font Generators   229
    Turbofonts   229
    Glyphix   229
    Softcraft Fontware   229
Desk Accessories and Utilities   230
    Sidekick   230
    Cruise Control   230
    Mace Utilities   231
    Perfect Exchange   231
Another Thesaurus   231
Seeing All of WordPerfect   232

Chapter 18 - Stylish WordPerfect

What is a Style?   233
Creating a Style   234
Naming a Style   235
Different Types of Styles   235
    Which One When   235
    Describing Styles   236
    Editing a Style   236
    The Enter Key   237
Using a Style   238
Other Style Options   238
    Deleting a Style - Option #5   238
    Saving a Style - Option #6   238
    Retrieving a Style - Option #7   239
    Updating - Option #8   239
Sharing Styles - A Style Library   239

Appendix A Setting up WordPerfect   241
Using the Setup Option   241
Backing up WordPerfect Files   242
The Cursor Speed   243
The WordPerfect Display   244
Fast Saves   245
Changing Initial Settings   245
    WordPerfect Beeps!   246
    Setting the Date and Time   247
    Summarizing a Document   248
    Setting Initial Codes   248

        Changing the Repeat Value   *250*
        Formatting Tables of Authorities   *251*
Defining the Keyboard   *251*
Locating other Files   *251*
Units of Measure   *252*

Appendix B WordPerfect Reveal Codes   *255*

Appendix C A Macro Library   *259*

Index   *315*

Introduction

Welcome to WordPerfect!

There's just no end to the number of word processing programs that are available. In a "blockbuster" review, *PC Magazine* rated 55 word processing systems from the most simple to the most complex, and found that WordPerfect was one of the best. Why? Just some of the reasons are it's clean, uncluttered screen, ease of learning, wonderful flexibility, and terrific technical support. And with the version you now have in your hands, 5.0, things have gotten even better.

If you are an accomplished WordPerfect user, the new WordPerfect features will make you an even more devout fan. For the new WordPerfect user, you'll be learning a tool that will improve your writing efficiency and maybe even its quality. In either case, WordPerfect is the choice when it comes to preparing a simple letter, a desktop published newsletter or a book. In fact, this book was completely written, designed and composed using WordPerfect 5.0. Even the table of contents and index were automatically generated.

As this book is being written, the WordPerfect corporation has sold well over 1,000,000 copies of various versions of WordPerfect for IBM and IBM compatible computers. And they don't intend to stop. WordPerfect continues to lead the way in providing a high end quality word processing system that anyone can learn to use. **The WordPerfect Expert 5.0** will help you along the way.

If You Are New to Computers

This book was written with two groups of people in mind. The first is the person who knows a little about computers, (such as how to turn one on, copy a file from one disk to another, and so on) and who is using any word processor for the first time. These people should begin with Part 1 of **The WordPerfect Expert 5.0** which will provide you with all the information you need to create, edit, and print WordPerfect documents.

If You Have Used WordPerfect Before

The second group who will find this book useful, are people who have already had experience with an earlier version of WordPerfect, such as version 4.1 or 4.2.

For them, Part 2 offers a detailed account of the many advanced features that set WordPerfect 5.0 apart from the competition. If you are an experienced WordPerfect user, you might begin with Chapter 6, which teaches you how to use one of WordPerfect's most powerful features - macros.

The WordPerfect Expert 5.0 will lead the beginner down the path to becoming an expert and will reveal the secrets and power of WordPerfect to those who already know how to use WordPerfect.

How the Book Is Organized

The WordPerfect Expert 5.0 consists of two parts: *Part 1 - WordPerfect Basics* and *Part 2 - Advanced WordPerfect*.

Part 1 introduces you to the basic features that WordPerfect offers beginning with Chapter 1 including instructions for setting up WordPerfect to fit your individual work habits.

Chapter 2 will show you how to create and edit text so you can begin writing and saving documents almost immediately.

Chapter 3 gets right to the stuff that dreams are made of - being your own publisher! While it may be unrealistic to think that you can turn out an award winning, or a best selling book design on your very first try, it is not unrealistic for you to use WordPerfect to be very competitive with many professional designers.

Either when documents are created or when they are edited, the format or appearance often is changed. You might want to switch from single to double spacing or from wide to narrow margins and it is in Chapter 3 that you will learn how to make these, and other, format adjustments.

Chapter 4 provides you with the information you need to print out a copy of your work, and Part 1 ends with a discussion of how to manage WordPerfect files in Chapter 5.

These five chapters are all you really do need to get WordPerfect up and running and to create a document and print out a copy. One of the fascinating things about using WordPerfect is that once you start with the simple features, you'll want to explore all of what WordPerfect can offer and so on to Part 2.

Part 2 picks up where Part 1 ends, beginning with an explanation in Chapter 6 of one of WordPerfect's most powerful and useful features, *macros*. These sets of stored keystrokes are time saving and fun to create and use. They're addictive, and once you learn how to use them, you'll find yourself asking, "How can I create a macro to do this or that"?

Another useful tool is the Merge feature discussed in Chapter 7, allowing you to combine two documents. The most frequent use of the merge feature is when a set of names and addresses are combined with a standard letter, so that each letter is personalized.

Chapter 8 is what you newsletter and document design people need when it comes to creating two columns of text for a publication. Both newspaper and side by side columns are easy to create and can provide a dramatic improvement in the readability and presentation of typed materials.

Short documents are relatively easy to get a good overview of, but if you are completing a book or a large report, then you will want to take advantage of WordPerfect's table of contents and index generation features explained in Chapter 9. With WordPerfect's new Master Document feature, you can generate an index for several long documents without having to first physically combine them.

Everyone misspells(!), and while WordPerfect cannot teach you to spell better, version 5.0 can certainly help you detect and correct those words that you may have typed incorrectly. And while you're working on spelling, how about finding that word that perfectly fits the situation (or circumstance, predicament, condition or state?)...that's the thesaurus working, which you'll also find out about in Chapter 10.

Chapter 11 introduces you to using outlines to help organize your writing activities including everything from simple lists to numbering paragraphs to reorganizing existing documents.

Information can often be presented in different ways and sorting lines for example (discussed in Chapter 12) in descending or ascending order (and then selecting special cases), often makes more sense out of things such as lists, or groupings of items.

In fact, there are times you may need to sort on numerical information. Once this is done, you can even use WordPerfect to perform mathematical calculations such as simple addition of columns and other spreadsheet functions covered in Chapter 13. Like any other perfect file, these can then be combined or merged with another Wordperfect file.

If you have ever tried to combine several shorter documents to produce one longer one then you know the problems that can be introduced. With WordPerfect's master document feature, discussed in Chapter 14, you can easily combine subfiles and use the newly created master document for generating tables of contents, indexes and so forth. What's best, is that this master document can then be "taken apart" and whatever changes were made in each of the files remains intact!

Here it comes! In Chapter 15 you'll learn about what may be WordPerfect's most attractive new change, the introduction of graphics to wordperfect. Creating and using graphics can add a new and fascinating dimension to your Wordperfect documents.

Among many of WordPerfect 5.0's new features are enhanced and greatly expanded printing capabilities. Chapter 16 covers these including details on laser printing and the printing of special characters such as these ß å and °, as well as redefining your keyboard.

No software package (or computer), not even WordPerfect 5.0 can do everything, so there are often other programs that help pick up what's needed. In Chapter 17 of **The WordPerfect Expert 5.0** several of these programs are covered such as WordPerfect Corporation's spreadsheet PlanPerfect and Library, Repeat Performance, and other commercial programs. You'll also learn about using files created with your IBM version of WordPerfect on a Macintosh computer.

Finally, in Chapter 18 you will learn about WordPerfect *styles*.

There you have it, the two parts and 18 chapters that make up your guide to WordPerfect.

Keyboard Instructions

Any book that contains instructional material uses diagrams, figures, and other tools to communicate information. In this book, you will find WordPerfect's keyboard instructions are presented as follows.

When You See...   *It Means...*

Characters or commands in bold, enter the characters or commands
                                    on the keyboard.

For example, if you see the line *Esc,<ret>* it means that you should press the Escape key and then press the Return or the Enter key.

Introduction

Characters that are separated by commas,   *enter these characters in sequence, one after the other.*

For example, if you see the line *Home,Home,Up Arrow* it means that you should press the Home key twice and then the Up Arrow cursor key.

Characters that are separated by an arrow   *hold down the first key while pressing he second.*

For example, if you see the line *Alt->F10* it means that you should press and hold the Alternate key while pressing the *F10* function key.

Function Keys

As you may already know, WordPerfect uses the 10 function keys (or 12 if you have an advanced keyboard) located on the left hand side or along the top of your keyboard in combination with the Control key (marked *Ctrl*), the Shift key (marked *Shift*), and the Alternate key (marked *Alt*). These three keys are located on the left hand side of your keyboard.

Function Key	Ctrl Key	Shift Key	Alt Key	No Key
F1	Shell	Setup	Thesaurus	Cancel
F2	Spell	Search Backward	Replace	Search Forward
F3	Screen	Switch	Reveal Codes	Help
F4	Move	Indent	Block	Indent
F5	Text In/Out	Date/Outline	Mark Text	List Files
F6	Tab Align	Center	Flush Right	Bold
F7	Footnote	Print	Math/Columns	Exit
F8	Font	Format	Style	Underline
F9	Merge/Sort	Merge Code	Graphics	Merge R
F10	Macro Def	Retrieve	Macro	Save

When these function keys are used alone, or in combination with the Control, Shift or Alternate keys, different operations are performed.

What follows is a listing of the 40 different combinations of function keys and what they do. This is the same information that is contained on the keyboard template that came with your WordPerfect manual.

Tips and Macros

Tips are helpful ideas, time savers, short cuts, and other ways of making WordPerfect work better for you. While they are related to the content that is discussed where they appear, they can stand alone and be used whenever need.

In addition, *Macros* are offered whenever appropriate. A macro is a set of stored keystrokes allowing you to perform many different operations with only one keystroke! Although Chapter 6 will teach you all you need to know about macros, specialized macros will be offered all along the way.

For example, when you first boot up your computer and begin using WordPerfect, you might want to automatically move to the end of the document. A simple macro can do this for you. Or, you might want to design a macro that marks a table of contents entry at a particular level without having to go through the five to 10 keystrokes that it takes each time.

You'll be able to tell when a macro is coming since it's is screened as this paragraph is. While these macros may be specialized, you'll learn how changing even the smallest step can make them applicable to many different WordPerfect tasks.

Hardware and Software Requirements

The Computer

WordPerfect 5.0 will work with the most basic of IBM PC, XT, or AT computers that have at least 512K of internal memory or RAM. These days, additional memory is so inexpensive that many computers come with 640K and we suggest you upgrade you computer to that level if it is not already there.

Software such as WordPerfect, works when your computer places all or part of the program inside certain storage units. The more room there is to store, the more quickly and efficiently the computer can work with the program. More important, when there is not enough storage room, you may have to "swap" one program disk for another since the computer may not even be able to hold all of the program's instructions at any one time!

If you have only two disk drives, you will have to swap disks when it comes time to use the thesaurus, certain dictionaries, and WordPerfect's graphics capabilities.

The Disk Drives

WordPerfect 5.0 can work just fine with one floppy disk drive, but this will certainly prove to be inconvenient. At a minimum, you should have two floppy disk drives so that you can have the program disk in one drive and a data disk in the other.

By far, the best arrangement is to have one floppy disk drive and a *hard* or fixed drive. A hard drive is a rigid (as opposed to floppy) disk of magnetic material housed in a sealed compartment that has increased storage capacity and speed.

For example, a single floppy can disk hold about 360,000 pieces of information (or about 150 pages of double spaced text) and you can get high density floppys that hold more than 1,000,000 bytes. A 20 megabyte hard disk holds an astounding 10,000 pages of text! Best of all, you can fit all of your WordPerfect program files on a hard disk all in one directory, so you don't ever have to "swap" disks in and out of drives! Hard disks are becoming so popular and are easily available. You can usually buy one for less than $300.00. If you are even thinking about getting serious about word processing then a hard disk is definitely the way to go.

The Printer

WordPerfect operates fine with a serial or a parallel printer. If you do not know what kind you have, ask your dealer or look in the owner's manual that came with your printer.

WordPerfect 5.0 supports *hundreds* of printers. If you updated from WordPerfect 4.2, then you were given the opportunity to indicate what printer you intend to use with WordPerfect 5.0 and your printer disks should contain the correct printer driver. If not, you will have to use the printer disks that came with 5.0 and find the printer you are using and then select it. This is an easy procedure that is described in detail in Chapter 4.

One of the wonderful improvements that you will find in WordPerfect 5.0 is special attention to different types of laser printers as well.

The Monitor

You can use a monochrome (black and white, amber, or green) or a color monitor. If you chose to purchase and use a color monitor, be sure that your computer has or will have any needed graphics enhancements. Color monitors alone may show beautiful colors, but since they are of different levels of quality, letters may tend to be grainy and difficult to read. Graphics enhancements such as EGA for "enhanced graphics adapter", make color monitors function with increased clarity and resolution.

While color is expensive, a good color monitor will make your word processing easier and more enjoyable. For example, a WordPerfect program can be easily set up so the screen shows light blue letters on a black background, with underlining in green, bolding in red, and underlining and bolding in dark blue. It not only looks nice, but at a moment's glance, once can see what is emphasized.

What's New about WordPerfect 5.0

So here you are, almost ready to begin working with what hundreds of thousands (and almost millions!) feel is the best word processor around.

If you've never used WordPerfect, then you have a treat in store learning all the various features it offers. If you have used WordPerfect in the past, here is a selection of just some of the things that you'll be able to do with the new version:

-easier to use page format menus,
-easier to use laser fonts including sizing,
-support for color printing,
-support for more than 250 printers,
-insertion of graphics files in text (wonderful!), and use of graphics tools such as line drawing,
-page previews so you can see the whole page at once, and even facing pages at once,
-comparison of multiple drafts of the same document,
-automatic cross referencing,

Introduction

-automatic redlining,
-extended column features, and much more.

The WordPerfect Expert 5.0 will cover all of these features.

When You Need Help

Don't think you're alone if you should run into a problem with WordPerfect that you just can't solve. There are several sources that you can rely on for help if you need it.

First of course, is **The WordPerfect Expert 5.0.** Use it as a tutorial or as a reference guide to the many features that WordPerfect offers.

Next, be sure not to overlook other people who are WordPerfect users. With so many users around, there is sure to be one in your town, in your department, on your block, in one of your classes, or even in your car pool! As any computer user can tell you, some of the best tricks (which never seem to be covered in any manual) are discovered by people who use the program intensively.

Next, you can use WordPerfect *Help,* an "on line" feature that comes along with the WordPerfect word processing program. To use help, you simply press the F3 function key and then the first letter of the command or operation you need to know more about. You'll learn all about help and how to use it in the chapter 2 of **The WordPerfect Expert 5.0.**

Fourth, WordPerfect Corporation leads the way by offering toll free telephone support open from early morning to late evening, and even on Saturdays. When you call (toll free) 1-800-321-5906, you will be greeted by a helpful and knowledgeable technical expert who can answer all your questions.

Incidentally, all WordPerfect Corporation products are supported through this toll free service.

Fifth, there are newsletters that focus specifically on word processing and one that focuses exclusively on WordPerfect products: *The WordPerfectionist.* This newsletter, published 6 times a year, costs $36 and is filled with information about the latest upgrades, ongoings at WordPerfect, tips on how to get more out of WordPerfect (and other WordPerfect products), book reviews, and more. Contact the publishers at

WordPerfect Support Group
POB 1577
Baltimore, MD 21203

Part 1
Getting Started

1
Getting Started

WordPerfect 5.0 is ready for use right out of the box. Along with the manual and other information (don't forget to send in your warranty card!), WordPerfect 5.0 will come to you as a set of ten 5 1/4" inch disks or three 3 1/2" disks.

This chapter is all about the basics you need to get WordPerfect up and running easily and smoothly. If you are new to WordPerfect, read through this entire chapter. If you are an experienced WordPerfect user, pick the sections that address your particular needs. Even if you have been using WordPerfect for years, you're bound to find something new and helpful in these pages.

Starting WordPerfect

Before you do anything else, expert or not, make a copy of each of your WordPerfect disks. As you make the copies, label each disk clearly and then place the originals in a dry, cool, safe place. Copies of the original disks are your insurance against a crash, power failure, or any other accident that would erase your originals and make you very unhappy!

Tip When you prepare disks to make copies of your original WordPerfect materials, use the following command:

format b:/s

This will format the blank disk in the B drive and place the operating system on that disk as well. That way, when you copy your WordPerfect files to the newly formatted disk, the system will already be installed and the disk is "bootable"!

We hope you never do this, but, you accidentally erase one of your original disks (which does happen otherwise I wouldn't be telling you to make backups!), send it to WordPerfect with an explanation and a copy of your receipt. They'll send you a new one for a small charge. Wouldn't it be more fun and a lot easier to make backups?

Once you have installed WordPerfect according to the installation directions contained in your WordPerfect owner's manual, you're ready to enter the letters *wp* at the system prompt (>*A* or >*C*) and begin with the opening WordPerfect screen.

Starting WordPerfect with Options

In addition to just "starting" WordPerfect, you can perform special functions when WordPerfect boots up. These can be made part of the batch file that automatically begins WordPerfect (called an autoexec.bat file which you can read about in your DOS and WordPerfect manuals), or you can insert them when starting from a floppy disk.

Here is a list and an explanation of each of these options. When an option is chosen, the command is placed after the characters *WordPerfect/* (don't forget the slash). For illustrative purposes, all of the examples below assume that you are starting WordPerfect from the A drive.

Retrieving a File Upon Start Up -*wp[file name]*

For example, if you are working on a file named "ch", the command

A>wp ch1

would start WordPerfect and retrieve that file all in one line. You're ready to work!

Setting the Timed Backup Option - *wp/b* [number of minutes between backups]

For example, if you wanted to have WordPerfect back up your word processing activities every 7 minutes (about the time it takes you to type one page perhaps?), the command

A>wp/b-7

would have WordPerfect create a backup every 7 minutes.

Changing the Overflow Drive -*wp/d* [drive]

For example, if you wanted to keep data files on a drive other than the one on which wp.exe is located, the command

A>wp/b

would make B drive active for the selection and saving of documents.

Starting a Macro -*wp/m* [the name of the macro]

You have created a macro (named news.wpm) that sets the margins, line spacing and column options for a newsletter that you produce. Upon startup, the command

A>wp/m-news

would place those formatting commands at the beginning of the document.

Getting Rid of the Flash! -*wp/nf*

Some systems produce a kind of flash that interferes with scrolling and makes it difficult to read the screen. If this is a problem, the command

A>wp/nf

will take care of it. This may especially be the case when WordPerfect is used with some IBM compatibles or with programs that use windows technology.

Loading WordPerfect into Memory -*wp/r*

Using this startup option loads about 300K of WordPerfect into RAM and allows it to operate much faster than otherwise possible.

Temporarily Returning to the Original Default Settings - *wp/x*

You might have changed the default settings for a particular project that you are working on and you want to return to the original settings only for this work session. The command

A>wp/x

will return you to the original WordPerfect settings that were on your program disk when you first opened the package. Remember, the use of wp/x is only a temporary change.

Defining the Screen Size -*wp/ss*

You might find that your system's configuration does not allow WordPerfect to identify the size of your screen monitor. If this is the case, you can use this startup function to do such.
For example, the

A>wp-24,80

provides for 24 rows of 80 columns.

Tip You can combine any and all WordPerfect startup options to further customize your word processing activities. For example, the command line

A>wp/ch1/m-date/b-10

will retrieve the file named "ch1", begin the macro named date (which dates the current version of chapter 1), and back up the file every 10 minutes. Easy? You bet. And fun.

The WordPerfect Screen

Once WordPerfect is started, you'll see the WordPerfect opening screen. You might have expected to see loads of messages and hints and other tidbits of information that more often than not confuse users, but don't expect to see them here. This screen is clean!

One of WordPerfect's trade marks is that it is a clean screen that has little clutter. It's almost as close as you can get to the metaphor of placing a piece of blank paper into a typewriter. Figure 1.1 shows a WordPerfect screen containing text from the first draft of this chapter.

What's on the Screen

```
Once WordPerfect is started, you'll see the WordPerfect opening screen. You might
have expected to see loads of messages and hints and other tidbits of information
that more often than not confuse users, but don't expect to see them here. This
screen is clean! One of WordPerfect's trade marks is that it is a clean screen that has
little clutter. It's almost as close as you can get to the metaphor of placing a piece of
blank paper into a typewriter. Figure 1-1 shows a WordPerfect screen containing
text from the first draft of this chapter.

C:WP/CH1                                              Doc 1 Pg 5 Ln 29 Pos 44
```

Figure 1.1 The WordPerfect opening screen

At the bottom of the WordPerfect screen is the status line which provides you with vital information about a document.

In the lower left hand corner of the screen is the name and complete path of the file that is currently active. In Figure 1.1, the name of the file is CH1 which is a file that is located in the directory named *WP5*.

In the lower right hand corner of the screen are four indicators. The first, *DOC* indicates the number of the active document. WordPerfect allows you to work with two documents at once and this indicator helps you keep track of which one is current.

Second, there is the *Pg* indicator, telling you the page on which the cursor is located.

Tip *If you every want to move to any page in a document, press the Ctrl->Home, key combination. The status line shows Goto and WordPerfect waits for you to indicate the page you want to go to.*

   Third, there is the *Ln* indicator, telling you the line on which the cursor is located.

   Finally, there is the *Pos* indicator, telling you the column position of the cursor. The Pos indicator also tells you some other things. First, when you depress the Caps Lock key, the Pos turns to *POS* and when you depress the Num Lock key, the Pos indicator blinks.

   This example shows the various indicators expressed in WordPerfect units (which are columns). Later on you'll learn how to change the unit of measurement to represent inches, centimeters and other measures.

That's the screen and the basics of getting WordPerfect up and running. It's now time to actually begin using WordPerfect and start on the road to becoming a WordPerfect expert!

2
Creating and Editing Text

It's time to actually start using WordPerfect and begin building on the experiences and confidence you'll need to be a WordPerfect expert.

Entering Text

The first step in any word processing activity is entering a set of characters. Since this chapter reviews fundamental WordPerfect skills (and practice makes perfect!), begin with a clean screen and enter the following letter (or any short text of your choice) so that you can use it to practice entering and editing text. Don't worry about typing errors. You'll learn how to correct those in a short while.

Dear Lew,

The news about the new baby was just wonderful. I know what it's like, since we have had six little ones and every one is different than the one that came before.

Best wishes to you and Linda,

Ron and Susan

As you type, several things happen on the screen. First, words automatically *wrap around* when they reach the end of a line. That's why you never have to press the return key when you use WordPerfect like you would do at the end of a physical line when using a typewriter.

You'll also notice that as you enter text, the Line and Position indicators in the lower right hand corner of the screen change. The Page indicator will change as well, but only when you either type enough to fill one page and move on to another, or when you tell WordPerfect to go ahead and begin a new page (called a *page break*) using the *Ctrl->Enter* key combination.

Continue typing until you enter all of the text that you want.

Tip When entering text you can either insert it or type over it. You toggle between the two using the Ins key. When you are in the insert mode, text is inserted between letters as it is typed. When you are in the type over mode, text is typed over what is on the screen. Try the two when you are correcting some errors to get a feel for the difference.

Correcting Simple Errors

The most simple way to correct an error is by using the *Delete* or *Backspace* key. The Delete key will delete the letter on which the cursor is located. The Backspace key will delete the character to the left of the cursor. Use the arrow keys to move the cursor to the second sentence in the text you created and try the Delete and Backspace keys to see what effect the keys have.

While these keys do not delete a large amount of text, they are quick and convenient to use.

Saving Text and Retrieving Text

Now that you have text on your screen, it's time to save it to a floppy disk or your hard disk.

Saving New Text

When you create a file and want to save it for the first time, follow these steps.

1. Press the *F10* function key, and WordPerfect will provide you with the prompt

Document To be Saved:

Creating and Editing Text 19

---

2. Enter the name you want to assign to the file. Remember that each document you save must have a unique name. Press the return key.

After a moment, the file name will appear in the lower left hand corner of the WordPerfect screen. The file is now saved under the name that you selected. The contents of the file will not change until you recall it and work with the text once again.

Using a Password

People who use word processors such as WordPerfect are often concerned about security and making sure that files are not readily available to others. If this is your concern, WordPerfect offers a password feature. To use it, select the *Ctrl->F5, 2* key combination.

When you do, WordPerfect will ask you for a password and whether you want to add a password, remove a password, or change it. Make a choice, enter a password, and press the Enter key. Your file (and all associated files such as dictionaries, etc.) are saved. When you try to retrieve that file, WordPerfect will ask you for a password.

Tip Be very careful when you use passwords and only use them when you must. Why? If you forget your password, there is no way to retrieve the file. Keep a written record of the passwords that you use in a safe place just in case. Remember, six months from now, it will be very difficult to remember the password associated with a file!

A Brief Visit With Macros

Now's as good a time as any to begin learning about macros. Chapter 6 will provide a detailed account of how macros work, the different kinds of macros there are, how to define them, and so on.

For now, you'll learn how to use one or two very simple macros to get an idea of their power and usefulness.

Some people see macros like medicine - they're good for you, but no one likes them. Now that you've entered some text, here are the steps (and what each does) in the construction of a very simple but useful macro that saves your file under an already assigned file name.

Here's how to create a macro that will save the current file.

The Keystrokes.....	What They Do.....
1. *Ctrl->F10*	1. Begins the definition of the macro.
2. *Alt->S*	2. Names the macro ALTS.WPM (the WPM stands for WordPerfect macro).

You will now see the WordPerfect prompt *Description:*. You can enter up to 39 characters describing the macro and what it does. In this case, enter *Saves existing file* and press the return. You will now see a blinking Macro Def message telling you that it is time to define the macro by entering the keystrokes in the step below. These are the exact keystrokes that will become the Alt->S macro.

3. *F10,<ret>,y*	3. Saves the current file under the previously used name.
4. *Ctrl->F10*	4. Ends the definition of the macro.

To use this macro after it has been created, just press the *Alt->S* key combination and the file will be saved.

Easy? Very. But remember that for this macro, the file must first be saved using the steps described earlier for saving a new file.

If you should make a mistake in creating a macro, use the *Ctrl->F10* key combination to end the macro definition and begin again.

Throughout **The WordPerfect Expert 5.0** look for macros appearing in the shaded or screened boxes to make your WordPerfect life easier.

Retrieving Text

Once you've saved text and you want to work with it again, use the *Shift->F10* key combination and WordPerfect will give you the Document to be Retrieved: message. Enter the file name and the document will appear on the screen.

Saving "Old" Text

One of the most attractive features of any word processing system is that you can recall existing text and work on it again.

Once the document has been worked with and changed, you will want to resave it. To save text that already exists and has just been changed, follow these steps:

1. Press the *F10* key, after which you will see the WordPerfect *Document to be Save*d: prompt, plus the name of the document such as

Document to be Saved:C:\wp\CH2.

2. Press the return key and WordPerfect will ask if you want to replace the current contents of the text (which may be different from that which was originally saved) or the same. Enter *Y,* and any changes that you made are now saved under the original name you used to save the file.

If you respond by indicating *N,* then WordPerfect will ask you for another name to use in saving the text.

Why would you want to save the "same" file under two different names? You might want to make two copies of the same document under different names and then alter only one. For example, you are writing a contract and almost all of the phrases and terms are identical except for one or two. It certainly doesn't make sense to retype the entire contract. Rather, you could save a copy of the contract under a different file name (such as *cont1*) and then go back and fine tune the content as needed for each individual client.

Saving a Document and Clearing the WordPerfect Screen

To save a document and clear the screens so you can begin work on a new WordPerfect document, press the

F7,<ret>,<ret>,y,n

key combination which will begin the exit operation, save the current document under its existing name, and clear the WordPerfect screen.

If you do not want to save the current document, use the

F7,n,y

key combination which will result in a clear WordPerfect screen without the document being saved.

> *Macro* Here's a macro for clearing the WordPerfect screen.
>
> 1. Ctrl->F10
> 2. Alt->x
> 3. clear the WordPerfect screen<ret>
> 4. F7,n,n
> 5. Ctrl->F10
>
> Use this macro any time you want to clear the WordPerfect screen.

Saving and Exiting WordPerfect

All WordPerfect Exit activities begin with the *F7* function key. To save a WordPerfect file and then exit the program press the

F7,y,<ret>,y

key combination which will begin the exit operation, save the current document, replace it with whatever changes have been made and then ask you if you want to exit WordPerfect.

> *Tip In trouble? When you have entered a command or have something on the screen you don't want, press the Esc key and you'll be returned to the document without executing any of the commands you started.*

> *Macro* This macro saves the current file and then exits WordPerfect.
>
> 1. Ctrl->F10
> 2. Alt->E
> 3. Save file and exit WordPerfect<ret>
> 4. F7,<ret>,<ret>,y,y
> 5. Ctrl->F10
>
> This macro can be your last WordPerfect command at the end of a work session.

Another Tip! *Be careful of double-documentitis, that dreaded disease that comes from retrieving one document while another is still on the screen. Remember to clear your screen of any documents before you retrieve another to work on.*

Editing Text

Once you create a document, you will probably need to edit it whether that includes fixing simple typos or inserting complete lines or paragraphs of new text.

Moving by Characters, Words, Lines, and Pages

The first things you need to know about editing text is how to move the cursor around the document in a quick and efficient way. Figure 2.1

To Move...	Press...
one character to the right	the right arrow cursor key
one character to the left	the left arrow cursor key
one line up	the up arrow cursor key
one line down	the down arrow cursor key
to the top of the screen	the - key (on the keypad)
to the bottom of the screen	the + key (on the keypad)
to the top of the file	the Home,Home,up arrow keys
to the bottom of the file	the Home,Home,down arrow keys
to the right end of line	the Home,right cursor arrow
to the left end of line	the Home,left cursor arrow
one word to the right	the Ctrl->right cursor arrow
one word to the left	the Ctrl->left cursor arrow
to a character or a page	Ctrl->Home key (plus the character or page)
up one page	PgUp
down one page	PgDn
to the end of the sentence	Ctrl->Home

Figure 2.1 Moving around a WordPerfect document

shows you what key or key combinations to use to move by a character, a word, a line, or a page.

For example, if you want to move to the top of the current document, press the *Home,Home,Up* arrow combination and the cursor will move to the top of the file whether it is 1 or 100 pages long.

Use these on the practice text that you entered until you feel comfortable with moving from one place to another.

Deleting Characters, Words, and Paragraphs

You've already learned how to delete a character either using the Delete or the Backspace key. You can use certain key combinations to delete much more than just one character.

Figure 2.2 shows you what key or key combinations to use to delete a character, a word, the rest of a page, and parts of lines.

To Delete...	Press...
one character to the left	the backspace key
character where cursor is located	the delete key
one word to the right	Ctrl->backspace key
one word to the left	Ctrl,left cursor key, backspace key
to the end of current line	Ctrl->End

Figure 2.2 Deleting text.

For example, if you want to erase everything to the right of the cursor on one line use the *Ctrl->End* key combination.

Use these on the practice text that you entered until you feel comfortable deleting text. Be sure that you saved the text before you begin practicing different key combinations that delete. Remember that once you save text after something has been deleted, it becomes a part of the file. The only way to restore it is through the undelete command.

Undeleting Text

Like everyone else, there will be times when you inadvertently delete text. WordPerfect undelete to the rescue!

To restore text, press the F1 function key. WordPerfect will then highlight the text that was most recently deleted and ask you if you want to restore it. If you want to restore the text, press Option #1. If you would like to see even more deletions (up to three back), select Option #2 and these other deletions will be made available from which you can pick.

Searching For Text

Another critical editing skill is being able to search through a document and find a set of characters. Once this is done, you can edit as you wish or automatically replace it with another set.

To search for a set of characters, press the F2 function key and at the ->*Search:* prompt enter the characters for which you want to search. You can search for up to 60 characters.

WordPerfect will move the cursor to the first occurrence of that string of characters following your command. If you want to locate the same string again, press *F2,F2* since WordPerfect remembers the last piece of text that it searched for.

To search through an entire document, you must begin at the top of the document. If, for example, you begin in the middle WordPerfect will only search from the middle on.

Tip *Want to search in a backward direction, say form the end to the front of a document? Use the Shift->F2 key combination in the same way as you would use the F2 function key.*

Search and Replacing Text

You may not only want to find a certain string of characters, but you might want to replace it as well. This operation is called search and replace.

For example, to search through a document and find the word "hte" and change it to the word "the", you would follow these steps.

1. Move to the top of the document.
2. Press the *Alt->F2* key combination and answer y if you want WordPerfect to stop at each occurrence and wait for confirmation to change, or n if you want all the changes to take place automatically.
3. Enter the string of characters you want to find at the *-> Search:* command. In this example the prompt would look like

->Search: hte

4. Press the F2 function key and WordPerfect will ask you for the characters you want to replace hte. Enter the and press the return key.
   WordPerfect will then locate and change each occurrence of "hte" to "the".
   A time saver? Yes! Fun? Yes! A potential disaster! Yes!!!! Why? Imagine coming across the word "thr" which you meant to type "the", and then using the search and replace feature to change the "r" to an "e". You then find that all the r's in the document are now e's! and unless you saved before the global change it can be impossible to reverse.

Tip *If you do a search and replace without confirmation, be sure to perform a save before hand. This way, if you do make some ridiculous substitution throughout your text, you can just clear your screen and retrieve the original.*

Another Tip *When replacing text, always replace the "largest" chunk you can. For example, if "thr" needs to be replaced, then search for that string of characters and not just the letter "r". Remember however, that "thr" is also a part of the words "three", "throw", and more! The moral? Save and confirm your substitutions!*

Doing a "Wildcard" Search

There may be a time when you are not exactly sure what the total string of characters is that you want to locate such as when you are unsure of the spelling of a word. When this occurs, use WordPerfect's wildcard feature, the *Ctrl->V,Ctrl->X* key combinations.
   For example, if you wanted to find all occurrences of the string of characters that start with *the*, you would enter:

F2,the,Ctrl->V,Ctrl->X,F2

Creating and Editing Text 27

---

which will search for words such as there, their, these, etc.

To form the "^X" character, first press the *Ctrl->V* key combination, then the *Ctrl->X* key combination.

Moving Sentences, Paragraphs and Pages

Another important editing feature is rearranging existing text. If the text that you want to move is in the form of a sentence, paragraph or page, the procedure for moving the text begins with the use of the *Ctrl->F4* key combination, which produces the following menu at the bottom of your WordPerfect screen:

Move 1 Sentence; 2 Paragraph; 3 Page; 4 Retrieve: 0

To move text, follow these steps.

1. Select option #1, #2, or #3 depending upon the format of the text you want to move and the position of the cursor. For example, if you want to move a sentence, you should have the cursor on the sentence that you want to move before pressing the *Ctrl->F4* key combination.
   Once the selection is made, the text is highlighted and appears in reverse color.
2. Indicate whether you want to move the text to another part of the document, cut (or delete) it from the document, copy it to another part of the document, or append it to an already existing file.
3. If you want to move or copy the sentence, paragraph, or page, WordPerfect will instruct you to move the cursor to the place where you want the text to appear. To complete the move, press the *<ret> or Enter* key. Remember that the first time you press the return key after you have selected text, the selected text will reappear.

> *Macro* This macro automatically moves the paragraph in which the cursor is located to the location of the cursor when the return key is pressed.
>
> 1. Ctrl->F10
> 2. Alt->P,<ret>
> 3. Move paragraph
> 4. Ctrl->F4,2,1
> 5. Ctrl->F10

If you *Cut* the text, it will be removed from the document, but you can still recall it if necessary. Since it is stored in buffer (a temporary storage location) use the *F1* undelete option.

Cut or copied text always remains in the temporary storage place (the buffer) until something else replaces it or until you turn your computer off.

Tip Keeping a list of ideas or notes to yourself as you work? Create a file called "ideas". Then use the Append block feature to add new ideas to the already existing list.

Using Blocks

What if the text you want to move is not a sentence, paragraph, or page? That's where WordPerfect's block capability comes in handy. A block is a portion of text, as long as you determine, that is defined using the *Alt->F4* (block on/block off) key combination.

Once this key combination is pressed, you begin selecting text at the location of the cursor. When you are in the process of forming a block, you will see a flashing "Block On" message in the lower right hand corner of the WordPerfect screen and the selected text appears in reverse video.

Once a block is selected, and text is highlighted, you can then do one of many things, such as

-using the *Ctrl->F4* key combination to move, cut, copy or
   append the block to another location,
-delete the block using the Delete or Backspace key,
-save the block as a separate file using the F10 key,
-underline or bold or center the block,
-convert the characters from upper to lower case or vice versa,
-print it,
-search through it, and more.

Any WordPerfect feature that is used on a standard file can also be used with a block.

Block is WordPerfect's most handy editing feature so try and use it whenever possible.

WordPerfect Reveal Codes

You've read several times that one feature of WordPerfect that many people like is the lack of a cluttered screen. Where some word processors insert all kinds of formatting and printing codes, WordPerfect's screen remains clean.

WordPerfect keeps these instructions on a hidden screen and you can see these reveal codes by pressing the *Alt->F3* key combination to produce a split screen and the set of codes like those you see in Figure 2.3.

```
Doc 2 Pg 15 Ln 3 Pos 5
{^^                        ]
[L/R Mar:5,11][Ln Spacing:2][Pg Numbering:Top Center][Pg Num:15]
Press Reveal Codes to restore screen
```

Figure 2.3 An example of WordPerfect reveal codes

For every one of WordPerfect's formatting features, there is a corresponding reveal code. For example, in Figure 2.3, you can see the following reveal codes and what they mean:

> *[L/R Mar:5,11] sets the left margin at 5 and the right margin at 69.*
> *[Ln Spacing:2] sets the lines spacing at double spaced.*
> *[Pg Numbering:Top Center] sets the page position number to 2, which is the top center of each page.*
> *[Pg Num:15] sets the new page number at 15, using arabic numerals.*

Every time you make a format change in a document, a corresponding reveal code is placed there as well, but you can only see it if you use the *Alt->F3* key combination.

A complete listing of reveal codes and what they indicate can be found in the appendix.

Deleting a Reveal Code

Deleting a reveal code is the same as deleting any set character. WordPerfect treats everything between the [and the] brackets as one character. If you want to delete a reveal code, place the cursor to the right of the code (use the *Alt->F3* key combination to see the codes) and press the Backspace key. Whatever reveal code you delete, the corresponding change will take place in the document.

For example in Figure 2.3, if the reveal code for spacing were deleted, the text would then be single spaced.

Searching and Replacing Reveal Codes

You can search and find reveal codes and replace them just like you can any other character, using the F2 key or the *Alt->F2* key combination.

The only difference is that you cannot directly enter the reveal code itself and search for that. The reason for this is that WordPerfect treats the reveal code as one character. In other words, if you are looking for where you placed a formatting code to change the margins to 5 and 20, you could not press the F2 key and then enter the individual characters [L/R] and then press the F2 key again. WordPerfect would search, but not for what you want it to.

Instead, once you press the F2 key, you would then press the *Shift->F8* key combination, which would give you the following menu of choices;

1 Line; 2 Page; 3 Other: 0

If you select option #1 for example (and you want to search for a formatting code that deals with lines), then WordPerfect will provide you with eight choices of codes to search for as follows:

1 Hyphen; 2 HZone; 3/; 4 Justification; 5 Line; 6 Margins; 7 Tab Set; 8 W/O: 0

You then indicate the code for which you want to search, press the F2 key, and WordPerfect will find that occurrence.

Tip *Want to delete all of one or the other codes? Just use the search and replace feature, find the reveal code you want and replace it with nothing!*

Creating and Editing Text   31

Using WordPerfect Help

In trouble? You can always call the WordPerfect support line or a friend of yours who is the resident WordPerfect expert. Before you try these, press the F3 function key and you'll see the opening invitation to use WordPerfect help as shown in Figure 2.4.

You'll also see the version and the date of your WordPerfect program in

```
Help                                              WordPerfect 5.0 04/15/88

   Press any letter to get an alphabetical list of features.


          The list will include the features that start with that letter, along with the
name of the key where the feature is found.  You can then press that key to get a
description of how thefeature works.

   Press any function key to get information about the use of the key.

          Some keys may let you choose from a menu to get more about
information about various options.  Press HELP again to display the template.

Press Enter or Space bar to exit Help.
```

Figure 2.4 The WordPerfect Help screen.

```
Underline on/off

Underlines text on the screen and at the printer.  While Underline is on, all type text
will be underlined.  Press Underline again to turn underlining off.
Pressing Underline with Block on underlines the entire block.
Note: When underline is on, the position number on the status line is
underlined as reminder.
```

Figure 2.5 An example of WordPerfect Help

the upper right hand corner. You can use WordPerfect help in two ways.

First, press any character that the WordPerfect feature with which you need help begins. For example, if you want to know about underlining, press the *F3,U* key combination. In a moment, you'll be directed to press the F8 which will provide you with instructions on underlining as shown in Figure 2.5.

If you already know what function key or key combination you want to use, simple use the F3,[key combination] and you'll see help on that topic almost instantly. The more you use WordPerfect the more familiar you will become with the various key combinations that are used and how easy it is to locate help on a specific function.

After you are finished with Help, press the space bar to return to your document.

Tip Want to see a neat reproduction of the keyboard template on your screen? Press the F3 function key twice. Then any of the function keys that you press will provide you with help about that key's functions.

In this chapter, you've learned all you need to know to get WordPerfect up and running and to customize it to your personal word processing needs. A little note of caution. When you first start using WordPerfect, don't get caught up in trying to change too many of the default settings or using too complex a combination of start up options. These can wait. Use WordPerfect as it comes, until you feel comfortable with what it offers and how it works - then you'll be ready to move on.

3 Formatting With WordPerfect

Even though the primary reason you learn to use a word processor is to create and edit text, you shouldn't forget that how things look, or the *format* of a WordPerfect document, is often as important as what's it says.

This chapter reviews some of the basic formatting features offered by WordPerfect such as changing the spacing of lines, the appearance of

```
Format
    1 - Line
        Hyphenation              Line Spacing
        Justification            Margins Left/Right
        Line Height              Tab Set
        Line Numbering           Widow/Orphan Protection

    2 - Page
        Center Page (top to bottom)   New Page Number
        Force Odd/Even Page           Page Number Position
        Headers and Footers           Paper Size/Type
        Margins Top/Bottom            Suppress

    3 - Document
        Display Pitch            Redline Method
        Initial Codes            Summary

    4 - Other
        Advance                  Overstrike
        Decimal Characters       Underline Spaces/Tabs
```

Figure 3-1. WordPerfect format options

pages, as well as working with the entire document. The major WordPerfect formatting options are accessed by first using the *Shift->F8* key combination, which produces the screen shown in Figure 3.1.

Formatting WordPerfect Lines

Formatting a WordPerfect line involves underlining and bolding, spacing between lines, setting margins and tabs, indenting, justifying and numbering the lines in a document. As you can see in Figure 3.1, the first

```
Format: Line

    1 - Hyphenation                 Off
    2 - Hyphenation Zone - Left     10%
                        Right        4%
    3 - Justification               No
    4 - Line Height                 Auto
    5 - Line Numbering              No
    6 - Line Spacing                2
    7 - Margins - Left              10
              Right                 10
    8 - Tab Set                     0, every 5
    9 - Widow/Orphan Protection     No

Selection: 0
```

Figure 3.2 The Format: Line submenu

option on the WordPerfect format menu is for formatting lines. Once this is selected, you can see the *Format: Line* menu shown in Figure 3.2.

Underlining with WordPerfect

Underlining (and **bolding**) text are essential tools in changing the appearance of a document.

There are two ways to underline text. The first is by pressing the *F8* key before you begin entering text you want to appear underlined and then by pressing the key once again when you are finished entering the text you what underlined.

> *Macro* This macro underlines the word on which the cursor is currently located. The cursor can be on any character but the first.
>
> 1. Ctrl->F10
> 2. Alt->U
> 3. Underline the current word<ret>
> 4. Ctrl-
> 5. Alt->F4
> 6. Ctrl->Right arrow
> 7. F8
> 8. Ctrl->F10
>
> With this macro, you can enter all your text and then go back and quickly underline as needed. WordPerfect treats a word as anything that has a space on each side, so punctuation marks (such as the period in "Dr." and the comma in "friends,") will also

The second way to underline text is to first enter the text, create a block of the text you want underlined, and then press the *F8* key. Which one for you? It doesn't make any difference, except that it is possible to forget what you wanted to underline, so don't wait too long to go back and create blocks if you don't underline as you enter the text.

Tip To draw a horizontal line, use the Esc key to repeat the spacing function. Press the F8 key, Esc (You'll see n=8 in the lower left hand corner of the screen), enter the number of spaces you want the line to be, press the space bar, press the return, and then F8 again. You will not see a line on the screen, but it will appear when you print.

Double Underlining

WordPerfect also offers the option to double underline text as shown in Figure 3.3 by selecting the *Ctrl->F8,2,3* key combination which elects double underlining from the *Appearance* submenu of the Font menu. Once this is done, any time that the F8 underline option is chosen, the text will appear with a double line underneath it.

<u>Single</u>	<u>Double</u>

Figure 3.3 Single and Double Underlining

There's one important difference between single and double underlining besides their appearance. To turn on double underlining you use the key combination shown above, and not the F8 key. When you are finished, you will have to turn it off as well, using the same combination of keystrokes.

Also, single underlining is the WordPerfect default. If you want to change that default to double underlining, you must reset the default options using the Setup menu accessed through the *Shift->F1* key combination.

Tip *As you can see in Figure 3.3, WordPerfect is set up to underline spaces. Want to change that? Use the Shift->F8,4,7 key combination to underline (or not to) underline tabs and spaces.*

Boldfacing Text

Boldfacing text follows the same procedure as underlining, only instead of the *F8* key, you use the *F6* key. As with underlining, you can bold

Macro As you might expect, here's the macro that boldfaces the word on which the cursor is located.

1. Ctrl->F10
2. Alt->b
3. bold the current word,<ret>
4. Ctrl->Left arrow
5. Alt->F4
6. Ctrl->Right arrow
7. F6
8. Ctrl->F10

As with underlined text, bold text will appear on a color monitor according to the display configuration you indicated when you set up WordPerfect 5.0 (see the appendix for more information about setting up WordPerfect).

Formatting With WordPerfect 37

before or after text is entered.

Indenting Lines

The *F4* key will indent five spaces (or the first tab stop) from the left hand margin and is the handiest way to indent the first line in a paragraph.

If you want to indent a number of lines from both margins, use the *Shift->F4* key combination and type away. Until you press the Enter key, WordPerfect will continue to indent from both margins as you can see in the following somewhat humbling quote.

Man with his noble qualities...with his godlike intellect which has penetrated into the movements and constitution of the solar system...still bears in his bodily frame with indelible stamp of his lowly origin.

-Charles Darwin

Setting Margins

Margins are the amount of white space that is between the left and right edges of the paper (or screen) and a line of text, and not the length of a line of characters.

To reset WordPerfect margins from the default settings of "1" and "1" (if you are using inches as the unit of measure), use the *Shift->F8,1,7* key combination which allows you to reset the margins as needed. If the unit of measurement you are dealing with is characters (u), it is helpful to know that the standard setting for most printers is 10 characters per inch.

Make whatever changes you need and then press the F7 key to Exit from the line format menu.

Tip *WordPerfect will change the margins from the location of the [L/R Mar] reveal code on. If things look screwy, it may be that you made changes in a location you didn't need . Check the reveal code and delete as necessary.*

Working with WordPerfect Tabs

Another formatting feature that makes the word processing life much easier is the use of *tabs*, which are pre-set stopping points along a line as you can see in Figure 3.4 accessed using the *Shift->F8,1,8* key combination. The "L's" in the Figure represent the tab stops that already have been set.

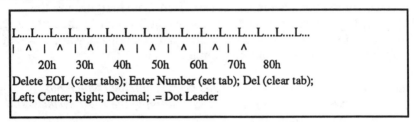

Figure 3.4 The tab setting screen

WordPerfect comes with tabs set at every .5 inches from columns 0 to 85 and has no tab setting from 85 through position 545 (!). When you want to reset tabs, you have several options.

Clearing Tabs

When you want to reset tabs, the first order of business is to clear the tab line of all existing tabs.

To clear the tab line, move the cursor over to position 0 (on the far left) and press the *Ctrl->End* key combination. This will clear all the tabs to the right of the cursor. Should you only want to clear part of the line, place the cursor to the left of that part before you use the *Ctrl->End* key combination.

Resetting Tabs

You can reset tabs in one of two ways.

The first is by moving to the column numbers where you want the tabs to be and then pressing the return key. For example, the numbers 5,15,35<ret> would set tabs at those columns. This is the ideal way to set one or two tabs, especially when they are not equally spaced.

The second way is used when you need to set multiple tabs that are

Formatting With WordPerfect 39

equally spaced. To do this, enter two numbers: the first is the column at which you want the tabs to begin, and the second is the spacing between tabs.

For example, the command *10,6* would place the first tab in column ten and tabs every six spaces. The command *0,5* would reset the commands to the original setting beginning in position 0.

Aligning Tabs

This is the feature you want to use when you need to vertically align text or numbers on a character. This is a very useful feature for people who want to present text and numbers in a columnar format as shown below.

Rent   234.67
Clothes 43.00
Food   125.00

To use this feature, set the tab stops where you want them and then use the *Ctrl->F6* key combination to set the align character. You'll see the *Align Char = .* prompt indicating that the decimal point is the current align character. Now enter text and then press the period (the default tab align character) and the remaining entries will appear to the left of the decimal.

To change the tab align character from a "." to some other character, enter *Ctrl->F6,[the new character]*. For example, you might want to use a diagonal to align text as in the following example.

Price/Earnings
23/11
6/3
124/54

Using Different Tab Styles

There are four different ways that you can set WordPerfect tabs to work. Each of these *Left, Center, Right,* and *Decimal* are available on the tab setting screen shown in Figure 3.4. The default setting is the Left tab style which means that any text that is entered after the tab key is pressed will move to the right. This is the way that any tab will work, such as when you use the tab key to indent the first line of a paragraph a certain number of spaces.

The *Center* tab style centers text in the middle of the page.

The *Right* tab style moves text to the right as it is entered, so that any text (as shown below) has a flush right margin (but not necessarily even with the right hand margin of the page).

> *Bid respectfully submitted,*
> *Steve Standing*
> *August, 1985*

Finally, the *Decimal* tab style is like the tab alignment character. Text that is entered moves to the left until you enter the decimal.

Tabs are wonderfully useful time savers but can be a disaster if you don't reset them and try to use them with other WordPerfect features such as columns. Be sure to check tab settings as you work, since you cannot undo a reformatting without changing the tab settings once again.

Setting Line Spacing

Line spacing can be set from 1 to any number in any increment you chose and is set using the *Shift->F8,1,6* key combination.

> **Macro** This macro takes you from whatever spacing you are using to single spaced lines.
>
> 1. Ctrl->F10
> 2. Alt->l
> 3. single space<ret>
> 4. Shift->F8,1,6,1
> 5. Ctrl->F10
>
> This could be used in double spaced documents for the entry of lists or quotes. Remember to switch back to double spacing if that was the original setting.

After you see the *Format: Line* screen, enter the new spacing number and press the F7 or Exit key.

Formatting With WordPerfect 41

Tip *If you do use spacing other than full lines (such as 1.25 or 3.5) the extra spacing will not show on the screen, but the Ln indicator at the bottom of the WordPerfect screen will show the new increments and the printed copy will show the new spacing.*

Using Subscripts and Superscripts

Some fancier line formatting for formulas and footnotes can be done with superscripts (above the line) and subscripts (below the line) as you can see in the following formula

$$a^2 = b^2 + c^2$$

To do super or subscripting use the *Ctrl->F8,1* key combination and select 1 for superscripting or 2 for subscripting before you enter the character that you want offset. WordPerfect will only super or subscript the block that is created

Justifying Lines

Most people have different opinions whether text should be justified (where the right edge is aligned) or not. The text in this book is not justified. Whether you justify text depends upon several factors including how you want the lines in your document to appear and the nature of the document.

WordPerfect's default setting is to justify text. To remove justification, use the *Shift->F8,3,y* key combination. From that point on, text will not be justified. When the justification option is turned on, you cannot see it on the WordPerfect screen.

Converting Characters

There are times when text that has already been entered needs to be converted from lower to upper case or vice versa. Say for example, you have typed the title of a document and you now want to change it from *Final Report* to *FINAL REPORT*.

To convert to all of one case, first block the text you want to convert and then press the *Shift->F3* key combination where you will see the following choices:

1 Uppercase; 2 Lowercase

Make your choice and the text that you blocked will be converted.

Formatting WordPerfect Pages

Once your lines look as you'd like, it's time to move on to formatting pages using the menu selected through the *Shift->F8,2* key combination that you see in Figure 3.5.

```
Format: Page
   1 - Center Page (top to bottom)    No
   2 - Force Odd/Even Page
   3 - Headers
   4 - Footers
   5 - Margins - Top                  6
               Bottom                 6
   6 - New Page Number                10
       (example: 3 or iii)
   7 - Page Numbering                 No page numbering
   8 - Paper Size                     85 x 66
       Type                           Standard
   9 - Suppress (this page only)

Selection: 0
```

Figure 3.5. The Format: Page submenu

Centering a Page Vertically

This first option on the *Format: Page* menu places an equal amount of space between the first and last lines of text and between the top and bottom edges of the defined page.

For example, Figure 3.6 shows you the cover page of report (slightly reduced) with the center page option (using the *Shift->F8,2,1* key Figure

> *Buying a House with a Friend*
> *by*
> *Michael Green*
> IBR Publishing

Figure 3.6. Centering a page

combination) turned on. WordPerfect will place a reveal code for centering a page *[Center Pg]* on the page on which the cursor is located and will center the text for only that page.

Remember that this option centers the *page* and not the text on any of the lines.

Doing Headers and Footers

A header (at the head of a page) and a footer (at the foot of a page) add additional information and really perk up the look of a document. You can see for example that the header on the odd page in this book is the chapter title and the header on the even page is the book title.

When you select a header or a footer, the same information will be printed in the same position on odd, even or alternating pages. Headers and footers are essentially the same (except for their placement on the page), so this section will only deal with headers.

To create a header, select the *Shift->F8,2,3* key combination upon which you will be asked to chose option #1 (an A header) or option #2 (a B header). You can have up to two headers on one page and header A is the first one you can define while header B is the second. Once this choice is made, you will see the following prompts on the bottom of your screen.

1 Discontinue; 2 Every Page; 3 Odd Pages; 4 Even Pages; 5 Edit: 0

Each of these provides an option for what you want to do with the header. Clearly options #2, #3, and #4 address how often and where you want the header to appear. Option #1 allows you to discontinue or turn off the header at any point in the document, and will continue to do so for the remainder of the document.

Once you have made your choice about which number header and on what pages it will appear, WordPerfect will then provide you with a screen to enter the header as you want it to appear on the page(s). You can use all the WordPerfect formatting tools available, such as underlining or bolding. When you are finished entering the header, press the F7 key and the reveal code for the header (plus the first 50 characters of the header) will appear in the reveal codes window.

Editing a Header or Footer

The only option that appears and not yet discussed is #5, *Edit*. Editing a header is like editing any other WordPerfect text. The only difference is that you first have to select Option #5 to bring the header up to the screen where you can work with it. Once this is done, and you have selected the header you want to edit, go about making changes as if it were any other WordPerfect document.

When you are finished, press the *F7* (Exit) key and things should be fixed with the new header appearing in your document as you have chosen.

Tip Headers really dress up text, but don't get carried away. If you chose to place more than one header on any one page, be sure that they are both short enough they don't overlap one another making a mess that is impossible to read.

Including the Page Number in a Header

It's a nice touch when a header contains the current page number such as:

Chapter 2 - The Early Years   *Page -56-*

To do this, simply use the *^B* (Ctrl->B) key combination, so that the actual header as entered would look like this.

Chapter 2 - The Early Years   *Page-^B-*

Each time WordPerfect sees the ^B character, it automatically enters the current page.

Setting Top and Bottom Page Margins

Lines have margins, which define their boundaries from where one line of text begins to where the same line ends. Pages also have margins, defining their boundaries from the top and bottom.

The default setting is one inch on the top and one inch on the bottom, or 6 lines. The more than you increase these margins, the more white space you will have at the top and the bottom of your printed page. You cannot see these page formatting changes on your regular WordPerfect screen, but you can see these changes using the *View* Document option (accessed by the *Shift->F7,6* key combination).

Assigning Page Numbers

WordPerfect does not automatically assign a page number since many documents such as letters, memos and such don't need such notations. In fact, pages are printed without them unless you specify otherwise. If you want to assign a page number, place the cursor on the page you want to begin with (which may not necessarily be page 1), and use the *Shift->F8,2,7* key combination. WordPerfect will now assign a page, but you need to indicate in which of the 8 positions you would like the value placed. For example, option #7 places a page number in the lower right hand corner of each page while option #4 places a page number in the upper right hand corner of odd numbered pages and the upper left hand corner of even numbered pages (pretty smart, eh?).

What a convenience when you are binding a large number of pages and there would be no room for the number to appear on the *gutter* side of the page.

Why would WordPerfect provide an option for assigning no page numbers? For the simple reason that people often do not want certain pages within a document numbered, such as the title page for a new part of a report, or the pages on which illustrations will be inserted.

Assigning New Page Numbers

Once directed, WordPerfect will automatically assign page numbers in sequence, but you may need to use a different numbering system (such as Roman numbers for an index) or even begin with a user defined number. In either case, place the cursor on the page where you want the new numbering to begin and select option #7 from the *Format: Page* menu. Now enter the number you want to begin with as well as the format, Roman (i, ii, iv, etc.) or Arabic (1, 2, 35, 117, etc.).

For peace of mind, most people who work on very long manuscripts do not store them as one file since there is too great a chance that if this one file is lost, so is everything along with it. Instead, people use separate files and then use the page numbering option to renumber them (chapter 1 from pages 1 through 56; chapter 2 from pages 57 through 91, etc.) before the final printing.

You can also use WordPerfect's master document feature which will be discussed later in **The WordPerfect Expert 5.0**.

Choosing a Paper Size

Once you had to chose between standard 8.5 by 11 inch paper and legal size 8.5 x 14 inch. Well, those choices are still here, but WordPerfect offers at least another 8 as you can see in Figure 3.7 accessed through the use of the *Shift->F8,8* key combination.

```
Format: Paper Size
   1 - Standard              (8.5" x 11")
   2 - Standard Landscape    (11" x 8.5")
   3 - Legal                 (8.5" x 14")
   4 - Legal Landscape       (14" x 8.5")
   5 - Envelope              (9.5" x 4")
   6 - Half Sheet            (5.5" x 8.5")
   7 - US Government         (8" x 11")
   8 - A4                    (210mm x 297mm)
   9 - A4 Landscape          (297mm x 210mm)
   O - Other

Selection: 1
```

Figure 3.7 The format paper size screen

These choices of paper size (and paper type) are available so that WordPerfect can match up the type of form you want to print with the appropriate type of paper.

Once again, the paper size that you chose depends upon the type of document with which you are working. For example, there is the standard page that measures 8.5 by 11 inches and the standard landscape page that measures 11 by 8.5. Same dimensions, but one is for printing vertically (standard) and the other, horizontally (landscape).

Tip As with any other WordPerfect features, if you will be printing out one size of page all the time, why not just set the default to that page size and leave it at that?

No Page Formatting at All

There will be times when you want to turn off those page formatting commands that are currently active. You can do this for many of the page formatting features that we have just discussed, but only for one page at a time, by selecting the *Suppress* (this page only) option from the *Format: Page* submenu. When the revcal code for this option is entered into a WordPerfect document, format features such as page numbering will be suppressed.

In this case, it means that the page number will not be printed. It does not mean that page numbering stops.

Formatting WordPerfect Documents

So far, you've learned how to change the format of lines and pages. There are more global format changes that you can make using the

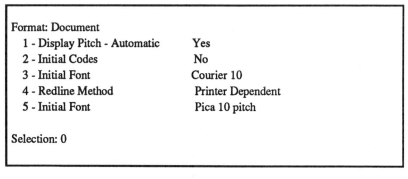

Figure 3.8 The format document menu

Format: Document submenu, which you access with the *Shift->F8,3* key combination as shown in Figure 3.8.

Changing the Pitch

The pitch of a character is the amount of space that each one takes up on the screen. As the pitch is increased, the space between characters is decreased. It's like spreading out the letters in a word or squeezing the letters closer together. The pitch in this sentence has been changed so that the letters are closer together than in any other sentence in this paragraph.

When might you want to change the pitch? When you use tabs or arrange other special spacing, such as columns, you may find that there are too many characters across the screen. To squeeze more information in on any one line (and therefore the entire page), you would increase the pitch. You can do this in one of two ways.

First, you can have WordPerfect set the pitch automatically and it will adjust the pitch to fit the individual characters for the font and printer combination that you after using.

Second, you can set the pitch yourself, by changing it from the default which is determined by your printer. Unless you know what the pitch needs to be, it's better to let WordPerfect do the setting for you.

Changing the Initial Settings

You may have already worked through *Appendix A - Setting Up WordPerfect*, where you learned that WordPerfect comes with a set of default settings such as single spacing, justification on, one inch margins and so on. You can use the *Shift->F1* key combination to change the default settings which will then be in force for every new document you create.

But what if you want to change some of the initial settings for only one document? For example, you might want this document to be triple spaced and have two inch margins. If you do want to change the initial settings for only the *current* document, use Option #2 on the *Format: Document* submenu. Any changes that you do make, will only be in force for the WordPerfect document on which you are working.

Creating a Document Summary

Wouldn't it valuable to know who typed the last draft of the report? Or

```
Document Summary                          System Filename
(Not named yet)
Date of Creation         May 17, 1988
1 - Descriptive Filename
2 - Subject/Account
3 - Author
4 - Typist
5 - Comments
```

Figure 3.9 A document summary.

what sections need attention? Or when the first draft of the first five chapters will be done?

All of this information and more can be made available in a *document summary*, as shown in Figure 3.9. To create a document summary, follow these steps.

1. Select the *Summary* option on the *Format: Document* menu using the *Shift->F8,3,4* key combination.
2. Enter the appropriate information by the corresponding number. Each of these informative categories can contain up to 40 characters and your comment can be up to 780 characters long.

The date and the system file name are automatically inserted for you. The date, is the original date that the document was created, not the date that the document was retrieved and revised. Document summaries are attached to the document, but are not printed.

If you want to see the document summary when you save the document or exit from WordPerfect, then you will need to enter the Setup menu (*Shift->F1*), select the initial settings option, and change it accordingly as discussed in Appendix A.

Changing the Font

Last, but not at all least on the *Format: Document* menu, are the options

```
Document: Initial Font

*Courier
 Compressed 17 pitch
 Compressed 17 pitch Italic
 Elite 12 pitch

1 Select; N Name search: 1
```

Figure 3.10 Some of the fonts from which you can select.

for changing the font from the default printer setting. Depending on the printer you are using, WordPerfect comes with a set of fonts such as some of those shown in Figure 3.10 for the Panasonic KX-P1092 with the default font (with the asterisk) being Courier 10 point.

Using this option, you can select the font (pica, elite, etc.) and pitch (6, 10, etc.). The type of printer you are using will determine what the default initial font will be that appears on the *Format: Document* submenu.

To change the font, use the up and down cursor arrows to move to the font you want to use and then select the *Select* option (#1).

Tip *When you change any format document attribute, no reveal code is entered since it is in force for the entire document. So when you change the initial font, for example, the font setting for the entire document is changed as well. You cannot change the initial font for only part of a document using the Initial Font option.*

There's one other option on the *Document: Format* menu named *Other*. These are document changes that don't readily fit into any of the other three categories on the Format menu and will each be covered individually as you work through **The WordPerfect Expert 5.0**.

That's it for formatting lines, pages and documents. You're ready now to move on to the next part of the basics; a brief discussion of printing out WordPerfect documents.

4
Printing with WordPerfect

After all is said and done with any word processor, the bottom line is usually sharing your document with others. By far, the easiest way to do that is through printed or hard copy as generated using the print feature. This chapter includes the important things you need to know about selecting a printer, using WordPerfect 5.0 to print your documents, controlling the printers operation and more.

The Print Menu

Before you begin any printing activity, look at the *Print* menu shown in Figure 4.1. You can see a series of options for printing certain amounts of text (such as printing the full document or only certain pages) as well as setting up options such as the number of copies you want to print and the quality of the text or graphics you want your printer to use.

What follows is a discussion of each of these WordPerfect features. More information about printing, including down loading fonts, and using a laser printer and other character sets will be discussed in Chapter 16 in Part 2 of **The WordPerfect Expert 5.0**.

Selecting a Printer

The first step in the printing of any WordPerfect document is the selection of the printer that you will be using. WordPerfect 5.0 has been designed so that the selection of a printer is simple and straightforward and should take you no time at all.

Even before you select a printer, you first have to add it to the list of all the printers that you might use in your WordPerfect travels. So, the first step is to add your model printer to the list by following these steps.

```
Print
     1 - Full Document
     2 - Page
     3 - Document on Disk
     4 - Control Printer
     5 - Type Through
     6 - View Document
     7 - Initialize Printer

Options
     S - Select Printer        Panasonic KX-P1091i
     B - Binding               0
     N - Number of Copies      1
     G - Graphics Quality      Medium
     T - Text Quality          Draft
```

Figure 4.1 The main Print menu.

1. Use the *Shift->F7,S* key combination to begin the selection process. If you have not listed any other printers, you should see a blank *Print: Select* Printer screen and on the bottom of the screen, several commands. Select option #2, *Additional Printers*.
2. Select option #2 once again, *Other Disk*, and WordPerfect will prompt you for the drive where you will be inserting one of the four printer disks that came along in your complete WordPerfect package. For example, Figure 4.2 shows the partial contents of the Printer 3.
3. Use the cursor arrow key to move to the printer you want to list. If your printer is not on the first disk that you inserted, take that one out and search through the others until you find your model number.
4. Once you have highlighted the model you want to list, press option #1, *Select,* and the highlighted printer will be added to the WordPerfect list of printers.
5. If this is the only printer that is listed, it will automatically be selected and used by WordPerfect 5.0 as the default printer. If you have more than one printer listed, you will have to use the cursor arrow keys to highlight the printer you want to use and then use the *Select* option to select that printer.

Printing With WordPerfect 5.0   53

These are the five steps to follow in the listing and selection of any

```
Select Printer: Additional Printers

Alps ALQ200/300/P2400C
Alps P2000/P2100
AMT Office Printer (Diablo)
AMT Office Printer (IBM Color)
Apple ImageWriter II
C.ITOH 8510 Prowriter
C.ITOH C-310 CP
C.ITOH C-310 EP/CXP
C.ITOH C-715F
C.ITOH C-815
C.ITOH ProWriter jr. Plus
Centronics 351
Citizen 120D
Citizen Tribute 224
Commodore MPS 1250
DOS Text Printer
Epson EX-800
Epson FX-80/100
Epson FX-86e/286e
Epson LQ-1050
Epson LQ-2500

1 Select; 2 Other Disk; 3 Help; 4 List Printer Files; N Name Search: 1
```

Figure 4.2 Some WordPerfect printers from which you can select.

printer. Remember that you can only select one printer at a time, but list several. You may want to list several so that you can switch back and forth between printers, depending upon the job at hand.

If you find that you no longer will be using a printer, just use the Delete (option #5) on the *Print: Select Printer* menu.

Printing the Document

Now that you have selected a printer, it's time to print a document. Enter some text on the screen now or retrieve one of the documents that you have created earlier.

If you want to print the complete document, use the *Shift->F7,1* key combination and the complete document, regardless of how many pages it is, will be printed.

If you only want to print the page on which the cursor is currently located, use the *Shift->F7,2* key combination and the page will be printed.

Printing from a Disk

In both of the above cases, you are printing a document that has been retrieved or is currently in the computer's memory. You can also print a file that has been previously created, and not currently in RAM (or resident memory).

To print a file that is located on a disk (either a floppy or a hard disk), follow these steps.

1. Select option #3 from the *Print* menu shown in Figure 4.1. When this is done, WordPerfect asks you for the *Document Name* (in the lower left hand corner of the screen).
2. Enter the name of the file you want to print and press the return key. You will now need to make the decision whether you want to print the entire file, or only part of it.
3. If you want to print the entire file, just press the return key once again when you see the *(All)* message.
4. If you want to print selected pages, you need to enter one of the following commands:

X (where X stands for a page number) will print a specific page. For example, if you enter the number 4, then page 4 will be printed.

X,Y (where X stands for a page number and Y represents another page number) will print both pages. For example, if you enter 4,7 then both pages 4 and 7 will be printed.

X- will print all the pages from X to the end of the document. For example, in a 27 page document, the command 23- will print pages 23 through 27.

Printing With WordPerfect 5.0 55

-X will print all the pages from the beginning of the document to the specified page. For example, in a 30 page document, the command -23 will print pages 1 through 23.

X-Y will print pages from X to Y. For example, in a 50 page document, the command 7-13 will print pages 7 through 13.

Tip Keep in mind that even if you don't have WordPerfect print page numbers, it keeps track of pages. Also, if you change the numbering (such as beginning a new chapter with the page 1 after another 45 page chapter) WordPerfect would see that first page as page 46.

What Can Your Printer Do?

WordPerfect 5.0 has many very sophisticated features, but there's always the question, What can my printer do?

To help you answer this, WordPerfect designers have included a special file named PRINTER.TST (located on the Learning disk that came in your WordPerfect package). If you retrieve this file and then print it, you will get a very clear picture (literally) of your printer's capabilities.

For example, some printers cannot print graphics while others cannot do double underlining. Examine the results of this printer test so you know the limitations of your own printer.

Controlling What the Printer Does

After you have become familiar with the printing of WordPerfect documents, there are some other WordPerfect options that will expand your use of the Print menu. These are the *Control* Printer options (#4) shown in Figure 4.3 where you can also see that three jobs are waiting to be printed.

The control printer option allows you to keep track of the progress of jobs being printed.

For example, if you are in the middle of printing a document and you want to cancel the operation, select Option #1 and WordPerfect will ask you if you want to cancel all of the jobs to be printed, or just the current one.

Or, if you are printing several jobs and want to push one up in its priority, then you can use the *Rush Job* Option to give priority to a particular job.

Tip *When you do cancel a printing job, it is likely that your printer will continue to print even thought your WordPerfect control screen says No print jobs. That's because there are still some printing characters left in the buffer (or temporary storage place) in your printer. To stop your printer, first press the on/off line button and then turn the power off. This will clear the buffer.*

```
Print: Control Printer
Current Job
Job Number: 1                    Page Number:  2
Status:      Printing            Current Copy: 1 of 1
Message:     None
Paper:       Standard 85 x 110
Location:    Continuous feed
Action:      None

Job List
Job  Document                    Destination     Print Options
1    C:\WordPerfect5\CH1         LPT 1           Text=Draft
2    C:\WordPerfect5\CH2         LPT 1
3    C:\WordPerfect5\CH3         LPT 1
Additional Jobs Not Shown: 0
```

Figure 4.3 Controlling the printer.

Using WordPerfect Like a Typewriter

Another WordPerfect feature that you may use quite often, is the *Type Through* (Option #5) on the *Print* menu which allows you to use your printer as a typewriter for those moments when you might want to type a simple memo or to fill in a form that needs to be completed.

When you select this option, you need to know whether you want to type through by line or character. Some printers cannot support either, and if this is the case, WordPerfect will give you that message.

If you choose *Line Type Through* the text that you enter will be sent to the printer when your press the Return key. You can use the cursor arrow keys and the space bar to actually move the printer head to the position you want it on the form, before you enter text. Not all printers however, can support this feature of Type Through.

If you chose the *Character Type Through*, text is sent to the printer (and printed) as soon as you enter the key which means that you can't edit any of the text before it is printed. This is something that you can do with the Line Type Through option.

Previewing a WordPerfect Document

Here is a simply wonderful option that has been added to WordPerfect 5.0. Using the *View Document* option on the *Print* menu, you can get a preview of what a document will look like before it is printed.

Using the *Shift->F7,6* key combination, you will actually see the current page you have been working on, only in a reduced form. On the bottom of the Preview screen, you will see other choices; *100%* which shows the document in its actual size; *200%* which doubles the size of the document; *Full* Size (which is the default and which you first saw when you chose the *View Document* option); and, *Facing Pages,* where odd numbered pages are shown on the right side of the screen and even pages are shown on the right.

Is this just another one of those add ons that are fun but don't do much in terms of helping improve word processing? Not at all. It's a good idea to preview all of your documents before you print them. It will give you an idea how headers and footers look, where pages breaks and page numbers occur, and a general idea about how paid out pages appear. This is especially important if you are printing a special document and want to make sure that it looks just right and if you are doing any desktop publishing.

Once you are in View Document, just use the cursor arrow keys and the various moving key combinations to move around and examine different parts of the document. You'll find that if you are in a particular part of a document (say page 3), and you exit View Document (using the F7 key), you will be returned to the place in the document where you were in the View Document mode.

The only drawback to this WordPerfect feature, is that you cannot do any editing while in View Document, but that's not what's it's there for anyway.

Changing the Quality of Graphics and Text

Different printing jobs require different qualities of print. For example, if you are working on a first draft of a paper for your eyes only, you might want to print in the draft mode which is fastest. On the other hand, when it comes time to do that important letter, then perhaps it's best to print as best as possible given your equipment.

One word of warning, however, laser printers do not know the difference between such words as draft and medium, so this information applies almost exclusively to those people printing with a dot matrix printer.

Using the *Graphics Quality* and *Text Quality* options on the print menu, you have three choices, *Draft, Medium,* and *High* from which you can chose. Simply select the one that you want to use before you begin printing.

Tip: The default for printing graphics is medium and for text is high and these cannot be reset. You can change the quality for any one document, but each time you begin a WordPerfect session and you want to print, you will have to change these settings if you don't want medium graphics quality and high text quality.

5
Managing WordPerfect Files

You already know that your computer system works by storing files in directories. When you enter the dir command at the system level for example, you're likely to get something like what you see in Figure 5.1 showing file names, their size and their date of creation. Your operating system (MS-DOS) contains all kinds of powerful commands to work with files at the system level, such as copying, deleting and renaming.

```
Directory of C:\MILE                      <DIR>    9-16-87  10:24p
  ..        <DIR>    9-16-87  10:24p
CH19        77036    2-02-88   8:28a
CH4         78396    2-02-88   8:29a
POL3         3868    2-01-88   9:37a
POL4         3507    2-01-88   9:37a
TC. NEW      2079    1-01-80   2:22a
TC           2705    2-01-88   9:36a
TC.OLD      12030    9-16-87  11:15p
CH4.BK!     78320    2-02-88   8:26a
CH19.BK!    77036    2-02-88   8:28a
    11 File(s)   7942144 bytes free
```

Figure 5.1 A directory of files

If you are working within an applications program (such as a word processing system like WordPerfect) you may, however, be at a loss to make those kind of changes. Not with WordPerfect. Using WordPerfect's List Files feature and the powerful file management tools that it offers, you can perform almost any kind of file management operation that is necessary. That's what this last part of this WordPerfect refresher is about; how to manage WordPerfect files while remaining within the

WordPerfect application.

The File Management Screen

In order to use the List File feature, you need to press the F5 function key. What you will see when you do this is shown in Figure 5-2.

```
05/19/88 08:29        Directory C:\WP5\*.*
Document size:   2545  Free: 7936000  Used: 656222   Files: 92

. <CURRENT>   <DIR>           .. <PARENT>  <DIR>
ALTA  .WPM    74 05/16/88 08:38   ALTC  .WPM   123 05/09/88 09:00
ALTD  .WPM    97 05/18/88 11:33   ALTE  .WPM    57 05/13/88 08:56
ALTI  .WPM    97 05/09/88 09:48   ALTL  .WPM   120 05/12/88 11:10
ALTM  .WPM    57 05/13/88 08:55   ALTP  .WPM    57 05/13/88 08:39
ALTQ  .WPM   108 05/12/88 08:34   ALTS  .WPM    96 05/09/88 08:49
ALTT  .WPM    57 05/09/88 09:37   ALTV  .WPM    57 05/13/88 08:55
ALTW  .WPM    89 05/13/88 08:28   ALTX  .WPM   117 05/09/88 08:51
ALTY  .WPM    67 05/13/88 08:41   APP   .A   17003 05/12/88 11:14
```

Figure 5.2 The file management screen

As you can see, this screen is full of information and here's your a guided tour.

At the top right hand corner of the screen is the date and time that the document you are working on was last saved.

As you read across, you'll see the name of the current directory for which this screen is listing files (in this case it's wp5), the size of the document that is active (2545 bytes), how much free space their is on the entire disk (a little under 8 million bytes), how much space in is use (all the files on the directory), and the number of files that are listed on the screen.

Below this information is a listing of each of the individual files within the current directory. Each listing contains the name of the file (such as ch1), its size (10049), and the time and date it was last saved (9/17/88 at 9:51).

If your directory contains more files than can fit on the screen, you can use the cursor arrow keys to move around the screen.

Managing WordPerfect Files 61

Tip *Want to print the directory? When List Files is active, just use the Shift->F7,1 key combination!*

The File Management Options

On the bottom of the List files screen, is the set from which you can pick one of 10 different file options. To use any of the options that are described below, you just follow these two simple steps.

1. Highlight the file of interest by using the cursor keys.
2. Select the menu option. It's as simple and straight forward as that.

Now on to the different options and what they do.

Retrieving a File

To retrieve an already created file, select the Retrieve item on the menu. The file will be retrieved and will appear on your WordPerfect screen in the location of the cursor. Keep in mind that whatever you retrieve, will placed on the screen (and into your computer's active memory) along with what is currently there. So if you have one document on the screen, whatever you retrieve will automatically be placed at the location of the cursor, whether at the beginning, middle, or end of the previous document.

A good work habit to develop is clearing the screen before you retrieve a new document. This is true unless of course you do want to retrieve documents in sequence to create a larger file such as with the chapters of a book or the parts of a report.

Deleting a File

When a file is deleted, it is removed from the directory. Because this can be an error on your part, WordPerfect asks you if you are sure that you want to delete the file by giving you the message

Delete C:\wp5\CH1? (Y?N) NO

WordPerfect even assumes that you do not want to delete the text and makes NO the default. If you do want to delete the text, enter the letter Y and the name of the file will disappear from the list files screen.

Tip If you accidentally delete a file don't panic yet! You probably have another copy of the file (with the extension .bk!, if you use the automatically back up function!) that you could rename or copy to get back to where you started.

Moving and Renaming a File

WordPerfect provides the option to move a file from one directory to another. For example, to move a file from the current directory to another directory named BOOK, you would select Option #3, and then enter the path for the new directory such as C:\BOOK. The file will then be moved.

When a file is moved from one place to another, the name disappears from the screen. The difference between deleting and moving a file is that when a file is deleted, it is removed entirely from any directory and is no longer available on that directory.

Renaming a file can have several important functions. First, as you just read in the tip above, you might want to rename a file from, for example, ch1.bk! to ch1 in the case of an accidental deletion. Second, you might want to do some housekeeping and rename files so they are more explicit in what their names represent, for example, from letter1 to springer.ltr. You can rename a file anything you choose, except a name that already exists on that directory or one that violates a system rule such as using more than eight characters for the name and three for the extension.

Printing a File

Once a file is highlighted and Option #4 is selected, it will be printed. Here you have the option to print the entire document (ALL), or just certain pages as discussed in Chapter 4. For example, to print the first 50 pages of the file named CH1, you would select the print item and then enter -50.

Working with ASCII Files (the Text In item)

An ASCII file is one that only consists of characters and hard returns and has neither printer nor format control codes. ASCII files are useful because almost any other word processing program can understand its contents.

If you want to create an ASCII file from an existing WordPerfect file, highlight the file and use the Text In (Option #5). When this is done, the ASCII file will appear on your screen. You should then save it under a new name, such as ch1.asc, so it will not get confused with the original WordPerfect file (named ch1 in this example).

ASCII fields are regularly used to important files from one application to another and to send via modem to other computers.

"Looking" at a File

You probably know that the more you use WordPerfect for any number of writing tasks, the more files you will create. Have you ever wanted to know the contents of a file without having to retrieve the entire file? That's what the Look option is all about.

When you highlight a file and use this option, you'll get a look at the contents of the file itself. You cannot edit a file in the Look option, but you can scroll through it using the cursor arrow keys to get an idea of its contents. If you have created a document summary, this will be the first thing you see on your WordPerfect screen when you use the Look option.

Changing a Directory

It's often important to be able to reach files from any directory or to change directories so you can work on a document that is located elsewhere. If this is the case, use the Other Directory option which will give you the

New Directory = c:\name of the current directory

where you can enter the name of the new directory to which you want to change. Once this is done, the list files screen will show the contents of the new directory.

Copying a File

You've already learned that you can move a file to another location but when you do that it is removed from the current directory. One of the List Files option, Copy, allows you to make a copy of the highlighted file and move it to another location or just make a copy of it on the current directory.

If you do want to move it to another location, you can use the same name for the file (as long as it goes to another directory). If you want to create another copy in the same directory, then you will have to give it a new name.

For example, you might have a five page form that needs to be sent to five different people and the only thing that needs to be changed is the mailing address at the top of the form. You could create five copies of the form, naming it form1, form2, form3, form4, and form5. While these may not be descriptive enough for you at this point, after you make whatever changes you need, you can then rename the files.

Searching for Words

Imagine this. You're a freelance writer who is constantly sending off correspondence about future writing opportunities, new contacts, completed projects, and so on. In any case, you have more than 300 letters on your disk. You get a call from an editor that you contacted several months ago about an assignment and need to send her some information but you forgot her address. Since you remember writing her a letter, you could find yourself in the "I know it's here somewhere" fix.

Instead, you can use the Word Search option on the List Files menu.

```
Search: 1 Doc Summary; 2 First Page; 3 Entire Doc; 4 Conditions:0
```

Figure 5.3. The word search menu.

When this is used, WordPerfect will search through various files to look for a certain string of words.

When you select Word Search, you'll see the menu shown in Figure 5.3 on the bottom on the screen indicating how the search can take place.

After you choose one of the options, WordPerfect will ask you for the words for which you want to search and will then mark the files on the List Files screen in which those words appear with an asterisk. If the words cannot be found anywhere that you told WordPerfect to search, you will get a *Not Found* message.

Doc Summary will search for words within any document summary that may have been created.

First Page will search for words on the first page of the document or through the first 4000 words.

Entire Doc searches through all the files that are currently available for searching on that directory.

The Conditions Option

The last option on the menu, Conditions, allows you even more flexibillty as shown in Figure 5.4. Here is a brief description of how each one of these can increase your search powers.

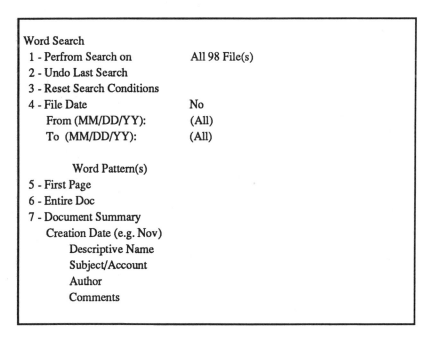

Figure 5.4 Setting up conditions for a word search

Perform Search all the files that will be included in the search and then list the number of files in which the words were located.

Undo Last Search will return the number of files in which searched for words were found on the last search operation.

Reset Search Conditions cancels any previous conditions that were specified. This is the choice you should make when you are switching directories or documents and want to clear the Conditions option.

Using File Date allows you to search more accurately and more precisely. For example, you might remember writing that editor between 6/1/88 and 6/15/88. Using the File Date option will speed things up rather than having to guess at the date the letter was written. WordPerfect assumes otherwise, that you want to search all the files through all the dates.

First Page searches the one page.

Entire Doc searches the entire directory and through all of the files for the words that you identified.

Document Summary allows you to specify what part of the document summary you would like searched such as a search for all the files that were typed by Doug or any documents with the comments "First draft prepared for B.G."

Wild Card Searches

You can use WordPerfect's wild card feature (and the * and ? symbols) to search for all words or phrases with certain characteristics. For example, if you want to search for all the phrases that begin with "During the past ten years", you would enter "During the past*years" which would recall the phrases "During the past ten years", and so on.

You can use the ? mark to represent a single character, so you could search for all four letter words that begin with t by entering t???, such as that and them, and this.

Finding a File

When you use the List Files option, all of your files are listed on the screen. If you know the name of the file that you want to locate quickly, you can use the Name Search option to highlight that file. For example, if you want to print the file named CH1, you would use the following sequence of keys

N,CH1,4,<ret>,<ret>

which would locate the file named CH1, select the print option, and print all the pages.

Tip Remember that when you search for anything in WordPerfect, provide as much information as possible. If you have 20 chapters, and files representing each one (CH1, CH2, CH3, etc.), you couldn't very well search for the word the and get what you want.

Working with Multiple Files

Everyone of the options listed on the menu at the bottom of the List Files screen performs some operation. Although you are more than likely to perform these on only one file at a time, you can also have WordPerfect act on as many files as you like.

For example, to print more than one file, place an asterisk next to each of the files that you want to print, and then press the Print option. Once this is done, WordPerfect will ask you

Print Marked Files? (Y/N) No

and by simply pressing Y, all of the files will be printed. You can do the same with deleting and copying files as well. Be especially careful when deleting more than one file at a time to be sure that each one that is marked (by an asterisk) is one you want to delete!

Tip When you do select more than one file as a batch of files, WordPerfect will perform a list files option (such as Print) in the order that it reads the file on the disk and not necessarily in the order in which you selected them. In other words, you cannot have WordPerfect print out a set of files in the order you chose using the List Files option.

To do this, use the Printer Control option (Shift->F7,4) and name each of the files you want to print using Option #3 (Document on Disk) in the order you want them printed.

That's it for the refreshers! You should be able to use WordPerfect 5.0 to create, edit, and save documents and even use some macros. Now it's time for you to start working on becoming a WordPerfect expert with a more detailed description of what macros are all about.

Part 2
Advanced WordPerfect

6
Using WordPerfect Macros

Earlier in **The WordPerfect Expert 5.0** you learned how macros can save you time and effort. In this first chapter on the more advanced features offered by WordPerfect 5.0, you'll learn about macros in more detail, including using different types of macros, having them pause for input from the user, and editing them if you should want to make a change, without having to re-enter all of the original keystrokes.

What is a Macro?

You use the WordPerfect word processing system for a very good reason: to make creating, storing, editing and printing documents easier and quicker.

As you probably know, however, there are often word processing tasks that can only be described as routine and have very little to do with the actual creation or writing of a letter, memo, or report. For example, directing WordPerfect to print out a full document involves the same combination of keystrokes whether you are printing out a 2 page letter or a 100 page final report.

Also, saving a document is *saving* a document!, no matter how you look at it. These are only two examples where using macros can be a real time saver.

A macro is a combination of keystrokes that WordPerfect stores as a separate file until the file is needed and retrieved. When you design a macro, you are the teacher and you tell WordPerfect what keystrokes to store (what the macro will do) and what the file of stored keystrokes will be named.

When you need to use a certain macro, you simply ask WordPerfect to perform it and whatever operations were indicated by the keystrokes will be automatically performed. It's that easy (and in fact turns out to be a lot of fun!)

When to Use Macros

The use of macros is really only limited by your imagination. You will surely find more uses than the ones listed later in this chapter, but these will give you some idea as to how people use macros in their everyday word processing activities.

Macros are especially useful for repeating a certain task that has to done several times. For example, you might want to go through a line of text and capitalize the first letter of each word. Or, separate every sentence in a paragraph into individual sentences. Both of these are easily accomplished with simple macros.

Another example of a time saving macro would be stopping the printer while a file is being printed which can take up to 8 separate keystrokes. This can be saved as a 1 or 2 keystroke macro, making this sometimes very needed command easy and quick to incorporate into your activities.

Not only can you save time by not having to enter multiple keystrokes, but you can assure the accuracy of your keystrokes as well. For example, when you design your stop printing macro using the correct sequence of keystrokes, the macro will always work. You not only save yourself keystrokes and time, but also the aggravation that comes with typos and the time and effort that is wasted correcting them.

Many people use macros to create *boiler plates* or standard portions of text that can be used in more than one document. For example, you might have a standard form or a clause in a contract or in an agreement or a standard format for a recipe that you want to follow. Save it as a macro and save yourself the time of having to re-enter it each time you need the format!

Not only can text be standardized, but so can the format of a document. For example, you might want each of your letters to begin with margins of 10 and 72, be double spaced and leave 2 inches at the top margin for a company logo. You can easily do this by defining these format conditions as a macro and invoking the macro before you begin writing your letter.

Converting 4.2 Macros

If you are an old hand at 4.2 macros, here's some encouraging news. On your 5.0 conversion disk is a utility that will convert many of your 4.2 macros so they work with 5.0. However, because of the changes in function keys and what they do, don't assume that any 4.2 macro will be converted keystroke for keystroke. If the macro does not work after you convert it, then you can either recreate it, or use the built in macro editor you will learn about later in this chapter.

The Four Basic Steps in Creating a Macro

By now, you should have some idea about what a macro is and how it works. Like thousands of others who just discovered macros, you'll probably find that your *Alt->S* macro created in Chapter 2, will get plenty of use and that you are busy on the hunt for more macros that are as convenient.

There are basically five steps in the definition of a macro:
- -defining the macro,
- -naming the macro,
- -describing the macro,
- -entering the actual keystrokes that make up the macro, and
- -ending the macro.

Starting and Defining the Macro

The first step in creating a macro is defining the macro. This is done by pressing the following key combination:

Ctrl->F10

As you saw when you created the save macro in Chapter 2, using this key combination produces the

Define Macro:

message in the lower left hand corner of your WordPerfect screen. Pressing the *Ctrl->F10* key combination is always the first step in defining any kind of macro, regardless of what the macro does or what you will name it.

Naming the Macro

The second step is naming the macro. Macros can be named in two ways.

The first is by using the *Alt->X* key combination where the X represents one of the 26 single letters on the keyboard. These are called *Alt Key* macros. These macros are especially handy to use (like the save macro you already created) since you only need to press the Alt key plus one other letter to start or invoke the macro.

To create an Alt Key macro, press down the Alt key and while holding it down, press the one letter that you would like to use to name the macro.

You can assign a full name to a macro by entering that name at the *Define Macro:* prompt and then pressing the return or enter key. This is called a *Full Name* macro. Using this method, you can assign a name of up to 8 characters long to a macro.

For example, instead of using the Alt Key combination to create *an Alt->S* macro that saves, you could have used the word *save*. WordPerfect would than save this macro as a file named SAVE.WPM rather than ALTS.WPM, if it were saved as an Alt Key macro.

Both the Alt Key and the Full Name methods are for permanent macros that are recorded as separate files on your directory.

Describing the Macro

Next, WordPerfect asks you to for a *Description:* of the macro. Here, you can enter up to 39 characters that describe what the macro does. Those of you familiar with WordPerfect 4.2 remember there was no opportunity to write a brief description and at times, it was very frustrating remembering what macro performed what operation!

Entering the Macro

The fourth step in creating a macro consists of entering the exact sequence of keystrokes that you want the macro to perform when it is invoked.

WordPerfect will remember these keystrokes since it stores as a *.WPM* file and will repeat them time and time again in the exact sequence that they were entered. Remember, once you have started the macro definition process and named the macro, any and all keystrokes that are entered become part of the macro. If you make an error and backspace or delete, these keystrokes will be entered as well.

Ending the Macro

After you have started the macro definition process, named the macro and actually entered the keystrokes that make up the macro, the last step is ending the macro definition process. The way that this is done is by using the same combination of keystrokes you used to start the definition process, *Ctrl->F10*.

Once the macro is completely defined, it is saved as a file and is ready to be used at any time.

What to Name Your Macros

What's in a name? In this case, almost everything.

When you create a document using WordPerfect you always assign a name to the document and save it as a file. You have probably already developed your own style for naming files including a set of separate extensions (such as *.ltr* for letter or *.rep* for report).

What do you chose for a file name? If you're like most people, you chose a name that comes as close as possible to describing the contents of the file. A file that contains a company report might be named *comp.rep* or a letter to your best friend Michael Green, might be called mikeg.ltr. Using such descriptive titles, you can easily determine the contents of a file before you spend the time retrieving or printing it.

It's no different in the case of macros. You need to name your macros in such a way that you can remember what the macro does by simply looking at the file name. The first and most important rule to follow then in assigning a name to a macro is to use a name that suggests the macro's function.

For example, a macro that copies a block of text might be called COPYB (for copy a block) or a macro that prints the current page might be called PP (for print page).

Alt Key versus Full Name Macros

Now the big question is whether to use the Alt Key method of assigning a name (which uses only one of 26 letters) or the Full Name method (which allows you to name a macro up to eight characters).

What are advantages and disadvantages of each? Let's take the Alt Key method first.

The Alt Key Method

The most striking advantage to using only one key to name a macro in combination with a key (such as *Alt->S)*, is speed and convenience. When you only need to use one key (or one key combination), you can set a macro into operation very quickly.

If you use Alt Key macros, you must be selective about what single letters you use to name what macros so you don't get confused. Few people could remember what all 26 (A through Z) Alt Key macros represent.

You also need to be careful about creating Alt Key macros that use keys that are physically close together on the keyboard and accidentally press one rather than the other. For example, an AlTD.WPM (delete current file) next to an ALTS.WPM (save current file) invites disaster. If you do create several Alt key macros, keep them physically separated if their functions clash.

Use the Alt Key method for assigning a name to a macro when it is a macro that you will use on a frequent basis and is one that does something that is suggested by its one character name.

The Full Name Method

The name method should be used in at least two circumstances.

The first is when you run out of single keys that are available to name macros!

The second is that using more than one letter to name a macro allows you the luxury to assign a name that gives you a clear and understandable clue as to what the macro does. Remember that you can only use up to eight characters in naming a macro. The second general rule for naming macros is to use as few letters as possible, but still convey some information about what the macro actually does.

You are the one who will be creating, naming and using macros. It follows, then, that you are the only one who really knows what they should be named. You might have your own system for developing and assigning names that might work best for you.

Where to Put Your Macros

When you create a macro, it is stored as a file with the extension .WPM in the current directory within which you are working. This means that a macro (or set of macros) is only available if you are working in a directory where those macros were created (or copied). For example, if you created the ALTS macro while working in the directory titled PAPERS, the macro will only be available within that directory.

The solution? You can do one of two things. You can either create your macros in the directory where your WordPerfect programs are stored or copy them to the directory from any other place they have been created. Since you may often work in different directories, you might find the second option more convenient, If so, at the end of each WordPerfect work session where you created a macro, just enter

*c> copy [current directory name] *.WPM [location of WordPerfect files]*

which will copy everything with a Wordperfect extension from one directory to another.

If you do this on a regular basis, you will have all of your macros in one location.

As another alternative, you can define a path for a macro library and include that in your autoexec.bat file.

Invoking a Macro

Invoking or starting a macro can be done in two basic ways.

If you want to invoke an *Alt Key* macro, you do so by pressing the Alt key plus the letter you used to name the macro. In the examples that were discussed earlier, the *Alt->S* key combination would be pressed to invoke the save macro and the *Alt->P* key combination would be pressed to invoke the print macro.

If you want to invoke a *Full Name* macro, you do so by pressing the

Alt->F10 key combination and WordPerfect will display the following message asking you to provide the name of the macro

Macro:

Once you enter the name of the macro you want to invoke and press the return key, the macro will begin.

Finally, you can invoke a macro when you first begin your WordPerfect work session by entering the following command at the system level

C> wp m-[macro name]

For example, you might want to take text that has already been entered but not checked for spelling and use the

C> wp m-spell

command to invoke a macro that checks the spelling of an entire document.

Stopping a Macro

If one of your macros is in the process of running and you want to stop it, press the *F1* key to cancel or abort the operation. This will return you to your WordPerfect document.

If you are in the middle of creating a macro and you made a mistake and want to stop and perhaps start over, you must press the *Ctrl->F10* key combination to tell WordPerfect that the macro has been completed, even if it isn't really what you want.

When you do this, WordPerfect will give you a message such as

ALTS.WPM is Already Defined. 1 Replace; 2 Edit: 0

You should chose option #1 so you can redefine the macro. Option #2 will be covered later in this chapter.

Remember than when you are creating a macro and you make an error, WordPerfect thinks that the error is part of the macro. So the *F1* key (a way to escape) becomes part of the macro itself! You cannot use these keys to cancel or escape while you are defining a macro.

Different Types of Macros

There are several different kinds of macros that you can use. Knowing which one to use for what task at hand will increase your efficiency and skills using 5.0.

Temporary and Permanent Macros

Temporary and permanent macros both do the same thing; they record a sequence of keystrokes that you can later recall. The primary difference between the two is that temporary macros are stored in the computer's memory and are not saved as a file. Therefore, temporary macros are best used for highly specific operations and only during the current WordPerfect session. Since they are not saved as a file, they disappear when your computer is turned off.

The ideas in most of this chapter focus on designing and using permanent macros (the kind you will probably most often use), so here's some information about temporary macros.

Using a Temporary Macro

To create a temporary macro, follow these steps:

1. Press the *Ctrl->F10* key combination to begin the macro definition (just like you did for creating a permanent macro).
2. Now instead of entering an Alt->[macro name here] key combination (such as *Alt->D)* or a full name (such as SPELL), use only one character to name the macro and press the return key.
3. Enter the set of keystrokes that you want to save as a macro.
4. Press the *Ctrl->F10* key combination to end the macro definition.
5. To invoke a temporary macro, simply use the *Alt->F10* key combination and when WordPerfect prompts you for the name of the macro, you enter the one character that represents the temporary macro and press the return key.

Tip You can have a permanent macro and a temporary macro that both are one letter macros, such as a permanent macro named ALTS and a temporary macro named S. The difference is that the permanent macro is invoked using the Alt+letter key combination without the return key being pressed and the *temporary is invoked using the Alt->F10, letter, return key combination.*

When you follow these steps, you will be creating a macro that is temporary and will not be stored as a permanent file on a floppy or a hard disk. When you turn your computer off, this macro will disappear. If you ever want to use it again, you will have to recreate it which is why you should only use temporary macros for very specialized tasks that will not be repeated again.

You can use any of the 26 letters of the alphabet to name a temporary macro, plus the return or enter key itself. In other words, you can even create a temporary macro that is invoked by simply pressing only the *Alt->F10* key combination and the Enter or the Return key!

Temporary Macros and Boilerplates

A frequent use of temporary macros is with standard bodies of text that need to be repeated within a specific document. These sections of text are often called *boilerplates*.

For example, if a contract were being drawn up that included two parties whose names are incorporated into the phrase

> the parties of Eisner residing at 123 Oak Way, Williams, MA and Gordon residing at 321 Elm Street, Old Town, ME have also agreed to the following;

Which could be saved as a temporary macro and then easily recalled in a passage such as the following (the boilerplate is underlined):

> As far as the responsibility for the everyday management of the business and other assets in the corporation, the parties of Eisner residing at 123 Oak Way, Williams, MA and Gordon residing at 321 Elm Street, Old Tow, ME have also agreed to the following;

Tip If you are going to create a macro that is used as a boilerplate and contains more than a few words of text, don't type in the actual text as part of the macro itself. Rather, first enter the text as a file, and then create the new macro by retrieving (Shift->F10) the file as a step in the macro. This way you can edit the text file as you go along and not worry about having to modify or restart the entire macro.

The Repeating Macro

There is a type of macro that will perform a specific function for as many times as it is necessary and then stop itself.

This type of macro is called a repeating macro and works by invoking itself until it can no longer find text that it can perform an operation on.

For example, here is a full name macro that will automatically underline the words Jerex Company in the paragraph shown below. Notice how the last step in the macro invokes the macro itself. (An explanation for each step is followed in parenthesis).

This is a good example of a temporary macro (which this one is) since it is so situation specific.

Step 1) Ctrl->F10 (begins the macro definition)
Step 2) j,<ret> (names the macro as a temporary macro)
Step 3) Underlines the word Jerex
Step 4) F2,Jerex (searches for JEREX)
Step 5) Home,<- (returns to first letter of the word Jerex)
Step 6) Alt->F4 (begins the block operation)
Step 7) Ctrl,-> (2x) (block the words Jerex Company)
Step 8) F8 (underlines)
Step 9) Alt->F10,j,<ret> (this is the step where the macro
        named j actually invokes itself)
Step 10) Ctrl->F10 (ends the macro definition)

Here's the paragraph after the macro was invoked.

Started in 1978, the <u>Jerex Company</u> has been expanding over the past five years and now has fifty Stores in more than 27 states. The <u>Jerex Company</u> is also planning <u>Jerex Company</u> stores in five other countries.

Any macro can become a repeating macro by having the macro invoke itself as the last step in the macro creation.

When a macro invokes itself, it will repeat until the condition that it is looking for is no longer present.

Chaining or Combining Macros

There's another kind of repeating macro that invokes a different macro as the last step in its keystroke definition. By placing more than one macro in a chain, you can combine different individual macros to accomplish a specific task.

For example, two steps in the development of a table of contents are the definition of a table of contents (how many levels of headings it will have and how it will look when printed, etc.) and the generation of the table of contents (where in the document you want the table of contents printed).

These two macros can be combined so that you can define and generate a table of contents in one macro. For example, here are the keystrokes and explanations for defining a table for contents:

Step 1) Ctrl->F10 (begins the macro definition)
Step 2) deftc,<ret> (names the macro)
Step 3) defines a table of contents,<ret> (this is the description)
Step 4) Alt->F5 (reveals the mark text menu)
Step 5) 5 (selects other options)
Step 6) 1 (selects define table of contents)
Step 7) 3,N (indicates number of levels and no wrap)
Step 8) <ret> (3x) (places the default heading at each level)
Step 9) Ctrl->F10 (ends the macro definition)

Here are the keystrokes and explanations for generating a table of contents.

Step 1) Ctrl->F10 (begins the macro definition)
Step 2) gtc,<ret> (names the macro)
Step 3) generates a table of contents,<ret>
Step 4) Alt->F5 (reveals the mark text menu)
Step 5) 6 (selects generate)
Step 6) 5,Y (generates a table of contents)
Step 7) Ctrl->F10 (ends the macro definition)

To chain or link these two macros together you would want to add another step to the macro DEFTC that invokes GTC.

Tip Rather than chaining these 2 together, you could create another macro that runs these two macros! You can "bury" as many macros as you want into how ever many levels as necessary and they will all still execute as designed.

Renaming and Copying Macros

You can rename or copy macros using the *F5* (list Files) feature of WordPerfect. When you rename or copy a macro, be careful that you are not assigning a new name that has already been used.

One other note of warning. If you are going to chain two or more macros together, it is a good idea to make a copy of the master macro or the one within which all the others will be embedded before you begin actually editing or modifying. This will insure that you do not accidentally name the new chained macro the same as the master macro. You might recognize this warning as one you might have heeded when you combined WordPerfect text files.

Repeating a Macro

You can easily create a macro that will repeat itself, but you can also control the number of times a macro repeats itself.

To repeat a macro, you use the Esc key to indicate the number of times that you want the macro repeated. Repeating a particular macro does not involve entering and changing the macro itself. The general steps in using the repeat feature are as follows:

1. Press the Esc key and WordPerfect will give you the default message of

Repeat Value = 8

indicating that unless another number is entered, WordPerfect will repeat this macro eight times. If you want to change the number of times you want the macro repeated, enter the value that represents the new number.

If you do not want to change the number, simply press the return key.

2. Invoke the macro as you would any other macro using either the Alt Key combination or the *Alt->F10* key combination and the full name. The macro will then repeat itself the number of times you have indicated.

For example, here are the steps that repeat the address macro (named ALTA) three times.

Step 1) Esc
Step 2) 3,<ret>
Step 3) Alt->A

When invoked three times, the *Alt->A* macro will produce the following.

Name
Address
City/State/Zip

Name
Address
City/State/Zip

Name
Address
City/State/Zip

A Macro that Repeats Itself or Repeat a Macro?

Remember that these are two different types of macro actions. The first, (a macro that repeats itself), invokes itself usually as the last step of the macro. The second, (using the WordPerfect Esc feature) does not make any changes in the macro itself.

Which one should you use? As with macros in general, there are so many ways to accomplish the same thing that it really boils down to personal preference. However, if you want to repeat a macro at some times and not others, then you should not use a macro that repeats itself. Otherwise, you would have to let the macro play itself out before it stops and change everything. In this case, just repeat the macro the number of times that you need it.

On the other hand, if you do need a macro that will always be applied to an entire document, than a repeating macro should be your choice. For example, if you are writing a book and use Latin phrases that need to be underlined (such as et al. or etc.) hundreds of times, you could use a repeating macro that will go through and underline every occurrence.

Macro Commands

The Macro Commands key combination *(Ctrl->PgUp)* allows you to create macros using WordPerfect's macro programming language. With

Using WordPerfect Macros

this feature you can do such things as see the steps actually executed as the macro is completed or have the macro pause for user input.

The first step in the Macro Commands is entering the *Ctrl->PgUp* keystroke combination which will produce the following menu at the bottom of the WordPerfect screen:

1 Pause; 2 Display; 3 Assign; 4 Comment: 0

Tip *The Ctrl->PgUp key combination produces these four options only when you are defining a macro. At other times, the key combination produces other outcomes.*

What follows is a discussion of each of these options.

The Pause Option: Macros with User Input

You have already seen how using macros can be a great convenience and some of the options that are available for designing the kinds of macros that fit your specific needs.

Regardless of the type of macro you use, there is one WordPerfect macro feature that really adds power to these tools: *user input.* When you construct a macro with a pause for user input, the macro waits until you enter the requested information, and then proceeds. These macros become customized.

For example, a macro that "asks" the user for margin settings or a macro that "asks" the user for the number of copies of a document that should be printed are two such applications of the pause and user input feature.

Pause (Option #1) on the Macro Commands menu will cause the macro to pause and wait for you to insert information. The macro will take keystrokes until the Enter (or Return key) is pressed. Once this occurs, the macro will resume execution.

For example, here is a macro (named space) that pauses for the user to indicate the number of spaces between lines.

Step 1. Ctrl->F10
Step 2. space,<ret>
Step 3. pauses for user input of spaces,<ret>
Step 4. Shift->F8,1,6
Step 5. Ctrl->PgUp,1,<ret>
Step 6. Ctrl->F10

When this macro is invoked (try it!), WordPerfect will wait for you to indicate the number of spaces that you want between lines. Enter the number, press the Enter key, and the spacing is set.

Seeing Your Macros Work

The second option, *Display* allows you to see the actual steps that take place as the macro is being executed. You will see the steps flicker by on the screen very quickly.

For example, if in the creation of the space macro listed above, you also included the following step between steps 3 and 4,

Ctrl->PgUp,2

the steps in the macro will actually be visible upon execution.

But since any macro is executed with almost lightening speed, in order to slow the steps display down, you need to set the speed of the macro execution, which will be discussed later in this chapter when the use of the Macro Editor is covered.

Assigning a Value to a Variable

The third option on the Macro Commands key combination allows you to assign a value to a variable. Here you can assign a variable to number such that routine phrases can be embedded into documents.

Inserting Comments

When a macro is created, you may have reason to attach a note to the macro itself that goes beyond the limited description that WordPerfect offers. For example, you might want to write a somewhat detailed description of the macro and mention what other macros are similar to the one being created.

If this is the case, simply chose the *Comment* option on the Macro Command menu and insert comments when prompted. These comments are ignored when the macro is executed, but will be available for your review when the macro is edited. These comments, like the steps in any

Using WordPerfect Macros 85

macro, can be edited using the Macro Editor.

The Macro Editor

What do you do when you have entered a long and complex macro and find out that you forgot just one step? Made an error on the last step? Included too many steps? Want to modify the macro to block one entire line rather than just one word?

Here's where WordPerfect's *macro editor* comes to the rescue. The WordPerfect macro editor allows you to directly edit macros. You can also use some of the powerful programming features of WordPerfect's macro command language.

Starting the Macro Editor

The macro editor is part and parcel of the WordPerfect 5.0 system and is one of the two choices you have when you try to begin creating a macro *(Ctrl->F10)* that already exists, as shown here:

ALTS.WPM is Already Defined. 1 Replace; 2 Edit: 0

If you chose to replace the macro (you will be using the same name but changing the macro's definition), you would chose Option #1. If you want to edit the macro however, you would chose Option #2.

When you chose option #2, you will see a screen similar to the one

```
Macro: Edit

        File              ALTS>WPM

    1. Description        Saves already named file

    2. Action
       ┌─────────────────────────────────────────┐
       │ {DISPLAY OFF}{SAVE}{ENTER}y             │
       │                                         │
       └─────────────────────────────────────────┘
```

Figure 6.1 The macro edit screen

shown in Figure 6-1 containing the name of the macro (in this case ALT5), the description, and a listing of the steps in the creation of the macro.

The first decision you need to make when editing a macro is whether you want to change the description of that macro. If so, selection Option #1 on the *Macro: Edit* screen and edit the description as necessary. Whatever you enter as a description will replace what was there before.

Next comes the heart of the macro editor, working with the actual steps that were used to create the macro in the first place which are shown in the box in the sequence in which they were entered. Each command, or separate keystroke operation, is separated by brackets, *{}*, and represents an individual keyboard action. For example, the entry {Enter} represents pressing the *Enter* key. Here's a list of some keyboard actions and the corresponding macro entry.

Keyboard Action	*Macro Entry*
Shift->F8	*{Format}*
Enter	*{Enter}*
F2	*{Search}*
Ctrl->F3	*{Screen}*

As you can see, the macro entry corresponds to the features of the function keys. In you have trouble understanding what keyboard action a macro entry represents, you can use the labels on the keyboard template to decipher what the macro entry means. For example, if you see the macro entry *{List Files}*, your template will tell you that the corresponding keystrokes are *Alt->F5*.

In Figure 6-1 you see the sequence of keystroke commands for saving an already named file.

The first command you will see is {DISPLAY OFF}. For all macros that are created with WordPerfect 5.0, WordPerfect assumes that you do not want to see the individual keystrokes displayed.

Next, the *{SAVE}* command corresponds to the F10 exit function key action, and *the{Enter}* that follows it corresponds to pressing the Enter key on the keyboard. Finally, the *y* indicating the file should be saved.

Editing a Macro

To actually edit the macro, chose Option #2, *Action*. When you are in this menu option, you are ready to actually edit the macro.

Any (and we mean any) keystroke that is now entered, will become part of the macro that you are editing, except for those keyboard entries that move the cursor around.

The first step in editing the macro is to move to the end of the macro using the cursor keys and press the *Ctrl->F10* key. When in the *Macro: Edit* screen, pressing this key combination immediately places you in the edit mode. Once in that position, each keystroke that you enter will become part of the actual macro itself. In other words, even if you make an error and enter a key combination that you don't want to be part of the macro, it will be entered as part of the macro.

Tip You can also enter new commands into an existing macro without using the Ctrl->F10 key combination, but not all. For example, if you are not in the macro edit mode and try to enter the F7 (Exit) command, it will not appear in the bracket, but rather begin the exit procedure from the macro editor.

When you use the *Ctrl->10* key combination, you will also see the following message at the bottom of the screen:

Press Macro Define to Enable Editing

To turn off the command insert feature, use the Ctrl->F10 key combination once again, and you will be able to delete keystroke commands you do not want to include in the new macro.

Here are the steps for editing the ALTS macro.

To clear the screen, enter the following keystrokes

F7,N,N

which on the macro edit screen will appear as you see in Figure 6.2 as

{Exit}

With this one line added, the macro will now save the file and then clear the WordPerfect screen without exiting the program.

```
Macro: Edit

        File              ALTS.WPM
    1. Description        Saves already named file
    2. Action

        ┌─────────────────────────────────────────┐
        │ {DISPLAY OFF}{SAVE}{ENTER}y{EXIT}        │
        │                                          │
        │                                          │
        └─────────────────────────────────────────┘
```

Figure 6.2 Adding the exit command

Using the Macro Programming Language

When you are comfortable with creating and editing relatively simple macros, you might want to explore the very powerful macro programing commands that WordPerfect offers.

These commands allow you a great deal of flexibility in creating macros that fit even the most individual task. For example, here are the steps in the creation of a macro that waits for user input (the name of the file to be retrieved) and takes advantage of one of the most often used macro programming commands, PAUSE.

1. Ctrl->F10 (begins the macro definition)
2. get,<ret> (assigns the name Get)
3. retrieves a user named file (describes the macro)
4. Shift->F10 (retrieve file function key sequence)
5. Ctrl->PgUp (pauses for user input)
6. 1 (chose the pause option),<ret>,
7. Ctrl->F10 (ends macro creation)

This macro waits for the name of the file and then retrieves it. If you look at the macro edit screen for this macro, you will see the *{PAUSE}* commands inserted between the *{Retrieve}* and *{Enter}* commands.

Zoom! Everyone is a little anxious when they first begin using macros. Have faith in yourself and stick to it. You can not now imagine the rewards for the little bit of practice and ground work that you invest.

   To get you started, we have included a library of macros in Appendix C in the areas of editing, formatting, special printing, graphics, and moving text. You already know how to edit macros, so you use these examples as a beginning point for building your own library.

7
WordPerfect Merge

If you asked 100 WordPerfect users the question, "What do you like best about WordPerfect?", there's a good chance many of them would answer with raves about the *merge* feature.

Merge - What It Is and How it Works

They have good reason to answer as such. At it's most basic level, merge allows you to combine two existing documents to produce a third. For example, you may combine a file that includes a form letter with a file that includes names and addresses to go with that form letter. More advanced applications of the merge feature include the preparation and printing of specialized forms, prompting the user for input from the keyboard, and having WordPerfect wait until you are ready to provide the information that it needs to complete its merge task.

WordPerfect merge works through the creation of two very specialized files. The first is called the *primary* file (or master file). This could be the form letter you've prepared, a contract without any specifics, or a loan form where the pertinent information needs to be filled in.

The second is called the *secondary* file. This is the file that contains the information that will be merged with the primary file. It is here that you would enter the names and addresses of people who will be sent the form letter. When directed to, WordPerfect will merge the contents of the secondary and the primary files, and produce a third merged file of form letters (in this example) that are completed and ready to be printed.

The Secondary File

Among the several applications you'll find in this chapter will be the creation of a primary and secondary file and the production of a merged file in the form of a letter indicating that an order has arrived.

The first step in this process is the creation of a secondary file, which contains the names and addresses, plus the member's co-op number. Each piece of information that is entered into a secondary file is called a *field*. In this case, the following information will be entered and repeated for each of the people who are to receive letters.

Field #1: Name
Field #2: Street Address
Field #3: City
Field #4: State
Field #5: Zip Code
Field #6: Name of Product Ordered

For illustrative purposes, two letters will be sent. There will be a set of entries for each of the letters. In this example, there are two records and six fields.

Tip *What you enter into a secondary file and use in a primary file depends on what it is you are going to do with the information. Information should be entered in the smallest "chunks" possible. For example, rather than enter city, state and zip code as one field, enter it as three. When you want to sort the secondary file, you can do so by the separate fields. If too many fields are combined, the option of sorting on a variety of fields is reduced and the flexibility is no longer available.*

When a secondary file is created, each of the fields and each of the records needs to be separated using special WordPerfect merge codes. The code that is used to separate fields from one another is the ^R code, which is entered at the end of each field using the *F9* function key, and not the "^" "R" key combination. This is a common mistake and WordPerfect reads it as two characters rather than as the special ^R code.

The F9 function key is used to indicate that this is the end of a field. When the F9 key is used, WordPerfect inserts the ^R code and automatically moves to the next line.

Once all the fields in a record have been entered, the special code that separates records from one another, ^E, needs to be inserted. This code is entered using the *Shift->F9,E* key combination. When this code is entered, a page break will also appear on your screen. WordPerfect assumes that whatever document you are doing, you will want the end of each document to end with a page break and WordPerfect inserts one for your convenience.

Here is a secondary file, consisting of two records each having six fields. Notice the use of the ^R code to separate fields and use of the ^E code to separate records. All of these records are part of a secondary file that will then be saved and called *names.sf*. While the .sf extension is not necessary, it helps you keep track of which files are secondary and which are primary.

Michael Greenwald^R
2775 Printers Row^R
New York^R
New York ^R
10158^R
#357^R
^E
Lewis Harvey ^R
8220 Wayside DRIve^R
Ann Arbor^R
Michigan^R
12345^R
#296^R
^E

Once this file is created it needs to be saved as a separate file.

Tip Use the same name for your primary and secondary files, but use different extension; .sf for a secondary file and .pf for a primary file. This way, you will not accidentally merge a secondary file with the wrong primary file.

Now on to the primary field with which the secondary file will be merged.

The Primary File

The primary file is the master document into which the information in the secondary file is merged. When you create the primary file, you

Macro This macro enters the ^R and the ^E codes into a list you want to use as a secondary file that consists of four fields ([1]name, [2]address, [3]city state and zip, [4]phone). This means you can take a name and address list (that contains no merge codes), invoke this macro and be ready to use it as a secondary file.

To use the macro, do not separate the records with any blank lines and place the cursor at the beginning of the first field. This macro will insert ^R and ^E codes for one record. Use the Esc feature to repeat the macro for the number of records you have.

1. Ctrl->F10
2. secfile,<ret>
3. Prepares information as a secondary file,<ret>
5. Ctrl->Right cursor arrow
6. F9
7. Delete
8. Ctrl->Right cursor arrow
9. F9
10. Delete
11. Ctrl->Right cursor arrow
12. F9
13. Delete
14. Ctrl->Right cursor arrow
15. F9
16. Shift->F9,E
17. Delete
18. Ctrl->F10

insert special codes that WordPerfect looks for. When it comes across one of these codes, it will enter the appropriate information from the secondary file. How does it know what information to enter?

WordPerfect keeps track of information in the secondary file by internally numbering it. WordPerfect does not print these numbers, nor does it indicate their number in any way. You know however, that the first field entered was field #1 or the name of the customer. Likewise, the last of the six fields entered is field #6, the number of the product ordered.

WordPerfect doesn't care if you don't use all the fields in a record in your primary file, but it is imperative that you place a code for each field in the primary document and you keep them properly sequenced. You'll

> May 26, 1988
>
> [Name]
> [Address]
> [City]
> [State]
> [Zip]
>
> Dear valued customer:
>
> It has come to our attention that we are out of stock of [number of product]. We expect a shipment within the next few days and will be mailing it out by June 5, 1988.

Figure 7.1 The draft for a primary file.

see in a moment how to tell WordPerfect to ignore a field.

The letter that will the primary file, including the placement of the different fields, is shown in Figure 7.1. No primary file codes are entered.

Defining Fields

When it comes time to actually enter the primary file, you need to include those special codes that were mentioned earlier. These are primary file codes, where the ^E and the ^R are secondary file codes.

To enter a primary code for the definition of a field, use the *Shift->F9* key combination and press the *F*. Upon doing this, WordPerfect will ask you for a *Field: number*. In this example, you will enter a number from 1 through 6 depending upon what field you want in what location of the primary file. In this straightforward case, the completed primary file is shown in Figure 7.2. Notice that fields 3, 4, and 5 are placed on the same line to read as city, state zip code.

Each of the fields in the primary file will be replaced with the corresponding field in the secondary file. The last step is to save the primary file. In this case, the file is saved as *names.sf*.

>
> May 26, 1988
>
> F1^
> F2^
> F3^, ^F4^ ^F5^
>
> Dear valued customer:
>
> It has come to our attention that we are out of stock of F6^. We expect a shipment within the next few days and will be mailing it out by June 5, 1988.
>
> Please accept out apology for any inconvenience this may have caused.
>
> Sincerely,
>
> F.V. Veck
> Operations

Figure 7.2 The primary file including field codes.

Merging the Primary and Secondary Files

Merging the two files together requires you to select the Merge option from the Merge/Sort menu using the *Ctrl->F9,1* key combination. When you do this, WordPerfect will ask you for the name of the primary file. After you enter the name of the primary file and press *Enter*. WordPerfect will then ask you for the name of the secondary file. Once you enter the name of the secondary file and press the Enter key, you will see the

Merging

message on the status line. This means that WordPerfect is now merging the two files.

When it is complete, your screen will be replaced with a set of the completely merged files. In this case, there are two letters, (the first one of which is shown in Figure 7.3) each with the appropriate information

May 26, 1988
Michael Greenwald
2775 Printers Row
New York, New York 10158

Dear valued customer:

It has come to our attention that we are out of stock of #357. We expect a shipment within the next few days and will be mailing it out by June 5, 1988.

Please accept out apology for any inconvenience this may have caused.

Sincerely,

F.V. Veck
Operations

Figure 7.3 A completed letter

entered for each individual.
You can now save this as a file itself.

Using Special Merge Codes

You just saw the most simple example of using the WordPerfect merge feature, which in itself may be just what you need.

WordPerfect holds in store many other possibilities, using some of the special merge codes that will be described in this section. Each of the these codes begins a special type of merge function.

Pausing for Keyboard Entries (^C)

You can direct WordPerfect to pause during a merge and allow you to enter information from the keyboard. For example, in Figure 7.3, the letter contained the greeting, "Dear valued customer". If you wanted to instead enter the customer's actual name, rather than leave this form introduction, the primary file codes would appear as follows:

May 26, 1988

^F1^
^F2^
^F3^,^F4^ ^F5^

Dear ^C:

It has come to our attention......

   As WordPerfect encounters the ^C code, it pauses and waits for your input from the keyboard. After the input is entered, the Merge (F9) key is entered, and the Merge operation begins once again.
   You can place a ^C code in a primary or a secondary file. In either case, WordPerfect will halt the merge operation and wait for keyboard input. If you only have a few form letters to write, you can entirely skip the preparation of a secondary file, especially if you would have very few fields in that file anyway. Just use the ^C code repeatedly to insert the information.

Inserting the Date (^D)

The current date (or time) can be inserted into a merge document by using the ^D code. Wherever the code is located in the document, the date that is currently in the system will appear. You'll remember that you can change the format of the date or the time using the *Shift->F5* key combination.
   In the case of the letter, the beginning of the primary document would look like this if the date were to be automatically inserted and if the greeting were under keyboard control.

^D

^F1^
^F2^
^F3^,^F4^ ^F5^

Dear ^C:

Using a Dummy Record (^N)

There may be times when you want WordPerfect to entirely skip a record in a secondary file or to avoid the page break that always occurs at the end of each form in a primary file.

For example, a good use of the ^N code in a secondary file is to have the fields defined at the top of the secondary file so that you can easily remember what information to enter and in what order it should appear. The secondary file in Figure 7.1 would than appear as
^N
F1 - name^R
F2 - Street Address^R
F3 - City^R
F4 - State^R
F5 - Zip Code^R
F6 - Product Ordered^R
^E

Be sure and notice that this record is set up like any secondary file record, including merge codes that separate fields and the ^E code that separates this record from the others. This is a handy reminder for letting you keep track of what goes where.

Including a Macro in the Merge (^G^G)

You already know that you can begin WordPerfect and invoke a macro as part of the same command (e.g. *c>wp m-[macro name]*), such as when you want to immediately begin checking the spelling of a document as it is first retrieved.

You can also incorporate a macro into a merge operation through the use of the ^G code. When the ^G code is used, it surrounds the name of the macro, such as ^GMERGE^G. This macro appears at the end of a secondary file and automatically begins the merge routine by asking you for the name of the primary and secondary files and then merging them. This saves you the trouble of having to enter keystrokes other than file names.

When WordPerfect encounters the merge command, it invokes the macro. The end of the secondary file that is being used throughout this chapter as an example, would look like this;

Michael Ott
POB 322
Table Rock
Arkansas
12345
222
^E
*^GMERGE^*

You could even customize the macro further to have it print the new file after the merge is completed.

There are a few things that you need to remember about the use of the ^G code in the merge routine.

First, when a ^G code is encountered, WordPerfect stores the macro and executes it when the merge is competed. In other words, you cannot invoke a macro in the middle of a merge operation. The macro will begin when the merge finishes.

Second, only one macro can be automatically invoked after the merge is finished. If you do have more than one appearing in a merge file, the one that appears last is the one that will be invoked.

Including a Message or a Prompt(^O^O)

When the ^O (for on screen) code is inserted into a merge file, a message containing the information within the ^O^O will appear on the status line of the screen. In other words, WordPerfect can prompt you for information as you work.

You might use the ^O code in the design of a set of prompts to have the user insert a specific type of information. For example, the design and completion of a primary file that records simple information as a registration form shown below.

REGISTRATION FORM
^O now enter name^O^C
^O now enter age^O^C
^O now enter address^O^C
^O now enter city^O^C
^O now enter state^O^C
^O now enter phone number^O^C
^O now enter hours available for work^O^C
^O now enter best time to call^O^C

WordPerfect Merge *101*

When the merge begins, the first prompt now enter name will appear on the screen. The ^C code included in the primary file allows for the entry of the name form the keyboard.

For someone who is unfamiliar with you system of entering data, a set of prompts like this could be very helpful. If you combined it with a macro that automatically inserts ^R and ^E codes after the record is complete, you could really automate the creation of secondary files from simple mailing lists.

Retrieving Primary and Secondary Files (^P^P)

Many merge operations require the inclusion of text from another file. If this is the case, then the ^P code can be inserted into the merge document before and after the name of the file that you wish to retrieve.

For example, you might use using a fixed paragraph (or a boilerplate) as part of one letter to a client and a different fixed paragraph as part of another so that certain people get one type of letter (a thank you) and certain people get another (an apology), depending upon their initial contact with you.

The primary document could look like this.

*^F1^*
*^F2^*
*^F3^*

Dear ^C:

Thank you for your recent letter to us concerning your order. ^Oenter file name here^P^C^P^O.

We will continue to try and respond too all your concerns and appreciate the opportunity to serve you.

The ^O^P^C codes will prompt for the file name, and wait for keyboard input to retrieve the appropriate file. One file might be named thanks and the other file named apology. Any name is fine as long as it conforms to DOS rules (no more than eight letters and the exclusion of certain symbols such as $ and -).

Here's the contents of the file named thanks.

It's always a pleasure to receive a letter like yours. Here, at Sabu enterprises we work very hard to earn your trust and your business.

The completed letter, with this file inserted, would appear as

*Dr. Moe Hodiri
1233 Stratford Avenue
Madison, WI 12345*

Dear Dr. Hodiri:

Thank you for your recent letter to us concerning your order.It's always a pleasure to receive a letter like yours. Here, at Sabu enterprises we work very hard to earn your trust and your business.. It's always a pleasure to receive a letter like yours. Here, at Sabu enterprises we work very hard to earn your trust and your business.

   You can create a library of boilerplates (or fixed passages of text) to use with letters or any other document. For those of you who complete legal documents or any form of agreement and often have standard words, phrases, or clauses that need to be inserted, this is exactly the way to do it!

Watching the Merge Happen (^U)

Inserting the ^U code within a primary file allows you to watch the operations of the merge on the screen as they occur. The combination of the ^U and ^C code (as ^U^C) will allow you to see the context in which WordPerfect is requesting keyboard input.
   For example, when merging a database file with demographic information from the keyboard, seeing what field was just entered can help assure the accuracy of entry of subsequent fields.

Printing Your Merged Documents Directly ^T

When you create a merged file, WordPerfect automatically sends the contents of the "new" file to the screen where you can see and examine it.
   There is one case however, where WordPerfect will send the output

directly to the printer and bypass the monitor altogether; the ^T merge code. When this merge code is inserted into a document, the output will go to the printer, up to the point of the ^T, and will not appear on the screen.

This code should be used when you do not have enough memory to store the results of the merge. For example, if you are merging thousands of names and addresses with a letter, a floppy disk will not be able to hold the entire merged file. Sending it directly to the printer will allow you to continue with the merge, but beware(!), once to the printer, the file is not saved. If you want to work with the merged file, you will have to recreate it and find a place that is large enough to store the contents.

Tip *If you have a very large secondary file and need to save the resulting merged file, divide the secondary file into parts and perform the merge, then save the file. That way, you will save the file and not have to use ^T to see your results.*

The ^T^N^P^P merge code combination sends a specified file to the printer and insures that there are no extra carriage returns. This combination will send a merged document to the printer, clear the document form memory, go to the next record and the print using the primary document.

Completing Special Forms

Almost all of us, at one point or another, have to complete a form that is already preprinted, or we have to design a form that other people need to complete.

Using the WordPerfect's merge feature and the ^O and ^C codes, this can be an easier job than first appears.

For example, the form that you see in Figure 7.4 was constructed using merge codes and completed as each field was requested from the keyboard. The text that appears in bold was entered from the keyboard.

```
┌─────────────────────────────────────────────────────────┐
│ Demographic and Test Information                        │
│                                                         │
│ Name: Sara James                         Date: 5/7/88   │
│ Street Address: 734 Indiana Street                      │
│ City: Carthage                                          │
│ State: MO                                               │
│ Zip: 12345                                              │
│ Phone: (123) 123-1234                                   │
│ Test #1 score: 92                                       │
│ Test #2 score: 88                                       │
└─────────────────────────────────────────────────────────┘
```

Figure 7.4 A sample form that can be completed using merge codes

Figure 7.5 shows what the actual primary file would look like to accomplish the above. The last line ^sub.dat^P recalls the primary file (named sub.dat) for the insertion of additional information.

```
┌─────────────────────────────────────────────────────────┐
│ Demographic and Test Information                        │
│                                                         │
│ Name: enter name                         Date:          │
│ Street Address: enter address                           │
│ City: enter city                                        │
│ State: enter state                                      │
│ Zip: enter zip code                                     │
│ Phone: enter phone                                      │
│ Test #1 score: enter score for test #1                  │
│ Test #2 score: enter score for test #2                  │
│ ^Psub.dat^P                                             │
└─────────────────────────────────────────────────────────┘
```

Figure 7.5 The primary file for the form shown in Figure 7.6

If you are designing a merge file to compete an already preprinted form (like you tax return or an application) then you will have to take some time to measure where the fields are on the printed form and set up your primary merge fields to correspond to the same position. You need to measure and practice, using a copy of the form that you will be printing on.

Tip *If you are entering information of preprinted forms, then be sure use the inches or pica units of measure option in WordPerfect setup. This will allow you much greater precision that if you use columns.*

Using Merge to Create a Report

Anytime you spend hours on preparing a secondary file of names and addresses for example, you would probably like to be able to do more than just generate letters. One way you can use the name and address file is to create a report. In one case it might be using names, phone numbers, and specialties listed in columns.as shown in Figure 7.8. Figure 7.6 shows two records for names and phone numbers of clients, plus their specialty both as part of a secondary file, and then as a merged file.The primary file is shown in Figure 7.7.

```
Dr. Bill Yellin^R
University of Missouri^R
Columbia, MO^R
(314) 123-4567^R
Radiation Physics^R
^E
Dr. David Brodski^R
Rutgers University^R
New Brunswick, NJ^R
(609) 123-4567^R
Clinical Psychology^R
```

Figure 7.6 The original secondary file

Name	Phone	Specialty
^F1^	^F4^	^F5^

Figure 7.7 The new primary file

Once the files are merged, the resulting printout would appear as shown in Figure 7.8.

Name	Phone	Specialty
Dr. Bill Yellin	(314) 123-3456	Radiation Physics
Dr. David Brodski	(609) 123-4567	Clinical Psychology

Figure 7.8 The merged files

The primary file in this example simply listed the column headings and could have listed any other information that you might have wanted to provide.

Printing Envelopes

You can easily use a macro to take the information from a secondary file and print it on an envelope. The macro shown here, selects the name and address from a secondary file and prints it on an envelope. Be careful when you create a macro of the following to be sure and place your field codes in the correct position and practice with a short secondary file before you begin printing a large number. The primary file might as follows;

$$^F1^$$
$$^F2^$$
$$^F3^$$

The macro assumes that the name and address for the label take up the first three lines in each record in the secondary file.

Here's the macro:

1. Ctrl->F10
2. ep,<ret>
3. envelope printer,<ret>
4. Shift->F10,address
5. Ctrl->F9,1
6. Ctrl->PgUp, name of primary file

7. Ctrl->PgUp, name of secondary file
8. Ctrl->F10

Macros and merge aside, your on your way to becoming a WordPerfect expert. Next you'll learn more about preparing WordPerfect text as columns, a format feature that you will find quite handy and free you from the "tab" blues!

8
Using Columns

There are many circumstances where it is necessary to organize your written material into columns. The most obvious, perhaps, is when you want to write a column of text that has a predefined set of margins and format such as a newspaper column. Another example is when you need to have multiple columns that are parallel to one another and may differ in size because of other page layout features and requirements.

WordPerfect provides you with two kinds of columns from which to chose, *newspaper style* columns (as shown in Figure 8.1) that snake from the end of one column to the top of the next, and *parallel* (or side by side) columns (as shown in Figure 8.2) that allow you to list related topics in columns that are set aside one another.

The definition of parallel columns is exactly the same as the definition of newspaper style columns, although in their use, there is one important difference. Here, (as you can see in Figure 8.2) there are two unequal columns, since the first columns only consists of 8 or so characters. Why	waste the space on an equal columns of two or three inches when only slightly less than one inch is needed? The Column Definition screen for both types of columns looks the same, except for the type of columns that was selected and the settings for the margins.

Figure 8.1 Parallel Columns

WordPerfect provides you with a great deal of control over the way your columns look. In fact if you should chose, you can have up to 24 snaking columns on one page!

Step 1	Open front and back doors
Step 2	Begin cleaning aisles and stocking shelves
Step 3	Assign other cleaning tasks
Step 4	Prepare registers

Figure 8.2 Side by side columns

Column Basics: Making Them Work

There are three basic steps to the creation and use of columns using WordPerfect.

First they need to be defined.

Second, once they are defined, you need to turn on the column function so WordPerfect knows when to begin to do its work.

Third, once the columns are defined and turned on, they then need to be generated. Let's go through each of these steps in the creation of a set of two newspaper style columns.

Once you have created or defined a column, you do not to do it again within the same document. This means that you can change from columnar to non-columnar and back to columnar material easily and maintain the same format.

> ***Macro*** Here are the simple steps for the definition of two newspaper style columns that are .5 inches apart.
>
> Step 1) Ctrl->F10
> Step 2) defnc,<ret>
> Step 3) defines newspaper style columns,<ret>
> Step 4) Alt-F7,4,F7
> Step 5) Ctrl->F10
> When this macro is invoked, the following reveal code will appear
>
> *[Col Def:2,1",3",3.5",5.5"]*

Defining a Column

When you define a WordPerfect column (or set of columns) you have to make 4 decisions;
- the type of columns (newspaper or parallel),
- the number of columns,
- the distance between columns, and
- the margin settings.

All of these decisions are made through the use of the *Alt->F7,4* key combination and the screen you see in Figure 8.3. The best way to decide on number of columns as well as distance between them, is to try different combinations until you achieve the look that you want. Keep in mind however, that the default of .5 inches between columns usually works quite well with 2 columns on a standard letter size page.

```
Text Column Definition

    1 - Type                            Newspaper

    2 - Number of Columns               2

    3 - Distance between Columns

    4 - Margins

    Columns   Left    Right    Column   Left    Right
    1:        1"      4"       13:
    2:        4.5"    7.5"     14:
```

Figure 8.3 The column definition screen

Defining Newspaper Style Columns

In Figure 8.1 you saw an example of a newspaper style columns. The *Column Definition* screen you see in 8.3 defines the characteristics of those columns; 2 newspaper style columns that are .5 inches apart. WordPerfect automatically defined the margins as 1 and 4 inches and 4.5 and 7.5 inches.

You can see that the text in these columns is right justified (set before the column definition took place).

Tip Unless you tell WordPerfect otherwise, it will automatically assign equal widths to the columns that you are defining. If you want unequal columns, select option #4 on the Column Definition menu and adjust the column margins as necessary.

Defining Parallel Columns

The definition of parallel columns is exactly the same as the definition of newspaper style columns, although in their use, there is one important difference. Here, (as you can see in Figure 8.2) there are two unequal columns, since the first columns only consists of 5 or so characters. Why waste the space on an equal columns of two or three inches when only slightly less than one inch is needed?

The Column Definition screen for both types of columns looks the same, except for the type of columns that was selected and the settings for the margins.

Turning Columns On

Once the column type has been chosen and other aspects of the columns' appearance have been decided, the next step is to turn the column function on. This is done through the

Alt-F7,3

key combination which turns columns on if they are off and off if they are on with either the

[Col On] or [Col Off]

reveal code inserted into your WordPerfect document.

Once you turn on the column function, it remains in force until you turn it off using the same key combination.

Producing Columns

Now that you have defined a format for columns and turned on WordPerfect's column function, it's time to generate columns. By simply entering text following the column definition and turning the column on, text will appear as the type of column that you indicated.

If you have planned the format of your document, you should first define and turn columns on and then enter the text.

Another choice is to enter the text first and then go back and place the cursor at the point after which you want columns to appear. Once you have defined the column and turned the column function on, whoosh, the text is formatted as a column.

Tip Do a lot of columns? Combine several macros so that you can produce them quickly. First, create a macro that defines the type of column that you want and also turns on the column function. Then enter the text that you want to form into columns, place the cursor at the beginning of the text, and invoke the macro. Instant columns!

Editing Columns Definitions

Let's say that you're basically satisfied with how things look, but you would like to explore the possibilities of redefining the column definitions that you just used. Perhaps you want to try more space between columns or even a change of the number of columns.

One way to do this, of course, would be to delete the column definition reveal code and begin anew.

A less painful way, is to place the cursor to the immediate right of the *[Col Def]* reveal code, and press the *Alt->F7,4* key combination. This will produce the current definition and allow you to change it without having to go through all of the steps that we have been discussing.

Two things you need to remember about changing any column format definition. The first is that you will not see any of the changes unless you reposition the cursor and WordPerfect has a chance to automatically reformat. The second, is that right before a column definition change (as before any format change) you should save your work so that you can revert back to it should you commit some ghastly act and lose everything!

Creating Parallel Columns

Working with newspaper style columns is relatively easy. You just enter the text and columns are automatically formed. Not so much the case with parallel columns.

With parallel columns, you need to tell WordPerfect when one column ends so that you can switch back to the other one. For example, in Figure 8.2, you can see how Steps 1, 2, 3, and 4 all have text to their immediate right. WordPerfect needs to know when the current entry for a set of parallel columns stops, and when it is time to go to the next entry.

When you want to switch from one column to the next when creating parallel columns, use the

Ctrl->Return

key combination. This will automatically take you from the end of one column to the top of the next. For example, in Figure 8.2, after the first entry in the first column was completed (Step 1), the
Ctrl->Return key combination, placed the cursor at the top of the right most column, ready to enter the text beginning with the words "Open front and back doors"

Whenever you want to change form one column to the other in a parallel column set up, use the *Ctrl->Return* key combination.

Tip WordPerfect is almost too easy to use in some ways, and one of them is in the creation and the use of columns. Plan your columns carefully, and don't create a format with 10 columns simply because you can. Instead, be sensitive to the white space that lies between columns and helps define them. Columns should be visually pleasing to the eye. Work with different plans and use the Page View option on the printer control menu to examine the results.

Editing Columns

Like any text, mistakes are made in the entry of text in a columnar format. To correct and edit text that is arranged in columns, you need to consider the text to be like any other WordPerfect text. For example, text that runs a total of two newspaper style columns that takes up a total of one page, is treated as one full page of text. If you use the down cursor arrow, once you get to the bottom of the first column, a push of the same key moves you to the top of the next column.

With that in mind, it is important to know about the cursor key movements that can be used to move you around either newspaper or parallel style columns. Figure 8.4 shows you what keys need to be pressed to get where you want to go.

If you want to go to:	Then press:
Top of the column	Ctrl->Home,Down cursor arrow
Bottom of the column	Ctrl->Home,Up cursor arrow
Left side of the column	Home,Left cursor arrow
Right side of the column	Home,Right cursor arrow
Column to the left	Ctrl->Home,Left cursor arrow

Figure 8.4 Moving through columns

Don't forget that once you have turned on the column definition, it is in force until it is turned off. Use the same key combination to turn it off *(Alt->F7,3)* as you used to turn it on and the text should appear as previously set.

A Note about Footnotes and Columns

Unfortunately WordPerfect does not allow you to create a footnote within a column, which may be shortcoming for some of you who use columns and footnotes.

If you do need to combine the two, it's best to turn the column definition off and then create the footnote. Then turn the column definition back on and resume the column format. If you are careful to watch spacing and word placement, you should not have any difficulty maintaining the continuity of the columns. Even though you cannot create a footnote (you also can't change the margin setting in the middle of a column), you can create an endnote.

Columns and Fonts

When you create a column in one font, and then change to another font, WordPerfect may have has to adjust the number of characters that will constitute the width of one column.

For example, if you change from Times 14 point to Times 9 point, you will obviously need more room for the former. Such changes can truly reek havoc on your document. Imagine a two page, newspaper style column document in Times 9 point that is reformatted to 12 point, representing a 33% increase in space. The letters need to go somewhere, and if you are planning your layout carefully, you could find yourself in trouble.

You can see in Figure 8.5 how to changing from one font to another (even of the same size) changes the nature of the column arrangement. The solution? The same as the one to many other challenges using WordPerfect 5.0 - planning things out before you finalize them. Use the preview function and print out drafts to be examined before you do any final production.

You can see in Figure 8.5 how to changing from one font to another (even of the same size) changes the nature of the column arrangement. The solution? The same as the one to many other challenges using WordPerfect 5.0 - planning things out before you finalize them. Use the preview function and print out drafts to be examined before you do any final production.

You can see in Figure 8.5 how to changing from one font to another (even of the same size) changes the nature of the column arrangement. The solution? The same as the one to many other challenges using WordPerfect 5.0 - planning things out before you finalize them. Use the preview function and print out drafts to be examined before you do any final production.

Figure 8.5 Using columns with different sizes

9
Creating Tables, Lists, and Indexes

WordPerfect is a time saver. There's no question about that. It allows you to do many of the things that would otherwise take hours or days to do "by hand." One set of time saving activities it does flawlessly is the creation of tables of contents, lists and indexes.

How WordPerfect Does Tables, Lists, and Indexes

There are three basic steps to the creation of a table, list or an index. First the text is *marked*. Second, the *format* of the table of contents, list or index is determined. Finally, the table, list or index is *generated*. Most of the steps that are discussed below begin with the selection of the *Mark Text* menu using the

Alt->F5

key combination. Then, depending upon what you are creating, different options are used from that point on.

Marking Text

The first step in the creation of a table, list or index is to mark the material that you want to include. This is done by locating the text, blocking it, then identifying what you want to mark it for (a table, list or index).

Defining the Table, List, or Index

Once the text has been marked, you need to define the nature of the table, list or index. For example, do you want page numbers included in the table of contents? How numbered? Leaders like these (.......) with page numbers or no leaders with page numbers in your index? All of these decisions (and more) are made when the table, list or index is being defined.

Generating a Table, List, or Index

Finally, you will want to generate the table, list, or index which WordPerfect will do automatically once you instruct it to do such. WordPerfect will generate the index, table of contents or list within your existing document at the position of the cursor.

Here we go with step by step instructions how to create a table of contents, a list, and an index.

Creating a Table of Contents

A table of contents is often the first thing that a reader looks at when first viewing a book or a report. It's a kind of road map, providing a quick overview of the contents as well as the order in which the contents appear.

Planning Ahead

The one thing you need to do even before you begin constructing a table of contents is to be sure of the level of headings that you want to assign to each topic.

For example, you might want to outline the headings for each section in the document to give you some idea which headings will assume #1 level status, #2 level status and so on throughout the entire document. This will allow you to speed up the marking and creation of a table of contents since you will not have to stop and think about what heading takes precedence among the other headings in the text.

Marking Text for a Table of Contents

In Figure 9.1, you can see a sample of material that will be used in the creation of a sample table of contents, a list and an index.

Chapter 1: Studying Children
The Role of Research
      Research is a very.....
What Theory Has to Say
      Although there are many different theoretical.....

                  Figure 1.1 Here

Judging a Theory
      There are a set of six criteria.....
Understanding Development
      Now that you have some understanding.....

                  Figure 1.2 Here

Chapter 2: Different Models of Development
The Basic Assumptions
      The most basic assumption.....
Psychoanalytic Theory
      More than 100 years ago in Vienna, Austria.....
Sigmund Freud
      The pioneering psychologist during these period of time.....
Erik Erikson
      While Freud's influence was great, the generative.....
Behavioral Theory

Figure 9.1 Sample materials for table or contents, list, and index.

You can see how the different levels are marked with level 1 headings being centered, level 2 being left flush, and level 3 being underlined. You'll also note that the sample material comes complete with the mention of Figures.

To mark text headings for a table of contents, follow these steps;

1. Block the text that you want to mark. In this case, the first text that will be marked is Chapter 1: Studying Children.
2. Select the *Alt->F5* key combination to see the *Mark Text* menu which will reveal the following list of options at the bottom of your screen.

Mark for: 1 ToC; 2 List; 3 Index; 4 ToA: 0

Select option #1, for table of contents.
3. Once this is done, the following prompt will appear at the bottom left hand corner of your WordPerfect screen;

ToC Level:

and it's time to identify the level at which the text should be placed. When the text is marked, the reveal codes surrounding the text (for a level 1 heading) look like this

[Mark:ToC,1]Chapter 1: Studying Children[EndMark:ToC,1]

> **Macro** It's kind of tedious to mark text for a table of contents entry if you have a bunch of headings. Instead, create a macro like the following one to save time. You'll notice that this only marks text for a level 1 table of contents heading and it is called *TC1*. You can create separate macros for different level headings or one that pauses so that you insert the heading level.
> When you begin this macro, be sure that you have placed the cursor anywhere on the line of the material that is to be blocked and assigned a table of contents entry.
>
> Step 1. Ctrl->F10
> Step 2 tc1<ret>
> Step 3. marks level one for tc<ret>
> Step 4. Home,Left cursor arrow
> Step 5. Alt->F4
> Step 6. Home, Right cursor arrow
> Step 7. Alt->F5,1,1
> Step 8. Ctrl->F10

The text is marked and when the table of contents is generated, *Chapter 1: Studying Children* will assume a level 1 status in the table of contents.

Defining a Table of Contents

Once the text is marked, it's time to define what you want the table of contents to look like. To define a table of contents, follow these steps.

1. Using the *Alt->F5* key combination, you can select *Define* (option #5) from the Mark Text menu that looks like this;

1 Auto Ref; 2 Subdoc; 3 Index; 4 ToA SHort Form; 5 Define; 6 Generate: 0

2. Once you chose the define options, you will see a the *Mark text: Define* screen as shown in Figure 9.2. To define a table of contents, select *TOC* (option #1) and you will see the screen shown in Figure 9.3.

```
Mark Test: Define

    1 - Define Table of Contents

    2 - Define List

    3 - Define Index

    4 - Define Table of Authorities

    5 - Edit Table of Authorities Full Form
```

Figure 9.2 The mark text menu

3. Select the number of levels you plan to have in the table of contents. In our example, there are 3 levels (planned out ahead!).
4. Decide on whether you want to have the last level entry displayed in "wrap around format". What this means is that WordPerfect will show the lowest levels in the table of contents (in this example, the number 3 level entries) as one unit.

5. Decide on how you want page numbers to appear in the finished table of contents (or if you want them to appear at all). You have the following choices:

```
┌─────────────────────────────────────────────────────────────────────┐
│ Table of Contents Definition                                         │
│                                                                      │
│     1 - Number of Levels                        1                    │
│                                                                      │
│     2 - Display Last Level in                   No                   │
│           Wrapped Format                                             │
│                                                                      │
│     3 - Page Numbering -        Level 1         Flush right with leader │
│                                 Level 2                              │
│                                 Level 3                              │
│                                 Level 4                              │
│                                 Level 5                              │
└─────────────────────────────────────────────────────────────────────┘
```

Figure 9.3 The table of contents definition screen

1 None - No page numbers appear at all.

2 Pg # Follows- The page number follows the table of contents entry such as;

> *Studying Children 1*

3 (Pg #) Follows The page number follows the table of contents entry such as;

> *Studying Children (1)*

4 Flush Right
The page number follows the table of contents entry but is flush right with the right hand margin such as;

> *Studying Children*   *1*

5 Flush Rt with Leader
The page number follows the table of contents entry but is flush right with a leader of dots or periods, such as;

> *Studying Children 1*

Which one you chose is of course up to you and the type of design features you want to include in your document. Keep in mind that if you have lots of 3rd, 4th and 5th level headings, then you might want to use leaders to help keep things in order and make them visually easier to read

Creating Tables, Lists and Indexes   *123*

than would otherwise be.

6. Press the *F7* key (twice) to exit the Table of Contents Definition screen and you will be returned to your document.

Generating a Table of Contents

Once you have the text marked for the table of contents and define what you want the table of contents to look like, you are now ready for generating the table of contents.

```
Mark Text: Generate

    1 - Remove Redline Markings and Strikeout Text from Document

    2 - Compare Screen and Disk Documents and Add Redline and Strikeout

    3 - Expand Master Document

    4 - Condense Master Document

    5 - Generate Tables, Indexes, Automatic References, etc.

Selection: 0
```

Figure 9.4 The generate menu

When WordPerfect generates a table of contents, it places the table at the location where the table of contents was defined. To generate the table of contents, select option #6 from the *Alt->F5* menu, which reveals the screen shown in Figure 9.4.

Now chose option #5. Since the table of contents format has already been defined, all you have left to do is wait and watch for your table of contents to appear! Be sure to note that when you define a table of contents, a list, or an index that WordPerfect automatically deletes all other references to table of contents and so forth.

In this example, the generated table of contents is shown in Figure 9.5.

You'll notice that just as the level 3 headings were underlined in the text, they are in the table of contents as well.

Chapter 1: Studying Children   1
The Role of Research   2
What Theory Has to Stay   4
Judging a Theory   6
Understanding Development 10
Chapter 2: Different Models of Development   12
The Basic Assumptions   13
Psychoanalytic Theory   18
Sigmund Freud   22
Erik Erikson   27

Figure 9.5 The sample table of contents

Tip *When Things Go Wrong...What is That? There are times when your first attempt at generating a table of contents will fail miserably and rather than just nice clean headings like you see in Figure 9.5, you have a mixture of text and headings.*

If this occurs, it's probably because you inadvertently placed mark codes some other place than at the beginning and end of a heading (such as at the end of a paragraph). If you suspect that this is the case, use the F2,Alt->F5,1 key combination to search for [Mark] in table of contents and find you where the mistake is. Delete the table of contents, the incorrect marks, and then remark the heading correctly. Finally, regenerate the table of contents.

Creating a List

Creating a list is much the same process as marking, defining, and generating a table of contents.

  First you block the text you want to include in the list, then mark it accordingly as to the list number, then define and finally, generate the list.

Marking Text

As earlier, we will be using the material in Figure 9.1 as the text for generating the list. The list that will be generated will be labeled "Figures" and will list each of the figures as well as the page number on

Creating Tables, Lists and Indexes 125

which they appear.

First the list entries (such as Figure 1.1 and Figure 2.1) are blocked. When the *Alt->F5,2* key combination is used, you will see

List Number:

prompt appear in the lower left hand corner of your screen.

You can have up to nine lists in any one WordPerfect document. Once you see this prompt, identify the list that you want to assign the marked text to, enter that value, and press the return key.

Each entry into a list must first be blocked and then marked for the list number (not the level) to which you want to assign it. Remember that whatever you block will appear on the list. If all you want on the listing is something like *Figure 1*, then just block that. If you want a title to the figure to appear as well, you must block that as well.

Tip *If you write large manuscripts that involve lots of tables and figures, you almost always need to have a listing of those in the table of contents or some other location in a document. Get into the habit of making list #1 a listing of tables and list #2 a listing of figures, or some such arrangement. It will save you the time necessary to find them all later on.*

Defining a List

Once all the entries that are to be included in the list are marked, the next step is to define the format of the list.

The first step in defining the list is to access the Mark Text: Define menu through the use of the *Alt->5,5* key combination. Once this is done, you will see the screen already shown in Figure 9.2. To begin defining a list, select option #2 on the *Mark Test: Define Menu*. When you do this, you will see the prompt

List Number (1-9):

and you need to enter the appropriate list number.

Once this is done, you will see the *List 1 Definition* screen as shown in Figure 9.6. You'll notice that this is the list definition screen for list number 1. If you created a second list, then there would be a screen for the definition list 2 as well and would continue for each of the lists that you are creating.

```
List 1 Definition

    1 - No Page Numbers

    2 - Page Numbers Follow Entries

    3 - (Page Numbers) Follow Entries

    4 - Flush Right Page Numbers

    5 - Flush Right Page Numbers with Leaders
```

Figure 9.6 The definition menu for list 1.

As you did with the definition screen for a table of contents, you must chose the type of format you want to use to display the page numbers (or not to display them should you chose) as shown on the List 1 Definition screen. Once this is done, a

[Def Mark:List1,2]

reveal code is inserted into the text, indicating List 1, option #2 (page numbers following entries) as follows will be shown when generated.

Figure 1.1   3
Figure 1.2   4
Figure 2.1   4

Working with Multiple Lists

When WordPerfect generates lists, it generates all of them in order. For example, list 1 will be generated first followed by list 2 and so on. If you want your lists to appear in places other than all together, mark the individual lists and move it to another location.

WordPerfect only knows to generate lists when the time comes, and does not distinguish between list numbers.

Creating an Index

Anyone who needs to find something fast in a book, knows that a good index can be a real time saver.

There are two ways that you can generate an index using WordPerfect. The first is through the use of the same steps that we have just outlined for a table of contents or for a list or set of lists. The second is through the use of a *Concordance File,* both of which we will address.

Marking Text

To create an index through marking the text, follow these steps.

1. Block the text you want to be an index entry.
2. Select the *Alt->F5,3* key combination and WordPerfect will show you what you intend to mark in the lower left and corner of the screen, For example, if the word *Index* was marked and identified as an index entry, you would see the following in the lower left hand corner:

Index heading: Index

Once you press the Enter key, WordPerfect will then ask you if you want a subheading for this entry by showing you the following prompt in the lower left hand corner;

Subheading:

If you want a subheading for the entry then enter it now and press the *Enter* key. Subheadings, which appear separated with a comma from the main heading, are also called nested headings. Here are what some might look like;

Index, nested entries
  using a concordance file
  without page numbers

Using a Concordance File

Creating and using a concordance file allows you to avoid having to mark the same word or phrase over and over again. In other words, all you need to do is to enter it once and you are in business.

A concordance file is list of words in a separate WordPerfect document that can be created like any other WordPerfect document. You need to name it and save it to be recalled later when WordPerfect needs to know the name.

For example, a concordance file for the information shown in Figure 9.1 could look as follows:

children
development
Erikson
psychoanalytic
research
theory

You'll notice that they are in alphabetical order and even though you are using a concordance file, *each one needs to be marked as an index entry with subheadings defined as well (a great time for a macro by the way!).*

When you define an index, WordPerfect will look for these words and will assign them as index entries wherever they are found. The only thing that you need to be sure of when creating a concordance file is that you include all of the words that you want to use as entries in the completed index.

Defining an Index

When it comes time to define the index, use the *Alt->F5,5,3* key combination and you will be asked to enter the name of the concordance file that you are using, In this case, the name is index.one, and would be entered as such.

Once you have entered the name of the concordance file (or the "=" (equal) sign if you are not using such a file), you will have to chose how you want the index formatted on the screen. You select page number format from a screen very similar to the one shown in Figure 9.5, except that it is labeled as an index, and not a list definition.

Generating an Index

Once the marking of the index (or the creation and identification of the concordance index is finished) and the index is defined, use the *Alt->F5,6,5* key combination to generate the index.
  For the text material in Figure 9.1, the index would look like this:

INDEX

children 3, 9, 14, 15
development 3, 4, 9, 14, 15
Erikson 4, 9, 15
psychoanalytic 4, 9, 15
research 3, 9, 14, 15
theory 3, 4, 9, 14

When you finish an index, be sure to place the heading INDEX at the top in the center of the first page. To finish things off nicely, place a header such as the only you see above at the beginning of the entire document.

The index at the end of this book was created using a (big) concordance file, but before the index was generated, the words that made up the file were checked for spelling (and typing) accuracy. Let's move on to that special WordPerfect feature now.

10
Using the Speller and Thesaurus

Wouldn't it be nice to be able to zip along at about 100 words per minute without any concern for misspellings or typos? If you're anything like the rest of us, it's not likely that this will happen soon, but...

That's why WordPerfect's spell check feature and the thesaurus are such handy tools. They can not only check your spelling (and even help improve it), but they can also help you to find just the right word, *term, expression, statement or utterance* (they're all from the thesaurus!) to express what it is you want to say.

How the Spelling Checker Works

When you request WordPerfect to check a document, it "stops" (although you can't see it doing so) at every word in a document and compares each of the words to the set of words contained in WordPerfect's main dictionary. This dictionary of around 200,00 words divided into a *main* word list and a *common* word list. WordPerfect first checks the common word list (containing such words as "the", "time", and "house") and if it does not find the word in the common word list, it then switches over and searches the *main* word list.

As you will learn later on in this chapter, you can create your own dictionary of specialized words that you can use to check a document as well. For example, you might be a statistician and use specialized terms such as *recursive* and *iteration,* and might often spell (or type them) incorrectly. You can create your own dictionary that WordPerfect will use to check these words along with checking the others in the document.

First, some things about using WordPerfect's spelling feature, as well as almost any other spell checker for that matter.

First, spell checkers correct your typing as much as they correct your spelling, so don't think that by the use of the spell checker you will automatically become a better speller. If you have absolutely no idea how a word is *spleld,* WordPerfect may be able to help you come close, but may not even be able to help at all. It can give you some ideas, but don't look for more miracles than WordPerfect already delivers.

Second, the dictionaries that WordPerfect uses to check words will simply not contain every one of the words that are contained in your document. What this means is that you may enter a word that is spelled correctly (especially proper nouns such as Erikson, Fuller, DaVinci) and WordPerfect will stop on that word telling you that it may be spelled incorrectly. You have to make the final decision!

Finally, if you do not use the correct word too express yourself, WordPerfect will not know the difference. WordPerfect "thinks" that the words *to, two, and too* are all spelled correctly, so it doesn't care how they are used.

There are some grammar checkers that can pick up on this problem but you have to know the difference between such words as to, too, and two, and their and there and other homonyms (words that sound the same but have a different meaning).

Checking a Document

To begin the spell checker, use the *Ctrl->F2* key combination. When this key combination is used, you will see the following screen as shown in Figure 10.1. Here, some sample text from Chapter 1 of this book is being checked.

I hope you never do this, but - If you accidentilly erase one of your original disks (which does happen otherwise I wouldn't be telling you to make backups!), send it to WordPerfect with an explanation and a copy of your erceipt. They'll send you a new one for a a small charge. Wouldn't it be more fun and a lot easier to make backups?

Check: 1 Word; 2 Page; 3 Document; 4 New Sup. Dictionary; 5 Look Up; 6 Count:

Figure 10.1 The choices from the spell check menu

You can see that there are six options at the bottom of the screen. Before we go an discuss each of the options, let's assume that you are interested in checking the entire document (as you probably will be in most cases). To check the entire document, you would chose *Document*

Using the Speller and Thesaurus 133

(option #3) and WordPerfect would proceed with the check and produce the screen you see in Figure 10.2.

```
I hope you never do this, but - If you accidentilly erase one of your original disks
(which does happen otherwise I wouldn't be telling you to make backups!), send it
to WordPerfect with an explanation and a copy of your erceipt. They'll send you a
new one for a small charge. Wouldn't it be mor emore fun and allot easier to make
backups?
-----------------------------------------------------------------------------------
A. accidentally          B. accidental              C. occidental
```

Figure 10.2 The spell check options

The Spell Check Options

WordPerfect begins and checks every word in the document against its dictionary file named WordPerfect {WordPerfect}EN.LEX and stops at a word that it does not recognize. The first of these words is accidentally. WordPerfect will now do one of two things. It will begin listing suggestions that among which might be the correct spelling of the word or it will indicate that it does not have any suggestions and that you're on your own!

In this case, you can see that WordPerfect has the following suggestions; *accidentally, accidental,* and *occidental.* Given a set of suggestions such as these, you now have 6 options as listed at the bottom of the screen in FIgure 10.2

Skip Once - Option #1

This option skips the word that is highlighted only once. This should be used when you might want to skip the spelling of a word (since it may be spelled correctly). Remember, however, that every time WordPerfect comes across this word, it will stop again.

This option is a good one when you are entering lots of proper nouns and may not spell the same one the same way throughout the document.

Skip - Option #2

This often used option skips a word throughout the rest of the document, whether or not it is spelled correctly. So if WordPerfect stops on the word Salkidn (which is the incorrect spelling of the word Salkind), and option #2 is chosen, WordPerfect will skip every occurrence of the word Salkidn, but will stop when it reads Salkind.

Add Word - Option #3

When option #3 is chosen, WordPerfect adds this word to the supplemental dictionary that it has created. This is the perfect place to add words that are used frequently such as your name, names of those you frequently write letters to and so forth.

When a word is added to the supplemental dictionary (which is the file WordPerfect{WordPerfect}EN.SUP) it becomes part of a list that WordPerfect checks against when it cannot recognize a word. This list can be edited like any other WordPerfect document, but it's best to make sure that the word is spelled correctly when you first add it to the supplemental dictionary and save yourself the trouble of having to go back and edit the file later on.

Edit - Option #4

This is your choice when WordPerfect can make no suggestions for corrections and when you have to actually edit the entry that was misspelled. You'll see this choice in action shortly.

Look Up - Option #5

WordPerfect is very forgiving. It not only allows you to make spelling errors and then helps you correct the error, but it even allows you to ask WordPerfect how to spell a certain word using the *Look Up* option.

For example, you might know that the word you want to use in a document is grammar, but you are not sure whether it is spelled grammar or grammar. When you chose option #5, you will see the following prompt in the lower left hand corner of your WordPerfect screen;

Word or word pattern:

WordPerfect is asking you to enter the word that you want to spell with as close an approximation as you can make to the correct spelling. Once you do this, you will how WordPerfect provides a series of possible spellings. Now the final decision (as always) rests with you, but at least you have some clues as to what the correct spelling might be.

Ignore Numbers - Option #5

The last option is when WordPerfect encounters a number and you want all words with numbers ignored.

For example, you are working on a long document that contains the names, addresses, phone numbers and zip codes of 500 people. Wow! Can you imagine WordPerfect stopping to check every one of those phone numbers or zip codes? Even if it would stop on each one, it can't possibly suggest a correction, so you end up with lots of skips. That's why the Ignore Numbers option is such a help.

Word Count - Option #6

When you want to know the number of words contained in a document, simply use the

Ctrl->F2,6

key combination and the number of words (not characters as some word processors will count) will appear on the screen. This is an especially useful took for freelance writers who often must stay within strict limits as to the number of words contained in an article.

Back to where we were when we started the spell check. WordPerfect stopped to check accidentally and suggests several words as you saw in Figure 10.2. Since choice *a* (accidentally) is the correct spelling (it's always up to you!), by simply pressing that key, you will replace the word accidentally with the word accidentally and every other occurrence of the same misspelling will be replaced throughout the entire document.

Using Wild Cards

But let's assume for a moment that you are very tired and can't even get close enough to use the look up option as you might like. If this is the case, then use WordPerfect's wild card feature which allows you to search for a word, when you only know part of its spelling.

For example, you might want to spell a three letter word that begins with the two letters *th*. If you enter the letters *th?* at the *Word or word pattern:* prompt, you will get a list of all the three letter words that WordPerfect has in its dictionary that begin with the letters *th*. What you'll see is shown in Figure 10.3, which is only three such words. The use of the *?* option is the one to use when you want to search when only one character is missing (such as *th?* or *?he*, or *t?e*).

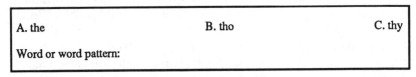

Figure 10.3 The three letter words beginning with th

Surprised that there are so few words that begin with th and end with one other letter? Don't be. Watch this.

The other wild card option is using the asterisk which represents *more* than one character. So if the set of characters *th** is indicated, WordPerfect will come back with the screen with such words as thai, thailand, thais, thalamencephala... Is this all there is? No, no, and no. If you press any key (*Press any key to continue* prompt), you will find out that WordPerfect has 38 (that's right, 38) more screens (not just 38 more words) with words that begin with the letter *th* and have some other number of letters!

Can you imagine who it is at WordPerfect corporation who is responsible for deciding what goes in the dictionary and what does not!

In any case, the * and *?* wildcard features can be a big help when what you need is simple help with looking up words that you have some idea about how to spell but are not quite sure.

When WordPerfect Isn't Perfect!

As we said before, WordPerfect cannot possibly recognize every misspelling but offers a solution. In the example in Figure 10.2, it stops on the word erceipt (which should be receipt) but there are times when WordPerfect cannot make any suggested changes..

It's now up to you to get out of your chair and find a dictionary that will provide you with the spelling of the word that you want to spell (receipt).

When you find the correct spelling of the word, then chose *Edit* (option #4) enter the correct spelling and press the *F7* (Exit) key. You will then see the word *erceipt* replaced with the word *receipt*. You just edited this word and can edit any characters on the line on which the cursor is located when you select the Edit option.

Other Menu Options

There is another menu that will pop up depending up the kind of word that WordPerfect encounters. The first is when WordPerfect finds that the same word appears twice, adjacent to one another, such as the a you see in the fourth line of Figure 10.2.

When WordPerfect finds double words you get the special line of options.

Options #1 and #2

These options will both skip the word. Double words are more often intentional than a mistake. For example, you might have a table with the labels

Column *Column* *Column*
   1   *2*   *3*

In this case, WordPerfect would identify the first pair of *Column Column* as a double word and stop. In this case, you would want to skip the pair.

Delete 2nd - Option #3

This options deletes the second word. When it was used in the text in Figure 10.2, the second *a* was deleted and the corrected text reads as follows:

I hope you never do this, but - If you accidentally erase one of your original disks (which does happen otherwise I wouldn't be telling you to make backups!), send it to WordPerfect with an explanation and a copy of your receipt. They'll send you a new one for a small charge. Wouldn't it be more fun and a lot easier to make backups?

Edit - Option #4

Here you can edit the words that WordPerfect stops to check as you did with the main set of options shown in Figure 10.3

Disable Double Word Checking - Option #5

This options turns off the WordPerfect double word check. In other words, when WordPerfect finds double words, it will not stop to indicate such. This would be an attractive option when you are working with text that contains intentional repetitions of words and you do not want to stop on each double occurrence.

The WordPerfect Thesaurus

The thesaurus is another kind of dictionary, only in this case, the words that are contained are synonyms for other words. In addition, the WordPerfect thesaurus provides antonyms as well.

A *synonym* is a word that has a similar meaning to the word under questions. For example, synonyms for the word *perfect* are complete, entire, intact and whole among others. Synonyms are often not exact substitutions for words, but since so many of us are inexact in our writing, then such substitutions can usually work just fine.

An *antonym* is a word that has an opposite meaning. For example, antonyms for the word *perfect* are partial, imperfect, bad, and flawed.

Using the WordPerfect Thesaurus

The thesaurus is incredible easy to use. When you want to work with a particular word, just place the cursor on that word (or in the preceding space) and press the

Alt->F1 key combination.

For example, in Figure 10.4, you can see the screen that results from placing the cursor on the word perfect and using the key combination just mentioned.

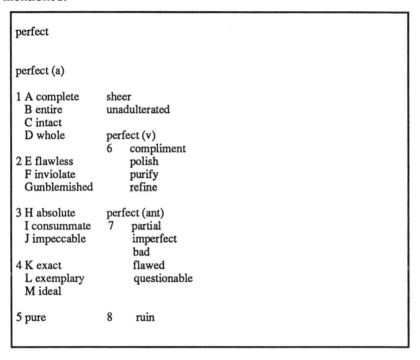

Figure 10.4 The thesaurus screen

The Thesaurus Screen

What you see in Figure 10.4 is the WordPerfect thesaurus screen for the word *perfect*.

What you see in the screen are listing of words first organized by part of speech. The word perfect can be an adjective (a) as in *It was a perfect dive*, or a verb (v) as in *We will have to perfect the formula*. You can see antonyms (ant) for the word perfect as partial, imperfect, etc.

These words are arranged in as many columns as the thesaurus needs. In this example, it is only two columns, but it could be three or more.

When more than three columns are filled, you can use the right and left arrow keys to go from column to column.

At the bottom of the thesaurus screen is the menu of options that are available.

Replace Word - Option #1

When you wan to replace a word with one that is in the list of words on the thesaurus screen, you begin by entering the number of the group to which the word belongs.

When you enter "1", WordPerfect will ask you for the letter of the word which represents the one you want to replace the word that originally started the thesaurus search (which in this case was the word perfect).

For example, if you wanted to replace the word perfect with the word exact, you would press the

1,k

key combination and the word exact would then appear in document.

But what if you wanted to replace the word *perfect* with the word *flawed* (which is in the second column that has no letters)? Using the right and left arrow keys, switches the alignment of the letters from one column to the next. So pressing the right arrow key once, could select letter J and the word flawed would replace the word perfect in your document.

View Document - Option #2

This is a terrific option. Ever notice that when you have to go to another WordPerfect screen that you would like somehow to be able to see what you are doing while you are making some kind of change?

Using the View Document option allows you to scoot around your document and see how a word is being used or get a feel for the context within which it appears before you make any decision about replacing it. In other words, this option suspends the actual operation of the thesaurus until you press the F7 key upon which WordPerfect returns you to where you were.

Use this option to check on what you intend to replace and where it is located so you are sure that you are making the substitution that you want.

Look Up Word - Option #3

You can extend your investigation into what is the correct word (or the one that sounds best) by using option #3 where WordPerfect looks up a word from the list of words on the thesaurus screen.

For example, let's take the word *perfect,* and lets look up the word whole. When this is done, WordPerfect considers the word whole to be a new word that the thesaurus is working on, and you see a compete listing for that new word.

You get the same result as if you used the *Alt->F1* key combination when the cursor was placed on the word whole.

Using the look up option you can continue to "tree" through sets of words until you find the one that you want and then use option #1 to place it into the text.

On any WordPerfect thesaurus screen some of the words have "bullets" (or solid circles) next to them and some do not. Words with bullets next to them are called *headwords*. You can only look up another headword from inside a thesaurus screen.

For example, *complete* is a headword but *unblemished* is not. If you tried to look up the word unblemished, you would get a Word not found message.

Clear Column - Option #4

Too much stuff on the screen! Want to get back to where you were? Use option #4 to clear the columns, which is handy if you want to begin with a new word (using option #3).

What good work. Now that you can spell and have almost 200,000 words at your fingertips, it's time to move on to using WordPerfect to create an outline, an often used tool for guiding or summarizing writing.

11
Creating an Outline

Remember those days in elementary school when you would have to an outline and you thought that you would go crazy trying to figure out what went under what and what went where?

Well, the elementary school days might be over, but your outlining days might not be. Outlines can be very valuable writing tools which can help you a variety of ways.

Why Outlines Are Important

There are at least three reasons why learning how to outline and using outlines in your writing activities can be of great benefit.

First, they can provide you with a framework or a guide to your writing. Many writers use outlines in this way by first creating an outline and writing from that.

Second, an outline can serve as a summary of a written document. Depending upon the number of levels in the outline and the degree of detail, outlines are often very effective tools for summarizing long documents.

Third, the very process of doing an outline can help you think through the different topics and issues that you might want to include in a document.

What WordPerfect's outlining feature can offer you is a quick and easy way to get ideas down in outline form and then be able to manipulate these ideas until you are satisfied that the form and format of the outline reflects its purpose.

What an Outline Looks Like

An outline consists of different levels that organize information in a hierarchical fashion. What this means is that information at a lower level is subsumed by the level or the section that it belongs to. WordPerfect allows you to have up to eight levels of information in an outline.

In Figure 11.1, you can see what the headings for an eight level outline would look like. Not only are lower levels set off from the ones that are immediately above them, but the level indicators for the outlines (the number or letter indicating the level such as I. or 3. or a)) change as well.

```
I. This is level 1.
    A. This is level 2.
        1.This is level 3.
            a. This is level 4.
                (1)This is level 5.
                    (a) This is level 6.
                        i) This is level 7.
                            a) This is level 8
```

Figure 11.1 The eight levels of a WordPerfect outline

Doing a Simple Outline

Figure 11.2 shows you a simple outline, which will be recreated here to illustrate the steps you would take in creating a WordPerfect outline.

```
I.Children and Families
        A.New Developments
        B.Theories of Family Development
        C.Methods for Studying Families
II.Understanding the Adolescent
        A.Physical Changes
        B.Intellectual Changes
        C.Social Changes
                1.Peer Groups
                2.Relationships with Parents
```

Figure 11.2 A sample outline

Creating An Outline 145

To create a simple outline, follow these steps.

1. Use the *Shift->F5* key combination to reveal the Date/Outline menu shown in Figure 11.3.
2. Select option #4, Outline.
3. Press the return key and you will see the first level indicator appear on your screen. Since WordPerfect's default outline style is a Roman numeral I for the first level heading that is what you will see. Enter the heading Children and Families and press the return key.
When you do this, WordPerfect will automatically insert the next first level headings which will be a II.
4. Since the next heading is a second level heading titled New Developments, press the Tab key once and WordPerfect will create a second level heading. In this case, the letter A. will appear on the screen and you should enter the heading, *New Directions*. Continue entering headings for levels B. and C. These are all second level headings which you access using the tab key after a hard carriage return (that is pressing the Enter or Return key).

```
1 Date Text; 2 Date Code; 3 Date Format; 4 Outline; 5 Para Num; 6 Define: 0
```

Figure 11.3 The Date/Outline menu for starting an outline

The general rule is that every time you press the Tab key when using the outline feature, you will move to the next lowest level heading.

Tip *If you accidentally go beyond the level that you want and for example Tab until level a. instead of level 1., use the Delete or Backspace key to move back to the previous level of the outline. You can also use the Shift->Tab key combination to accomplish the same thing.*

5. Once you have entered all of the levels of the outline as shown for example, in Figure 11.2 you are finished. Use the

Shift->F5,4

key combination to exit the outline feature.
Congratulations! You've shown your WordPerfect expertise through the creation of a simple outline.

Working with an Outline

Even though you completed an outline and perhaps saved it, you may not yet be finished. Perhaps you want to edit what is there, change levels, or insert or delete existing levels and topics. Once you finish an outline, WordPerfect provides many different tools to work with and modify that outline.

Editing an Outline

You can edit an outline as you can any other WordPerfect document using the cursor keys. There is one important thing however, that you have to keep in mind.

WordPerfect numbers outline headings as if they were paragraphs. If you delete a heading, either the entire line or just the heading level indicator itself (such as I. or 1. or a), then the outline will automatically renumber itself.

Deleting a Section

For example, in Figure 11.4, headings II.A. and II.B. were deleted. As

```
I. Children and Families
        A. New Developments
        B. Theories of Family Development
        C. Methods for Studying Families
II. Understanding the Adolescent
        A. Social Changes
                1. Peer Groups
                2. Relationships with Parents
        B. Political Concerns
```

Figure 11.4 Automatic renumbering of levels.

you can see, what was level C. is now A. and what was level D. is now B. WordPerfect will automatically renumber headings as you delete others.

Inserting a New Section

There is always additional information to add to any document and outlines are no different. For example, let's say that you wanted to add an additional second level heading called Emotional Development, after IIB. Intellectual Changes in the original outline shown in Figure 11.2. Once this is done, Emotional Development becomes IIC. and Social Concerns becomes IID. and so on.

To add a new level to an outline, follow these steps.

1. Place the cursor at the end of the line after the heading which you want to insert the new level and press the return.
2. Turn on the outline feature using the *Shift->F5,4* key combination.
3. Use the tab key to go to the level you want,, which in this case is the second level.
4. Enter the new heading, Emotional Development.
5. Use the Down arrow cursor key to scroll through the different levels as you do, they will automatically renumber.

Once again WordPerfect automatically renumbers when new headings are inserted as you can see in Figure 11.5.

```
I.Families
        A.New Developments
        B.Theories of Family Development
        C.Methods for Studying Families
II.Understanding the Adolescent
        A.Physical Changes
        B.Intellectual Changes
        C.Emotional Development
        D.Social Changes
                1.Peer Groups
                2.Relationships with Parents
        E.Political Concerns
```

Figure 11.5 Inserting a new topic.

Moving Sections

There may also be times when you will need to move a section of an outline from one place in the outline to another. It's probably no surprise to you that when you do move the section, WordPerfect will automatically renumber things to fit the new order.

For example, in Figure 11.6 the entire second section was moved by creating a block, using *Ctrl->F4,1,1* key combination, relocating the cursor to the top of the outline, and then pressing the Return key. Voila! The section was moved and renumbered.

```
I.Understanding the Adolescent
        A.Physical Changes
        B.Intellectual Changes
        C.Social Changes
                1.Peer Groups
                2.Relationships with Parents
        D.Political Concerns
II.Children and Families
        A.New Developments
        B.Theories of Family Development
        C.Methods for Studying Families
```

Figure 11.6 Moving sections within an outline.

Unlike other cases, when you move things, you do not have to have the outline feature turned on for WordPerfect to automatically renumber the headings.

Promoting an Outline Section

You can not only change the order of items in a paragraph, but you can also promote an item from one level to the next highest level.

For example, in Figure 11.7 the second item in the outline

I.A. New Developments

will be promoted to become item II. by following these steps.

1. Turn on the outline feature.
2. Place the cursor on the level indicator. In this case, it is the letter A.
3. Now use the Backspace or Delete key (once in this case) to move from a level 2 heading (A., B., C. etc.) to a level 1 heading (I., II., III., etc.).
   When this is done, you will see how the item has been promoted.

> I. Children and Families
> II. New Developments
>   A. Theories of Family Development
>   B. Methods for Studying Families
> III. Understanding the Adolescent
>   A. Physical Changes
>   B. Intellectual Changes
>   C. Social Changes
>   1. Peer Groups
>   2. Relationships with Parents
>   3. Political Concerns

Figure 11.7 Promoting an item.

Demoting an Outline Section

You may also need to demote an item from one level to the next lowest level as well as promote it.

For example, in Figure 11.8 the last item in the outline II.D. Political Concerns will be demoted to become item II.C.3. by following these steps.

1. Turn on the outline feature.
2. Place the cursor on the level indicator. In this case, it is the letter D.
3. Now use the Tab key (once in this case) to move from a level 2 heading (A., B., C. etc.) to a level three heading (1., 2., 3., etc.).

When this is done, you will see how the item has been demoted.

```
I.Children and Families
        A.New Developments
        B.Theories of Family Development
        C.Methods for Studying Families
III.Understanding the Adolescent
        A.Physical Changes
        B.Intellectual Changes
        C.Social Changes
                1.Peer Groups
                2.Relationships with Parents
                3.Political Concerns
```

Figure 11.8 Demoting an item.

More Than One Outline?

You may find that you need to create more than one outline in the same document. For example, let's say that you have the outline shown in Figure 11.2, and you want to begin a new one on an entirely different topic.

Oops! When you begin the outlining process, you will find that the first level will be III, and not I. That's because WordPerfect thinks that you are just continuing the existing outline!

What you need to do in this case is use the

Shift->F5,6,1,1

key combination to begin the sequence at the first level of the outline. This will allow you to begin all of your outlines anew.

Outline Styles

Perhaps you don't like the default outlining indicators shown in Figure 11.1 and want to try some others. That's fine since WordPerfect offers you a variety of styles.

Choosing a New Outline Style

As you know, WordPerfect defaults to the outline style that you see in Figure 11.2. To select a different outline style, follow these steps.

1. Move the cursor to the top of the completed outline.
2. Use the *Shift->F5,6* key combination or reveal the *Paragraph Number Definition* screen.
3. Select the definition you want to use.
4. Press F7.
5. Return to your document and move the down cursor arrow. Boom! A new set of markings.

You can assign new definitions either before you begin creating an outline, or after you are finished. The 5 steps that were just described was used to change the definition after an outline was already created. This may be your choice if you want to experiment with different styles of headings.

Numbering Paragraphs

Numbering paragraphs is a great deal like working with outlines. It's for that reason that both outlining and paragraph features use the same reveal code in a WordPerfect document

[Para Num: Automatic]

In Figure 11.9, you can see how there are three paragraphs that were automatically numbered by WordPerfect. To number paragraphs, as they are entered, follow these stops.

1. Use the *Shift->F5,5,<ret>* key combination to turn on the automatic paragraph numbering. When you do this, you will see the I. indicating the first paragraph.
2. Begin entering the text of the first paragraph. Use a hard return when you are finished with the first paragraph to move to the next line.
3. Repeat step 1 each time you want to add a new paragraph. Instead of a I. you will see a II. on the screen and you are ready to enter your second paragraph. WordPerfect automatically renumbers paragraphs, but you have to tell it each time to begin the paragraph numbering operation.

> I. This is the first paragraph.
> II. This is the second paragraph.
> III. This is the third paragraph.

Figure 11.9 Numbering paragraphs.

That's all there is to simple numbering a set of paragraphs.
If you need to, you can change the level, by using the same techniques that you learned for promoting and demoting outline entries.

Inserting a New Paragraph

When it comes time to insert a new paragraph, follow these steps.

1. Place the cursor at the position you want to insert the new paragraph.
2. Use the *SHift->F5,5,<ret>* key combination to turn on paragraph numbering. You will see the next number in the sequence of paragraphs.
3. Enter the new paragraph.
4. When you move the cursor down or rewrite the screen, you will see all of the paragraph numbers change so that are in sequence.

You can also number paragraphs after they have been entered. Just place the cursor at the beginning of the paragraph and begin paragraph numbering. At each paragraph, WordPerfect will assign a number in sequence.

Numbering Styles

Just as with outlines, if you do not like the scheme being used for numbering paragraphs, you can change it with option #6 on the Date/Outline menu.

Simply select a style (or define your own) the definition screen. For example, in Figure 11.10, you can see two styles of numbering paragraphs, the default and the legal style (option #4 on the Paragraph number definition screen).

> *The Default Option*
> I. This is paragraph 1.
> II.This is paragraph 2.
>   A. This is sub-paragraph 1.
>
> *The Legal Option*
> 1.This is paragraph 1.
> 2.This is paragraph 2.
>   2.1This is sub-paragraph 1.

Figure 11.10 The default and legal options for numbering paragraphs.

Numbering Other Things; Figures and Lists

Outlines and paragraphs are really just "things" that WordPerfect knows to number and renumber. For example, WordPerfect does not know or care if a paragraph is one or 1,000 lines long as long as it ends with a hard return.

Because of this, you can use the paragraph numbering features to assign numbers to items in a list or figure or tables in a manuscript and not worry about adding or deleting a figure since each one will be changed accordingly.

For example, let's say that you have Figures 1, 2, and 3 in a chapter. You could use the paragraph numbering feature. Each time you do so, WordPerfect enters a reveal code and keep[s track of numbers. What this means is that the addition of a new Figure (using the appropriate key combination which is *Shift->F5,5)* turns on the paragraph numbering and the next number will be inserted. This is a great time saver for people who are always adding and deleting tables figures, drawing, etc,. from a manuscript and who have a difficult time keeping track of numbers and such.

12
Sorting

If you have ever needed to alphabetize a long list of names, or references, or a numbered set of items then WordPerfect's sort feature is the saving grace you've been looking for. WordPerfect can take any number of lines or paragraphs and sort them either alphabetically or numerically in ascending (from, a to z or from 1 to 10 for example), or descending (from z to a or from 10 to 1 for example) order.

Basic Sorting

WordPerfect begins the sorting routine when you use the

Ctrl->F9,2

key combination to produce the menu that you see in Figure 12.1.

```
1 Merge; 2 Sort; 3 Sort/Order: 0
```

Figure 12.1 The initial sort menu

Before we explore some of the options that are opened to you when you sort (and use it with the merge feature), let's first go through a simple sorting of a list of items things from the hardware store. Here's the list of 10 items, presented in unsorted order.

nails
glue
sandpaper
hammer
saw
rope
seed
paint
brush

Let's also assume that this list exists as a separate file that is now active (that is, it has been retrieved and is on your screen). To sort this list, follow these steps.

1. Use the *Ctrl->F9,2* key combination to begin the sort operation.
2. When you begin the sorting operation, you will see a prompt in the lower left hand corner of your screen:

Input file to sort: (Screen)

You need to indicate whether you want to sort what is currently on the screen (the active file) or you want to specify another file.
   For our purposes, hit the Enter or Return key since the material on the screen is to be sorted.
3. Once this is done, another prompt

Output file for sort: (Screen)

appears, asking you where you want the sorted list to be placed. If you want it returned to the screen, press the return key. If you want it to be sent to another destination (such as another file) enter the file name and press the Enter or Return key.
4. Once you have told WordPerfect where the text to sort comes from and where it is going, you will see the sort screen shown in Figure 12.2.
5. Now press option 1, *Perform Action* and WordPerfect will sort the list in ascending order so that it looks like this

brush
glue
hammer
nails
paint
rope
sandpaper
saw
seed

Simple? You bet.

```
nails
glue
sandpaper
hammer
saw
rope
seed
paint
brush
                                                                Doc 3 Pg
1 Ln 1" Pos 1"
{                                                                      }

-------------------------------Sort by Line-------------------------------
Key Typ Field Word    Key Typ Field Word    Key Type Field Word
 1   a   1    1        2                     3
 4                     5                     5
 7                     8                     9

Action                 Order                 Type
Sort                   Ascending             Line Sort

1 Perform Action; 2 View; 3 Keys; 4 Select; 5 Action; 6 Order; 7 Type: 0
```

Figure 12.2 The sort screen

The Sort Screen

In Figure 12.2, you see the sort screen that acts as central control for all sorting activities.

In the simple that you just completed, you sorted by line in ascending order which will be the default if you have not yet done any other sorting operations. Let's go through the 7 different options that are available on

> ***Macro*** Here's a macro to just that for sorting by line in ascending order.
>
> 1. Ctrl->F10
> 2. sortla,ret
> 3. sort in ascending order
> 4. Ctrl->F9,2
> 5. <ret>,<ret>
> 6. 1
> 7. Ctrl->F10

the sort screen that illustrate the power of this feature.

Perform Action - Option #1

This option will perform whatever set of instructions you provide WordPerfect after decisions such as order of sorting (ascending or descending, line or paragraph, etc. have been made).

View - Option #2

Remember in Chapter 10 how you could use the View feature to examine the context within which a word appears when using the thesaurus?

The view option on the sort screen is used the same way. When using View, you can scroll through a document to see what is contained, for example, in the list or set of paragraphs that are to be sorted.

Keys - Option #3

WordPerfect will gladly sort a list of items, and will do so using the first character in each of the items on the list. What if you want to sort on something other than the first character of the first word or number? That's where the Keys option comes in.

For example, in Figure 12.3 is a list of first and last names. You want to sort by last name. What you need to tell WordPerfect is what word you

Sorting 159

want to sort on. WordPerfect considers each set of characters separated

---

Before Sorting

Sara Salkind
Joy Friedman
Jon Ott
Mohammed El-Hodiri
Phil Montgomery
Ed Morris
Debbie Altus
John Poggio
Leni Welitoff
Phyllis Retsky

After Sorting

Debbie Altus
Mohammed El-Hodiri
Joy Friedman
Phil Montgomery
Ed Morris
Jon Ott
John Poggio
Phyllis Retsky
Sara Salkind
Leni Welitoff

Figure 12.3 Sorting on last name

by a space to be a separate word. To use the key option, follow these steps.

1. Use the *Ctrl->F9,2* key combination to begin the sort operation.
2. Select option 3, Keys.
3. Now you need to decide whether you are sorting on alphanumeric information (which we are in this case since they are names beginning with letters) or numerical information. The default is alphanumeric so TYP (for type of field) can be left alone.

4. You can sort on up to 9 different key types (alphanumeric or numeric), fields, or words.

In this example, there is only 1 field consisting of 2 key words (the first and last name). Use the cursor arrows to move to the word Word on the first key and replace the 1 with a 2 since you want to sort on the second word in the first field. Press the F7 key to return to the sort screen you see in Figure 12.3.

```
Sara Salkind 2 13
Joy Friedman 2 13
Jon Ott 1 21
Mohammed El-Hodiri 1 24
Phil Montgomery 1 7
Ed Morris 1 12
Debbie Altus 2 31
John Poggio 1 27
Leni Welitoff 2 29


Doc 3 Pg 1 Ln 1" Pos 1"
{
                                          }
-------------------------------Sort by Line-------------------------------
Key Typ Field Word                Key Typ Field Word
Key Typ Field Word
1   n   1   3                     2   n   1   4
3
4                                 5
6
7                                 8
9
Select
key1=2 * key2>15

Action                            Order
Type
Select and sort                   Ascending
Line sort

1 Perform Action; 2 View; 3 Keys; 4 Select; 5 Action; 6 Order; 7 Type: 0
```

Figure 12.4 Using the select option

4. Now select Option 1 which will sort the list in ascending order using the second word in the first field as a key.

Select - Option #4

WordPerfect is a thinking person's word processor and the select sort feature lets you select out certain cases based on their attributes.

For example, in Figure 12.4 you see a list of names, codes for their sex (1 if they are male and 2 if they are female) and their age. In this list, first and last name are key words 1 and 2, sex is key word 3, and age is key word 4.

Here are the steps you wold follow to select all females who are over 15 years of age.

1. Use the *Ctrl >F9,2* key combination to begin the sort operation.
2. Select Option 3, Keys and designate the first key you want to sort on as numeric, word 3. Now designate the second key you want to sort on as numeric, word 4.
3. Select the select option, and enter the following

$$key1=2 * key2>15$$

Here's what you are telling WordPerfect to d:;
Select all of those records where sex (which is key 1) equals 2 and all those records where age (which is key word 2) is greater than 15. You can see the final sort command in Figure 12.5. The * in the select statement represents the word AND.

4. Press the F7 key.
5. Select option 1 for Perform Action and the sorted list will appear as shown below:

Leni Welitoff 2 29
Debbie Altus 2 31

Here's a listing of the major operators and what they do:

If you want to select	Use
11 and 13 years olds	key2=11+13
only 24 year olds	key2=24
only males	key1<>2
those older than 24	key2>24
those younger than 13	key<13
those 13 or older	key>=13
those 13 or younger	key<=13

Words and Fields

As we pointed out earlier, in a record, words are defined as those strings of characters that are separated by a space. A field, is defined as those strings of characters that are separated by tabs. If you wanted the list of names, sex, and age shown in Figure 12.5 to be aligned along a tab stop, such as;

Sara Salkind   2   13
Joy Friedman   2   11

use the tab key to separate information *but not spaces.*

When you do this however, you need to define the keys as field and not words. For example, the same sort operation as was performed in Figure 12.5, would have key 1 sorted on field 2 and key 2 sorted on field 3, since the first and last name are field 1 (since they are only separated by a space).

Action - Option #5

If you want to select records without sorting them, use option 5. For example, you might want to select all the females in the list shown in Figure 12.4, but not be concerned about he order in which they appear you would select option 2 on the Action menu, which is Select only.

Order - Option #6

You can sort in either ascending or descending order. Ascending order is from a to z if you are sorting alphanumerically and 1 to 100 (and above) if you are sorting numerically. Descending order is from z to a if you are sorting alphanumerically and 100 (or above) to 1 if you are sorting numerically.

WordPerfect's default is to sort in ascending order, popularly known as alphabetically.

Type - Option #7

Up to now, all of the sorting that has been done has been by line. You can also sort by paragraph if you select option 3 on the Type menu. Before we go through an example, you have to remember that

---

Before sorting by paragraph

Finkelhor, D. and Korbin, J. (1988) Child abuse as an international issue. Child Abuse & Neglect, 12, 3-23.

Vikan, Arne. (1983) A note on the formal operational interpretation of adolescent psychological development. Scandinavian Journal of Psychology, 24, 339-342.

Rauh, V., Achenbach, T., Nurcombe, B, Howell, C., and Teti, D. (1988) Minimizing adverse effects of low birthweight: Four-year results of an early intervention program, Child Development, 59, 544-553.

After sorting by paragraph

Finkelhor, D. and Korbin, J. (1988) Child abuse as an international issue. Child Abuse & Neglect, 12, 3-23.

Rauh, V., Achenbach, T., Nurcombe, B, Howell, C., and Teti, D. (1988) Minimizing adverse effects of low birthweight: Four-year results of an early intervention program, Child Development, 59, 544-553.

Vikan, Arne. (1983) A note on the formal operational interpretation of adolescent psychological development. Scandinavian Journal of Psychology, 24, 339-342.

Figure 12.5 Sorting by paragraph.

WordPerfect defines a paragraph by any set of text that is followed by two hard carriage returns.

For example, a very common use for sorting by paragraph is when you want to alphabetize a set of references that might belong at the end of a paper. Figure 12.5 shows three references in unsorted and sorted order.

Tip When WordPerfect sorts, it remembers the configuration of the last sort that it did. It does not reset itself to a simple line sort with only 1 fields or key. If you are going to do more than one sort, remember that each of the sorts needs to be redefined from the beginning.

Sorting and Blocks

When you first started to sort lines, you needed to tell WordPerfect what was to be sorted and where the sorted material was to go. You saw these prompts on the screen since the assumption was that everything in the file needed to be sorted. In many cases, however, you might only want to sort part of a file, such as a list contained in a document.

To sort only part of a document, simple create a block of the material you want to sort and the press the *Ctrl->F9* key combination and you will go right to the sort screen.

13
WordPerfect Math

The WordPerfect Corporation offers a terrific spreadsheet or electronic ledger named *PlanPerfect* that you can use to keep track of numbers and manipulate numerical information. But, if you don't have this software package, you can always turn to the *math* feature of WordPerfect to get many of the same things done.

Math Basics

There are six steps in the use of WordPerfect's math feature.

First, you need to move the cursor to the place where you want to use the math function and then set a tab for each of the math columns that you are going to create.

Second, define the characteristics of the math columns through the use of the *Alt->F7,2* key combination.

Third, turn on the math feature using the *Alt->F7,1* key combination.

Fourth, enter the information that you want into the set of columns. This includes both numbers and text.

Fifth, enter the formulas and the operators that you want to use to act on the information in the math columns.

Finally, turn the math feature off using the *Alt->F7,1* key once again.

Let's look at each of these in detail as we set up a personal budget for a three month period shown in Figure 13.1.

	January	February	March
Income	2,343	2,343	2,343
Total	2,343	2,343	2,343
Expenses			
Rent	225	225	225
Food	185	185	185
Car	325	325	325
Fun	125	125	125
School	65	65	65
Insur	52	52	52
Misc	75	75	75
Total	1,052	1,052	1,052
Grand Total	3,395	3,395	3,395

Figure 13.1 A personal budget for three months.

Tip *Before you begin working with WordPerfect math, always plan ahead and be sure what you want to use as column headings, what data will be entered and so forth. It's much easier to do this than to have to go back and begin editing text and numbers.*

Setting Columns

The first step is to set the tabs at the columns you want to define the information. In this case, tabs will be set at columns 30, 40 and 50 using the *Shift->F8,1,8* key combination as discussed in Chapter 3.

Once this is done, it's clear what the matrix will look like. You can see in Figure 13.1 how labels were entered down as well as across and different categories of budget items were inserted.

Defining the Math Columns

The first step in defining math columns is to select option #2 from the Math menu that you see in Figure 13.2.

---
1 Math On; 2 Math Def; 3 Column On/Off; 4 Column Def: 0

Figure 13.2 The math menu

Once Option #2 is selected, you will see the Math *Definition* screen shown in Figure 13.3. Using the options available on the screen, you will define each of the columns. Since this math matrix has three months across, you will need to define three of the columns, A, B, and C.

Math Definition		Use arrow keys to position cursor	
Columns		A B C D E F G H I J K L M N O P Q R S T	
Type		2 2 2 2 2 2 2 2 2 2 2 2 2 2 2 2 2 2 2 2	
Negative Numbers Number of Digits to the Right (0-4)		) 2 2 2 2 2 2 2 2 2 2 2 2 2 2 2 2 2 2 2 2	
Calculation Formulas	1 2 3 4		
Type of Column: 0 = Calculation	1 = Text	2 = Numeric	3 = Total
Negative Numbers			

Figure 13.3 The math definition screen

Types of Columns

In WordPerfect math, you can define any columns as one of four kinds.

The first is *Calculation* (0) and is used to perform a calculation of some kind across a row of columns (not up and down).

The second is *Text* (1) which is used to enter the description for a row of information. That's how the various row entries that you see in Figure 13.1 were entered. You'll note that there are a total of five columns, the first two of which are text and the last three of which are numeric.

The next kind of column *Numeric* (2) is the most often used. Here numbers are entered into columns as was the information in Figure 13.1.

Finally, the last type of column you can define is a *Total* (3), used to display totals.

The math definition for the screen that you see in Figure 13.1 has five columns, two of which are text (A and B) and three of which are Numeric (C, D and E). The math definition screen for this configuration is shown in Figure 13.4.

Math Definition	Use arrow keys to position cursor
Columns	A B C D E F G H I J K L M N O P
Type	1 1 2 2 2 2 2 2 2 2 2 2 2 2 2 2
Negative Numbers	)) - - -)))))))))))
Number of Digits to the Right (0-4)	0 0 0 0 0 2 2 2 2 2 2 2 2 2 2 2

Figure 13.4 The math definition screen for the budget

You can also see in Figure 13.3 that negative numbers can be stated in parenthesis (45.65) representing -45.65, or simply using a minus sign before the number. You just have to tell WordPerfect what you intentions are. In most financial dealing, the parenthesis are used to indicate a negative number. In mathematical calculations, a minus sign is used.

Second, you need to define that number of digits that will be to the right of the decimal point, from 0 to 4 in the final calculated results. For example, for most financial transactions, large numbers are rounded off so there will be no digits to the right of the decimal. If you were working with numbers and wanted to include dollars and cents, you would have two digits to the right of the decimal, such as in the numbers 45.32 and 67.66.

Tip Don't include $ when using WordPerfect math. WordPerfect tries to read it as a number and cannot do so successfully.

Once you have defined the columns that will be used, the type each one is, how negative numbers will be expressed and how many digits will be shown in the final calculation, press the *F7* exit key to return to the math menu.

Turning Math On

Now that you are back to the math menu, just select option #1, *Math On*, and you will see the Math On message in the lower left hand corner of the screen.

Entering Information

OK. Now you're ready to begin entering column and row headings and entering the information. Don't forget to use the *Tab* key to move from row to row.

The column headings (January, February and March) were first entered. Then the row headings, beginning with Income and Expenses and then the subcategories were entered as well. As you can see, the subcategories were offset one tab space and they make up their own column (Column B on the math definition screen shown in Figure 13.4).

Using Operators

As you can see in Figure 13.5, there are some +'s and ='s operators entered into the rows of figures.

These are operators and tell WordPerfect to perform some kind of an operation on the row of numbers of which they are a part. They are all operators that total up a set of numbers.

The plus operator (+) tells WordPerfect to create a subtotal of all the numbers above it. So placing a + in the column below income totals will sub-total that category of values. Likewise, the + under Total (for Expenses) will produce a total for that category.

The equal sign operator (=) totals sub-totals. In other words, the = sign at the bottom of the math sheet will total the sub-totals of the income and expense categories and provide a total sum of both.

The third operator, the asterisk (*) generates a total from other totals. It's relationship to the = operator is the same as the relationship between the + operator and the + operator; both the = and the * total totals from some other source.

	January	February	March
Income	2,343	2,343	2,343
Total	+	+	+
Expenses			
Rent	225	225	225
Food	185	185	185
Car	325	325	325
Fun	125	125	125
School	65	65	65
Insur	52	52	52
Misc	75	75	75
Total	+	+	+
Grand Total	=	=	=

Figure 13.5 The budget with operators

You can see in Figure 13.5 that you want to total income, then total expenses, and then total those values.

Calculating Values

Once the math sheet is constructed, and all the information and operators are present, it's time to calculate totals.

Simply use the *Alt->F7,2* key combination and WordPerfect will calculate values and show them on your screen as you can see in Figure 13.6. The operators show on the screen, but do not actually print when you produce a hard copy. There you have your basic math sheet, with calculations included.

Tip Make an error? If you entered the wrong value in a category, just edit the value and then recalculate using the Alt->F7,2 key combination. WordPerfect remembers everything else and will change all the other values that are dependent upon that one.

	January	February	March
Income	2,343	2,343	2,343
Total	2,343+	2,343+	2,343+
Expenses			
Rent	225	225	225
Food	185	185	185
Car	325	325	325
Fun	125	125	125
School	65	65	65
Insur	52	52	52
Misc	75	75	75
Total	1,052+	1,052+	1,052+
Grand Total	3,395=	3,395=	3,395=

Figure 13.6 After the calculation

Working with Calculation Formulas

A formula is a set of operators that perform a certain calculation and you can have up to four of them associated with any math definition screen.

In order to use a formula, you first have to go back into the math definition screen redefine some columns. Be careful! You are not proposing a new math definition, but only editing the existing one. For this reason, you need to place the cursor after the *[Math Def]* reveal code and before the *[Math On]* code, and then select *Math Def* (Option #2) from the Math menu.

Here a column will be added that totals the amounts across the three months for all categories. The new math definition screen is shown in Figure 13.7. To add a formula, follow these steps:

1. Return to the math definition screen by using the *Alt->F7,2* key combination. Remember to be sure that your cursor is after the *[Math Def]* reveal code so that you are redefining the correct screen.
2. Define column F (the new sixth column) as a Calculation with an 0.
3. When you do this, you will see under Calculation Formulas (of which

```
Math Definition                    Use arrow keys to position cursor

Columns                            A B C D E F G H I J K L M N O P Q R

Type                               1 1 2 2 2 0 2 2 2 2 2 2 2 2 2 2 2 2

Negative Numbers                   ) ) ) ) ) ) ) ) ) ) ) ) ) ) ) ) ) )

Number of Digits to                0 0 0 0 0 2 2 2 2 2 2 2 2 2 2 2 2 2
the Right (0-4)

Calculation            1    F    C+D+E
Formulas               2
                       3
                       4

Type of Column:
        0 = Calculation    1 = Text      2 = Numeric      3 = Total

Negative Numbers
        ( = Parentheses (50.00)          - = Minus Sign  - 50.00

Press Exit when done
```

Figure 13.7 The math sheet with a defined formula

you can have up to 4) a F next to the 1. That shows that column F is being defined. Now enter the formula

$$c+d+e$$

indicating that you want to add the values of column c and column d and column e.

4. Press the *F7* key and you have redefined the screen.

Now that the screen is redefined, turn math back on (if it was for some reason turned off), and place the cursor at the end of the last column of numbers (Column E - March). Now, each time you press the Tab key, WordPerfect knows that it is a calculated column and will insert a ! sign indicating such.

You final step is to recalculate the entire sheet using the *Alt->F7,2* key combination and you will see the final math sheet with all totals as shown in Figure 13.8.

WordPerfect Math

	January	February	March	
Income	2,343	2,343	2,343	
Total	2,343	2,343	2,343	7,029.00
Expenses				
Rent	225	225	225	675.00
Food	185	185	185	555.00
Car	325	325	325	975.00
Fun	125	125	125	375.00
School	65	65	65	195.00
Insur	52	52	52	156.00
Misc	75	75	75	225.00
Total	1,052	1,052	1,052	3,156.00
Grand Total	3,395	3,395	3,395	10,175.00

Figure 13.8 The math sheet with all calculations

Tip Want to average across columns? Define a formula as you just did and use the

+/

key combination in the appropriate Calculation Formulas spot. When you turn math on and recalculate, you'll find that the +/ combination produces an average or mean value across the columns where it is placed. When you are all done, just turn math off and you can treat your created math sheet as any other file, ready to be edited as you see fit.

On now to controlling those very big WordPerfect documents that used to be absolutely impossible to work with, but with WordPerfect's master document feature, they are a pleasure!

14
The Master Document

One of the reasons why WordPerfect is such a popular word processor is because it has features for people who work with very long and complex documents, such as lengthy reports, books with lots of chapters, and so on.

Picture this. You have worked long and hard on a very difficult project and you are ready to print it out. After you retrieve each individual file and "chain" them together so that all 400 pages are intact, you discover an error in one part of the manuscript. Should you correct it there and ignore it in the file where the error was originally created? Go back and correct the original and then rebuild the entire 400 page file (a tedious and painstaking task)? Read on - WordPerfect has a wonderful solution.

One of the golden rules of word processing when long documents are involved is to work in several small files and not to work on the entire document as one huge file. The best reason for this is that if you should make a fatal error (such as forgetting to save) or your computer crashes, then you will only lose the amount of work that you are currently working on rather than the entire project. Another reason is that shorter files save faster and save you time.

But, a major shortcoming of many word processing systems is the inability to combine files while still maintaining the integrity of each individual file. In addition, when you are finished, you would like to be able to generate a complete and assembled document for which you can do such things as generate a tale of contents or an index, print out all at once, or any one of many different formatting operations for *all* the files together.

That's where WordPerfect's *Master Document* feature comes in.

What is a Master Document?

A *master document* is a file that consists of a set of *subdocuments*. A *subdocument* is simply a file that becomes part of a master document.

For example, here are the file names that have already been created that make up a five chapter book, including a preface, a table of contents, and an index.

>*pref (Preface)*
>*toc (Table of Contents)*
>*c1 (Chapter 1)*
>*c2 (Chapter 2)*
>*c3 (Chapter 3)*
>*c4 (Chapter 4)*
>*c5 (Chapter 5)*
>*index (Index)*

Each of these files becomes a subdocument which will be used to create the master document that will be called *book*.

By far, one of the most attractive features of using a master document is that it will always represent the set of subdocuments no matter what is changed in any one subdocument. What this means is that you can make all the changes you want in any one of the subfiles, and the master document will chang as well.

In addition, after the master document is created, you can even make changes in that and WordPerfect will automatically make the corresponding subdocument chanes as well! Talk about smart!

Creating a Master Document

Creating a master document consists of inserting subdocuments into a file and then saving that file under a new name.

Follow these steps to create a master document for the files that were listed above.

1. Select option #2 (SubDoc) from the *Mark Text* menu using the *Alt->F5,2* key combination. When you do this, you will see the prompt

>*Subdoc Filename:*

in the lower left hand corner of the monitor. WordPerfect is asking you for the name of the first file that you would like to insert either into another existing file or to use to begin a new master document.

In this example, the first file name is *pref*. When that file name is entered, WordPerfect inserts the subdocument at the cursor location as a box (as you can see here:

Subdoc: Pref

2. Next, use the *Alt->F5* key combination for the Subdoc Filename prompt and then enter the name of the next subdocument that you want included. Continue to do this until all of the subdocuments you want to insert into the master document have been entered.

3. Finally, save the master document under some unique name using the regular F10 save steps.

Great! You have now created a master document.

> *Macro* Here's a macro that automatically gives you the SubDoc Filename: prompt and allows you to enter the name of the file. You'll notice that in step 6 the macro calls itself. This will allow you to enter as many subdocuments as you wold like. When you are finished, use the F1 button to cancel the macro operation.
>
> 1. Ctrl->F10
> 2. sub,<ret>
> 3. prompts user for subdocument name 4. Alt->F5,2
> 5. Ctrl->PgUp,1,<ret> (pause for name of subdocument)
> 6. Alt->F10,subdoc,<ret>
> 7. Ctrl->F10

Working with Subdocuments

Once you have created and saved the master document using a unique file name, you can then begin to work with it. The two reveal codes for any subdocument are

[Subdoc Start:] The subdocument content goes here [Subdoc End:]

Editing within a Master Document

You can use all of WordPerfect's editing features within a master document. For example, you can delete a subdocument by placing the cursor after the [Subdoc End] reveal code and backspacing.

Any text that is included inside of a subdocument when expanded can be edited in the normal fashion. You can block text and move it to another subdocument, and so forth.

Expanding a Document

A master document is convenient because you can use it to easily arrange a large set of subdocuments containing a great deal of information. There will also come the time when you need to work with the contents of the master document, such as when you want to assign page numbers or generate a table of contents or search and replace throughout a master document rather than doing it for each subdocument.

When you want to work with the contents of a master document, you need to *expand* the document revealing the contents of each subdocument.

To expand a master document you first need to retrieve the master document file. In this case, the file named "book" was retrieved and would appear on the screen.

Next, use the

Alt->F5,6

key combination and you will see the *Mark Text: Generate* screen shown in Figure 14.1. Here you can see that option #3 expands master documents.

When you select option #3, WordPerfect will give you a message on the status line as each of the individual files is expanded. When the master document is expanded, the contents of each of the subdocuments is revealed. You'll note that each of subdocuments also has an on screen start and end message that is labeled *Subdoc Start:* and *Subdoc End:*.

```
Mark Text: Generate

    1 -     Remove Redline Markings and Strikeout Text from Document

    2 -     Compare Screen and Disk Documents and Add Redline and
    Strikeout

    3 -     Expand Master Document

    4 -     Condense Master Document

    5 -     Generate Tables, Indexes, Automatic References, etc.

Selection: 0
```

Figure 14.1 The mark text screen

This is an expanded master document and the contents of it can be worked with as you work with any WordPerfect document.

Saving an Expanded Document

Once you have expanded a master document and edited its contents, you will want to save it as you would any other document. When you press the *F10* key to save, WordPerfect will give you the message;

Document is expanded, condense it? (Y/N) Yes

If you press *N*, WordPerfect will not condense the document.
If you press *Y*, then WordPerfect will condense the master document and in the process of doing so, save any changes that were made in documents as well as the entire master document. When WordPerfect does this saving, it gives you the status line message

Save Subdocuments (Y/N)? Yes

If you respond *N*, then WordPerfect will not save any of the subdocuments.
If you respond *Y*, then WordPerfect will ask you if you want to replace each of the subdocuments with the new version (if you made any

changes in the subdocument). The message you now see on the status line will be

Replace PREF? 1 Yes; 2 No; 3 Replace All Remaining: 0

If you chose option #1, whatever changes that were made in the subdocument called PREF will replace the old version of PREF. If you chose option #2, PREF will not be replaced. Want to be on the safe side? Chose option #3 which replaces all the remaining subdocuments with any that have been changed. While this might take a bit longer, it will save you from having to sit and enter Y's every time you are asked whether you want to replace a subdocument.

However, if you do have subdocuments where you don't want to replace them with the changes you made, then it's best to go through each one individually.

Condensing a Document

OK, so you've created a master document, and then you saved it for some work at a later time. Now you've retrieved it and worked on it again. You're now ready to condense and save that master document.

When you condense a master document using option #4 on the *Mark Text: Generate* menu (as you see in Figure 14.2), WordPerfect will ask you the same series of questions that it asks when you save a master document. It wants to know if you ant to replace the individual documents, or replace all of the remaining ones. Again depending on what it is that you need to do, select the option that best fits.

> Macro Here's a macro that condenses the current master document and replaces all the remaining files.
>
> 1. Ctrl->F10
> 2. cmd,<ret>
> 3. condenses a master document,<ret>
> 3. Alt->F5,6
> 4. 4,y,3 (here's where the document is condensed and all the subdocuments are replaced.
> 5. Ctrl->F10

More Subdocuments

You've seen how a master document consists of several subdocuments. There's no reason however, why a master document cannot become a subdocument of yet another master document.

For example, you might be assembling a series of tables, all of which are subdocuments that will then be placed in a master document titled *Tables: 1980-1985*. You might also create another set of subdocuments and place them into a master document titled *Tables: 1986-Present*. As a last step, you would create a third master document called *Tables: 1980-Present*, and the two subdocuments that would be placed into this master document would be *Tables: 1980-1985* and *Tables: 1986-Present*.

You can construct as many levels of master documents and subdocuments that you need. Just be sure you know where you are keeping things so that they do not get lost.

Printing a Master Document

A master document must first be expanded before the contents of the subdocuments will be printed. If you try to print out the contents of a master document before it is expanded, the only thing that will appear on your hard copy will be the listing of the subdocuments.

Generating Tables, Indexes and Lists

One of the great time saving features of using a master document is being able to generate a table of contents, for example, from a group of subdocuments.

When you do generate tables, indexes and lists WordPerfect will automatically expand the master document before the actual generation takes place.

15
WordPerfect Graphics

If there is any one thing that sets WordPerfect apart from the other word processing programs that are available, is the ease with which you integrate graphics into your WordPerfect documents.

As you work through this chapter keep the following in mind. WordPerfect does not create graphics. It creates a box or a space into which the graphic can be retrieved.

Let's Get Right To It!

This stuff is so much fun, (and you've waited so patiently up to now), let's jump right in and retrieve a graphic. You will learn about the nitty gritty of editing and such after this simple demonstration. To retrieve a graphic, follow these steps.

1. Use the *Alt->F9* key combination to begin WordPerfect Graphics.
2. Select Option #1 - Figure.
3. Select Option #1 - Create.
4. Select Option #1 - Filename and enter the following:

phone.WPG

This is the name of a WordPerfect graphic that came on your Font/Graphic disk. Be sure to provide the correct path where all of the *.WPG* (WordPerfect graphics) files are stored.

5. Now use the *Shift->F7,6* key combination to view the graphic as you see in Figure 15.1.

You probably notice that on your WordPerfect screen, there is a box marked FIG 1. This is how WordPerfect shows you the approximate location of the figure within the document. Whenever you create a figure, regardless of the its kind (figure, table, etc.) you will see something on your WordPerfect screen indicating that it has been created and where it is located.

Figure 15.1 The phone.wpg

That's basically all there is to it. Now it's time to settle in and learn about the more detailed aspects of working with
WordPerfect graphics.

One note of caution before we begin. WordPerfect is designed so that you can see graphics on your screen regardless of whether or not you have a special graphics card. If you do not have such a card then the images may appear somewhat rough and jagged. To print graphics however, you must have a printer that supports graphics printing, otherwise you will not be able to produce an image of the hard copy.

Also, you will not be able to see text *plus* graphics on your regular WordPerfect screen. You will need to use the *View Document* option on the *Print* menu to do this. That's OK, since you have to use this option anyway to do any kind of editing (as you'll learn about later) of the image.

How WordPerfect Graphics Works

Using WordPerfect graphics feature consists of the following steps.

First, you must select the *Alt->F9* key combination which produces the menu shown in Figure 15.2. This menu shows you that there are five different types of graphic elements that you can produce; figures, tables, text boxes, a user defined box, and lines.

```
1 Figure; 2 Table; 3 Text Box; 4 User Defined Box; 5 Line: 0
```

Figure 15.2 The Graphics menu

Second, once the box type has been selected (by selecting one option from Options #1 through #4), you will be shown the menu in Figure 15.3 which is an example of the menu for creating a figure. This menu is exactly the same for a figure, table, text box, or a user defined box. Creating lines as a graphic element requires other menus and will be covered later in this chapter.

```
Figure: 1 Create; 2 Edit 3; New Number; 4 Options: 0
```

Figure 15.3 Creating a figure graphics box

Third, the box needs to be defined using the *Definition: Figure* screen you see in Figure 15.4. Here you will define the type of figure, assign captions when desired, position the figure on the page, and edit the figure

```
Definition: Figure

        1 - Filename

        2 - Caption

        3 - Type                      Paragraph

        4 - Vertical Position         0"

        5 - Horizontal Position       Right

        6 - Size                      3.25" wide x 3.25" (high)

        7 - Wrap Text Around Box

        8 - Edit
```

Figure 15.4 The figure definition screen

once it has been incorporated into your document and more.

Fourth, use the *Shift->F7,6* key combination to view the graphic and examine it's placement and so forth. You can then go back and edit it as you see fit.

Using Different Types of Boxes

You don't actually create a graphic in WordPerfect. Instead, you create a *graphic box* into which a graphic is retrieved. Since WordPerfect knows that graphics will be used for many different features, it allows you to create one of four types of boxes, figures, tables, text, and user defined boxes.

While these boxes are treated basically the same way when it comes to creating and working with a WordPerfect graphic, the type of box does not refer to the contents of that box. In other words, you can place the same WordPerfect graphic in a text box as in a figure. The reason why there are different boxes is to make it easier for you to keep track of which independent list of graphics each of the boxes belongs to.

Throughout the remainder of this chapter, a figure graphics box will used in the various examples.

For example, when you create three figure boxes, they are numbered Figure 1, Figure 2, and Figure 3. When you create three table boxes, they are numbered Table 1, Table 2, and Table 3. You can then use WordPerfect's List feature (see Chapter 9) to easily and automatically create a list of tables, figures or other text boxes.

So, a figure box would be created for a figure (such as a drawing), a table box could be created for a table of numbers and such, and a text box could be created for a quote or a sidebar.

Creating a Graphics Box

Let's get into more detail about the creation of a graphics box and the completion of a graphic through the *Definition* screen that you saw in Figure 15.4. Here is a brief discussion of the various options and what they do.

Filename - Option #1

Here you can enter the name of any graphics file that was generated using a format that is compatible with WordPerfect, of which

WordPerfect supports several different types. You can find a list and extensive description of the formats that WordPerfect supports beginning on page 446 of your manual. You already used this option when you retrieved the *phone.WPG* graphic.

To use any graphic, such as phone.WPG simply enter the name of the graphic and press the return key. Remember that if the graphic image is not located on the current directory, then you have to provide the entire path. For example, here is the path command for retrieving a graphic image created in *IMG* format:

c:\figures\duck.img

The graphic image named duck is located on the C drive in the directory named images.

If you are creating a figure anew, you will still need to use the Definition screen, but you will not be defining an already created graphic.

Caption - Option #2

Adding a caption to a figure is as important as adding a title to a report. This lets the reader know what it is you are presenting and helps provide the information that allows the visual information to have the desired impact.

When you create a caption, WordPerfect automatically provides the first part of the caption title such as Figure 2 or Table 4. WordPerfect also keeps track of the number as well. All you need to is to enter the actual text of the caption.

Tip You can create a text box each time you need to enter information that you need numbered in sequence, even if it is not a "graphic." WordPerfect will help you by keeping track of the number and it will be easy to generate a list of these entries later on.

Type - Option #3

There are several types of graphics that can be specified. In general, type refers to the positioning of the graphic image in regard to the text. You can chose paragraph, page or character.

Paragraph means that the graphics box will stay with the text that surrounds it no matter where the text is moved. This means that the graphics box travels with the text when text is moved. This is probably your choice if you want to be sure that the information in the text is closely related to any illustration that might accompany the text. You want them physically close to one another regardless of what kind of editing takes place.

Page means that the graphics box will stay in a fixed position on the page it was created, regardless of whatever other type of activity takes place within the document. In other words, if a graphic box is located at the top of page 3, then you can add or delete any amount of text and the position of the graphics box will not change. This may be the choice when the graphics that are being used are relatively unrelated to the text (such as in headings, special symbols, and other graphic illustrations).

Finally, *Character* type boxes are used to tie them to a particular character such as when you would use a graphic in a footnote.

Vertical Position - Option #4

Vertical position refers to the offset that is associated with the top of whatever it is that you tied the graphic box to. It's the up or down position on the page and it depends on the type of box that you have chosen to create. For example, if you selected a paragraph (which is the default setting) then the 0" that you see in Figure 15.4. means that the graphics box will be placed even with the top edge of the paragraph.

If you tied it to a page, and set the vertical position for 5", it means that the top of the graphic will be placed five inches from the top of the page regardless of what text is on that page.

When you chose this option, you will see the following prompt for the setting in the lower left hand corner of your screen:

Offset form top of paragraph: 0"

which is the default unless WordPerfect is directed otherwise.

Horizontal Position - Option #5

Horizontal position refers to the position of the graphic between the left and right margin on the page.

WordPerfect Graphics

The horizontal setting also depends upon the type of graphic defined (paragraph, page or character). When you select this option (for a paragraph) you will see prompt for the setting in the lower left hand corner of your screen:

Horizontal prompt: 1 Left; 2 Right; 3 Center; 4 Both Left and Right: 0

These settings position the text to the left, right, or center, and can be used to encompass the width of the entire page if you chose option #4. If you chose page, then the prompt looks as follows:

Horizontal Position 1 Margins; 2 Columns; 3 Set Position: 0

These setting position the text on the left or right margin (option #1 - Margins), aligned with a column margin or in between columns (option #2 - Columns) or specify the exact position of the page graphic using option #3 - Set Position.

Size - Option #6

The size option allows you to define the size of the graphics image. WordPerfect will always default so that some text surrounds the image. When you chose this option, you'll see the following prompt on your screen:

1 Width (auto width); 2 Height (auto height); 3 Both Width and Height: 0

The auto width setting for both width and height (the first two options) means that when you specify a width, then the height will automatically be adjusted so that it is proportionate to the original height setting. For example, if the original settings are for a width of 5 inches and a height of 2 inches, then changing the width to 7.5 inches will automatically cause in an increase in the height to 3 inches (both a 50% increase). The same is true for the automatic height setting.

If you want to change the setting for both height and width with them being independent of one another, then select option #3 and you will be prompted to set both the height and the width.

Wrap Text - Option #7

When this option is used, WordPerfect allows you to either reserve all of the space in the box just for graphics *(Yes)* or allows you to actually enter text into the graphic box *(No)*.

You might want to enter text into a graphics box when you want to label part of a graphic or you want to place the caption into the box itself.

Edit - Option #8

The edit option allows you to work with a figure, changing it size and position on the page among other things. We'll go into editing a graphics box in more detail later on in this chapter.

Graphics Options

Once a graphics box is created and a graphics image in placed into the box, you can select option #4 - Options, that will allow you to further design certain attributes of the graphic image. When you select this option, you will see the *Options: Figure* screen shown in Figure 15.5. Here you can further change the appearance of a graphic box and it's content with one of nine separate options.

Border Style - Option #1

This option allows you to change the style of the border of the graphics box. Here are some of the border styles available:

Single	———————————
Dotted	. . . .
Thick	▬▬▬▬▬▬▬▬▬▬▬
Extra Thick	■■■■■■■■■■■

By specifying which type of border style you change the border that surrounds the graphic. Figure 15.6 shows you the same graphic with two

```
Options: Figure

1 - Border Style                        Single
       Left                             Single
       Right                            Single
       Top                              Single
       Bottom                           Single

2 - Outside Border Space                .016"
       Left                             .016"
       Right                            .016"
       Top                              ,016"
       Bottom                           .016"

3 - Inside Border Space
       Left                             0"
       Right                            0"
       Top                              0"
       Bottom                           0"

4 - First Level Numbering Method        Numbers
5 - Second Level Numbering Method       Off
6 - Caption Number Style                [BOLD]Figure[bold]
7 - Position of Caption                 Below box, Outside Borders
8 - Minimum Offset from Paragraph       0"
9 - Gray Shading (% o Black)            0%
```

Figure 15.5 The figure options screen

different border styles (a single and a double solid line). As you can see, the size of the graphic and the content can often look better or worse depending upon your purposes.

Figure 15.6 Two different borders around graphics

Outside Border Space - Option #2

When WordPerfect places a graphic, it automatically places .16 of an inch between the border of the graphic and the beginning of the text.

Using this option, you can place the text very close to the figure (be decreasing the amount of outside border space) or place the text at an increased distance form the border on one or more sides.

Inside Border Space - Option #3

Where you can set the space between the figure border and the text (outside of the graphic's box), you can also set the space between the figure and the border within the graphic itself.

You can make the border come very close to the figure using this option or separate the border from the figure. More complicated figures might require more "white" space to help the reader see the figure more clearly.

Numbering Methods - Options #4 and #5

When you create a figure (regardless of the type), WordPerfect automatically assigns a number in a sequence. For example, the first user-defined box you create is numbered as 1 and the second as 2 and so on.

Using this option, you can change the method for which figures are numbered. When this option is chosen, you will be able to chose form the following menu:

1 Off; 2 Numbers; 3 Letters; 4 Roman Numerals: 0

Once you specify a choice, the graphic boxes will be numbered accordingly, such as 1, 2, 3, or 4 or I, II, III, or IV.

Number Style - Option #6

How would you like the caption that goes along with your graphic boxes to appear? Here are some choices that WordPerfect offers:

Figure 1-2
Figure 3.4
Figure 5*5

These (and others) are possibilities using this option.
 As you can see in Figure 15.5 the default is

[BOLD]1[BOLD]

What this means is that the first numbering method (see options #4 and 5) will be bolded. If the Caption Number Style was changed to this:

[ITAL]2[ITAL]

it would mean that the second numbering method would appear in italics. This option only sets the style of the number method, regardless of the content of the caption.

Position of the Caption - Option #7

Here the position of the a caption can be set from below the box to above the box, with the difference shown in Figure 15.7.

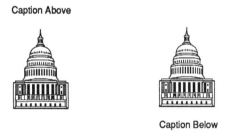

Figure 15.7 Different caption positions

Why would you want to go through the trouble of changing the position of the caption and not keep it as a constant? Probably the best reason is when text from your document interferes with the caption and you find both the figure and the text more readable and informative when the caption is not in competition with other text.

For example, you can place the caption at the top of the figure when the figure appears at the top of a new page and at the bottom of the figure when the figure appears at the bottom of a page.

Offset from Paragraph - Option #8

If the graphics box that you want to retrieve into your document is offset so that a paragraph is too close to the bottom of a page, then WordPerfect will reduce the offset in an effort to keep the text and the box together on the same page. If it cannot be reduced enough so that they can both fit on the same page, WordPerfect will move the graphics box to the top of the next page.

Gray Shading - Option #9

Here's how you can add shading (sometimes called screening) to your graphic. The range of shading is from 0% (no shading) to 100% (black) shading and is often used for different effects.

In Figure 15.8 you can see a graphics with several different levels of screening (0%, 10%, 40% and 70%). This is one of those nice touches that stays nice unless it is overused. For example, an 70% screen may not be very readable nor could you very effectively screen an entire page of text. It would be difficult to read and the shading loses its value as an effect.

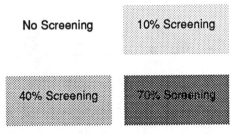

Figure 15.8 Different levels (%) of screening

Using Lines

If you were a version 4.2 user, you probably remember that you can use the *Ctrl->F3,2* key combination to use the cursor keys to draw lines. Version 5.0 supports this feature as well, but also offers a lines option as part of the graphics package.

The line option is available through the *Alt->F9,5* key combination which produces the following prompt:

1 Horizontal Line; 2 Vertical Line:0

Once you make the choice, you then have to insert the information WordPerfect needs to draw the specific line.

Whether you are drawing a horizontal or a vertical line, you need to provide WordPerfect with the position of the line, the length of the line, the width of the line, and the shading of the line.

Drawing Horizontal Lines

When you select Option #1 from the line menu, you'll see the Graphics: Horizontal Line screen shown in Figure 15.9.

When you chose Option #1 on the Horizontal Line menu you will see the following set of choices as to how you want the line offset from the left

```
Graphics: Horizontal Line
    1 - Horizontal Position          Left & Right
    2 - Length of Line
    3 - Width of Line                0.01"
    4 - Gray Shading (% of black)    100%
```

Figure 15.9 The horizontal line screen

margin:

Horizontal Pos: 1 Left 2 Right 3 Center 4 Both Left & Right 5 Set Position:0

If you chose Option #5, then WordPerfect will ask you for the amount of the offset that you want between the left margin and the beginning of the line.

The following line was created using Option #4, which means that the line will automatically go from the left to the right margins of the defined space. When this option is chosen, you cannot set the length of the line since it is automatically defined by the margins. On the other hand, if we were to center (Option #3) as shown here, then size would be set (which is 2 inches, one half inch wide, and 50% shading.

The reveal code for the line would appear as

[HLine:Center,5",0.01,100%]

WordPerfect lines will always be placed in alignment with the bottom of the current line of text. You have to be careful then about the placement of horizontal lines and the use of spaces to be sure that they are adequately separated from the text of the document.

Macro Here's a macro that inserts a centered line 4 inches long and one-half inch wide that is 25% shaded.

1. Ctrl->F10
2. hl,<ret>
3. shaded centered line,<ret>
4. Alt->F9,5,1
5. 1,3,2,4,F7,3,.5,F7,4,25,F7
6. Ctrl->F10

Drawing Vertical Lines

Drawing a vertical line is not much different from a horizontal line. If you look at Figure 15.10, you will see the *Graphics: Vertical Line* menu and how it differs only in the addition of one other option, number 2 which defined the vertical position of the line.

WordPerfect Graphics 197

```
Graphics: Vertical Line
    1 - Horizontal Position          Left Margin
    2 - Vertical Position            Full Page
    3 - Length of Line
    4 - Width of Line                0.01"
    5 - Gray Shading (% of black)    100%
```

Figure 15.10 The vertical line screen

The default is for a full page line, which means it runs the length of the page as you can see has been done on this very page with the default being aligned with the left hand margin.

As with a horizontal line, you can position vertical lines using option #1. The horizontal positions are as follows:

Horizontal Position: 1 Left; 2 Right; 3 Between Columns; 4 Set Position: 0

A vertical line can be placed a little to the left of the left margin (option #1), a little to the right of the right margins (option #2), between columns that you have created (option #3), or you can set the offset of the vertical line from the left hand margin of the page. The line that you see running through the middle of the text on this page was offset 2 inches and is four inches long.

Figure 15.11 show you the use of a line when placed between two columns of text.

Vertical Position

When you draw a vertical line, you have to specify the vertical positioning of that line, which is option #4.

When you select this option, you see the following menu:

Vertical Position: 1 Full Page; 2 Top; 3 Center ; 4 Bottom; 5 Set Position: 0

Your selection determines the position of the line relative to the top and

WHEN TO USE MACROS	
The use of macros is limited only by your imagination. You will surely find more uses than the ones listed later in this chapter, but the following descriptions will give you some idea of how people use macros in their word processing activities.	*accuracy* of your keystrokes as well. For example, when you design a macro to center all the titles in a report, using the correct sequence of keystrokes, the macro will always work. You'll avoid the aggravation of typos and the time and effort wasted correcting them should you have to do each one by hand.
Macros are especially useful for *repeating a task*. For example, you might need to go through a document and change the letters "wp" to "WordPerfect". You could use the search and replace feature that WordPerfect offers, but why not just create a macro called "WordPerfect" and use that instead?	Many people also use macros to create *boiler plates*, which are standard portions of text that can be inserted into another document. For example, you might have a standard form or a clause in a contract or a standard format for a recipe that you want to follow. Save it as a macro and save yourself from having to re-enter it each time you need the text!
This can be saved as a one or two keystroke macro, making this operation easy to incorporate into your word processing activities.	Not only can text be standardized, but so can the format of a document. Say you want your letters to be formatted with margins of 10 and 72, be double-spaced, and leave two inches at the top margin for a company logo. You can do this easily
Not only can you save time by not having to enter multiple keystrokes, but you can ensure the	

Figure 15.11 A vertical line between columns

bottom margin. For example, a Full Page line runs the length of the page from the top to the bottom margins, while a bottom position (Option #4) anchors the vertical line on the bottom margin.

The line drawing tools allow you to do many things that can be used to highlight your text. For example, in Figure 15.12 you can see how a vertical and horizontal lines was placed as borders as part of the design of a newsletter.

Editing a Graphic

Once an image is retrieved, it can easily and quickly be edited.

For example, the image that was shown in Figure 15.1 is shown as it was retrieved into a WordPerfect figure box. Using WordPerfect's editing features, it can be moved to another position on the page, scaled in the

WordPerfect Graphics

The Macro Newsletter	
Volume 13 #2	October, 1988

Macros and You

Remember the time you turned on your first computer? Or the first time you saved a file using WordPerfect and then recalled it to work on it again? These new experiences can be a little anxiety provoking, but that's only because they're new. If you are like the millions of other WordPerfect users, you know how much a part of your work and play WordPerfect can become. It's almost addictive!

Well, you can expect the same thing to happen once you start using macros. Even if you have never had any other WordPerfect experience beyond simply writing short memos, you will find yourself searching for opportunities to use macros whenever possible. In fact, like your favorite word processor, book, or shortcut home, you'll wonder how you ever did without them.

What is a Macro?

You use the WordPerfect word processing system for a very good reason: to create, store, edit, and print documents more easily and quickly. However, there are many word processing tasks that can only be described as routine. They have very little to do with actually creating or writing a letter, memo, or report.

For example, directing WordPerfect to print out a full document involves the same combination of key strokes whether you are printing out a 2-page letter or a....................

Figure 15.12 Using lines for design

horizontal or vertical direction, rotated from 0 to 360 degrees, and switched (or inverted) where black on white becomes white on black).

Editing a Graphic Image

Once a graphics box is created, it only takes a few simple keystrokes to edit the image.

1. Use the *Alt->F9* key combination to select a figure, table, text-box or a user defined box to edit, depending on what kind of a graphic you created.

For example, if you created a Figure graphics box, then you would chose option #1 - Figure.
2. Select option #2 - Edit and you can change such things as the vertical position of the graphic, the horizontal position and the caption.
3. Now chose option #8 - Edit and you will see the graphics edit screen. Along the top and the bottom of the screen you can see how different components of the image can be modified.

The Edit Options

Here's a discussion and examples of the four options for editing a graphic image.
  Each of the options (move, scale, rotate and invert) can be done whether using a combination of certain keys and cursor arrow movements, or by entering the exact numerical value of the editing command you want to make.

Move

Moving a graphic means that you move the horizontal and vertical position of the image in the graphics box. The easiest and most direct way is to simply use the up, down, left and right arrow key to reposition the graphic image in the graphic box that you created. This allows you to move the image in one of four directions quickly and easily.
  Using the cursor keys works great, but just how much is a move when the right cursor arrow key, for example, is pressed? The answer can be found in the lower right hand corner of the WordPerfect graphics edit screen. If the value (10%), indicating that any editing move using the cursor arrows will move the image 10%.
  For example, one press of the left hand cursor arrow will move the graphic 10% to the left of its current position.
  But this value is not fixed at 10%. Through the use of the *INS* key, the value of the change can be set to 1%, 5%, 10%, and even 25%. What this means, is that you can move the position of the graphic in increments of 1, 5, 10, and 25 percent by using the *INS* key in combination with the cursor arrow.
  The second way to move the graphic image is to select option #1 on the Edit screen. When you do this, WordPerfect will ask you to provide a horizontal and vertical amount of space that you want the image moved.

If you specify 1 inch for horizontal and 2 inches for vertical, then the graphic image will be moved that about within the graphics box. If you move it outside of the borders of the graphic box, then only that portion that remains will print. Remember, WordPerfect will print what you see when you view *(Shift->F7,6)* the document.

Scaling a Graphic

Scaling an image lets you change the size of an image by expanding or contracting the image in the horizontal direction (making it "fat" or "skinny") or in the vertical direction (making it "tall" or "short").

The quick key way is by using the *PgUp* and *PgDn* keys which changes both the horizontal and vertical scale proportionately according to the percent indicated on the screen. For example, if the percent indicator (in the lower right hand corner) is 15%, the one press on the PgUp key will increase the scale of the figure in both the horizontal and vertical direction 15%.

The more precise way of scaling an image is through the use of option #2 on the Edit screen. When you select this, WordPerfect asks you to set the actual horizontal and vertical measurements that you want to use to scale the image. Here, you enter the exact value you want to use to scale the image at the *Scale X:* and *Scale Y:* prompts. Entering the values you want rescales the image to fit the space provided for it in your document.

For example, in Figure 15.13 you can see a graphic that was scaled twice the number of units on the X (or horizontal axis) as on the Y (or vertical) axis.

Tip Made an error and want to return to the original image? Just use the Ctrl->Home key combination (the Goto command) and the graphic will reset. This Goto option is on your screen but is not on the edit screen shown on page 163 of the manual.

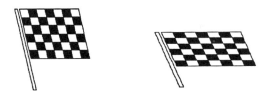

Figure 15.13 Scaling a graphic image

Rotating a Graphic

The last physical editing option that can be made with an image is through the use of the Rotate option. The quick key way uses the + and - keys on the numeric keypad which rotate the figure according to the percent indicator. For example, pressing the - key when the indicator is set at 25% will rotate the image 90 degrees (or 25% of 360 degrees) in a clockwise direction. To rotate the image in a counter clockwise direction, use the + key.

More precise rotations can be done when you select option #3 where WordPerfect wants you to enter the exact number of degrees you want to rotate the image. When you select this option and enter the number of degrees you want to rotate the figure, WordPerfect will also ask you if you want to reverse the image (as in a mirror image). When you do this, you will see the image rotate the defined amount. If you do not want to reverse the image, just say no!

Figure 15.14 Rotating an image 90 degrees

Switching or Inverting an Image

Using the Invert option displays the complementary colors of the image in your graphics box. For example, in Figure 15.15 you can see both the original as well as the inverted figure (which is white on black). The only thing you need be aware of when using this option is that it only works on bit-mapped, and not line drawn images. WPG images (such as those that came with WordPerfect are line drawn. Graphics from other programs than WordPerfect can use are bit mapped.

Figure 15.15 Inverting an image

Wrapping Text Around Graphics

Guess what? You can't. WordPerfect does not allow you to wrap the text of a document completely around a graphic unless you have created columns and placed the image in between them as you can see in Figure

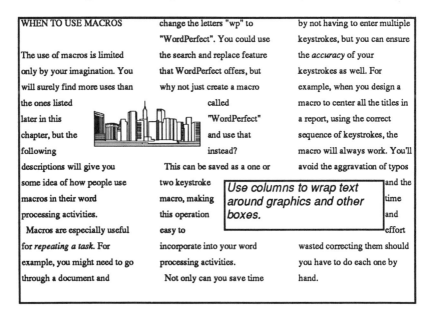

Figure 15.14 Wrapping text around graphics

15.14. But there is a way to get around this shortcoming.

You can create a graphics box and literally type around it. To do this, place the box in the middle of the page and then use the cursor keys to move from the beginning to the end of the box and enter the text that you want to use.

That's it for graphics. The real challenge to you, however, is to be brave enough to try some of these things in your documents.Graphics are great fun, so use the *View Page* option frequently to experiment and see what you come up with before you print out!

16
Advanced Printing

WordPerfect has changed in so many ways to make the program more powerful and easier to customize to your specific needs. A major change, and the focus of this chapter, is the way that WordPerfect supports new printing options. In Chapter 4 you learned about some of the basics of printing with WordPerfect. In this chapter you'll begin where you left off, changing the appearance of a document using the variety of fonts available to you.

Selecting Fonts

When Marshall McLuhan said that the medium was the message, he well anticipated how a document's appearance can often be as important as what the document says. Look at the contrasting headlines shown in Figure 16.1. The upper one looks busy and disorganized. The lower one looks focused, is easy to read, and makes a point.

H a w k s   W i n   I t   A l l !

Hawks Win It All

Figure 16.1 Contrasting headlines

While there are many factors that account for a document's appearance, the fonts that are used are probably the most important.

Selecting Fonts and Font Attributes

For our purposes here, a *font* is any family of characters of the same design. The font and the way you use these characteristics is almost solely dependent upon your purpose. For example, in Figure 16.2, you can see examples of three different fonts.

```
This is Courier
```

This is Helvetica

This is Times

Figure 16.2 Different Fonts

More specifically, Figure 16.3 shows you two families of fonts, Times Roman and Helvetica. Times Roman is a *serif* font, or one that has lines that cross the main strokes of the character. *Sans serif* fonts, such as the

Times Roman 12 point plain style.
Times Roman 12 point bold style.
<u>Times Roman 18 point plain style underlined.</u>
Times Roman 12 point plain style shadow.
Times Roman 12 point plain style$^{\text{with superscript}}$.

Helvetica 12 point plain style.
Helvetica 12 point bold style.
<u>Helvetica 18 point plain style underlined.</u>
Helvetica 12 point plain style shadow.
Helvetica 12 point plain style $^{\text{with superscript}}$.

Figure 16.3 Two families of fonts

very popular Helvetica, have no serifs. These families of fonts can appear quite different from one another depending upon the WordPerfect options that you select.

Selecting how characters appear when printed is as simple as selecting any other WordPerfect feature; you use a menu and select various options. Remember, however, that you must first be sure to have selected the printer that you want to use as was described in Chapter 4 so you can make these choices.

Selecting a font and changing its attributes begins with the use of the *Ctrl->F8* key combination where you see the Font menu shown in Figure 16.4.

---
1 Size; 2 Appearance; 3 Normal; 4 Base Font; 5 Print Color: 0

Figure 16.4 The Font menu

Base Font - Option #4

We hope you don't find it too disconcerting to see option #4 being discussed first, but we're doing so since it is basic to understanding some of the features on other attribute menus such as size (small, large, etc.) and appearance (italic, shadow, bold, etc.).

The *base font* can be defined in two ways. First, it is the font that you are currently using. Second, it is also the font that WordPerfect defaults to when you first chose a printer. In either case, the base font can be changed using the *Ctrl->F8,4* key combination which produces a menu of the different fonts that are available given the printer that you are using. Figure 16.5 shows you what these fonts are for the NEC LC 890 laser printer where the base font (the one with the asterisk) is Times Roman.

Changing Base Fonts

To change the base font, use the *Ctrl->F8,4* key combination and move the cursor arrows until the font that you want to change to is highlighted. Once this is done, WordPerfect will ask you to chose a *point size* for the font by prompting you with

Point Size:

```
Base Font

      Helvetica Narrow Oblique
      Helvetica Oblique
      ITC Avant Garde Gothic Book
      ITC Avant Garde Gothic Book Oblique
      ITC Avant Garde Gothic Book Demi
      ITC Avant Garde Gothic Demi Oblique
      ITC Bookman Demi
      ITC Bookman Demi Italic
      ITC Bookman Light
      ITC Bookman Light Italic
      ITC Zapf Chancery Medium Italic
      New Century Schoolbook
      New Century Schoolbook Bold
      New Century Schoolbook Bold Italic
      New Century Schoolbook Italic
      Palatino
      Palatino Bold
      Palatino Bold Italic
      Palatino Italic
      Symbol
  *   Times Roman
      Times Roman Bold
      Times Roman Bold Italic
      Times Roman Italic
```

Figure 16.5 The available fonts for the NEC LC890 laser printer

A *point* is 1/72 of an inch. The *text* in this book (not the headings which are set in Helvetica) is 11 point Times Roman. WordPerfect allows you to chose from 1 to an upper limit defined by your printer, which for many printers is 127 points (which produces big letters!).

For example, the NEC LC890 allows characters up to 140 points. A sample of what some of these sizes looks like is shown in Figure 16.6.

You can also chose a new base font by using the *Name Search* feature, or option #2 on the Base Font screen. Here you need to select this option (by pressing the letter *N*) and then enter the name of the font which will then be highlighted.

Whatever you select as the base font, remains the base font unless changed. In sizing other font options, WordPerfect will refer to this base font for a starting point. More about this is a moment after we discuss the size option on the font menu.

Advanced Printing

> 18 point Times
>
> # 36 point Times
>
> # 72 point

Figure 16.6 Some different size fonts

Size - Option #1

When the first option is selected, WordPerfect provides the size menu that is shown below and in Figure 16.7 shows you can see an example of the different sizes of type that you can use with WordPerfect. The font used in these examples (and was used in this book) is Times.

1 Suprscpt; 2 Subscpt; 3 Fine; 4 Small; 5 Large; 6 Vry Large; 7 Ext Large; 0

> This is superscripted text.
> This is subscripted text.
> This is fine text.
> This is small text.
> This is large text.
> This is very large text.

Figure 16.7 Available font sizes

There are two ways that you can use the size options to change the size of type.

The first is through the selection of the size option that you want to use before you begin entering any characters. For example, If you want text to appear as superscripted above other text, enter the base text, select the *Ctrl->F8,1,1* key combination and enter the text that is to be superscripted. Whatever is typed form that point on will be superscripted. Here is what the reveal codes for the text $a^2 + b^2 + c^2$ looks like:

a[SUPRSCPT]2[suprscpt] + b[SUPRSCPT]2[suprscpt] + b[SUPRSCPT]2[suprscpt]

The second way is to block the text that you want to change in appearance and then select the size change you want. The big advantage of the second method is that you do not have to switch back to the font that you were using when you changed to superscript. For example if Times Roman 12 point is your base font and you block text and change it to Extra Large, then only that text will appear extra large. If you were to use the first method, you would then have to switch back to the base font.

> **Macro** This second way makes it very easy to change to a frequently used size when the following macro is used. This macro changes normal text to subscripted text, once it is blocked.
>
> 1. Ctrl->F10
> 2. sub,<ret>
> 3. changes blocked text from normal to subscripted,<ret>
> 4. Ctrl->F8,1,1
> 5. Ctrl->F10
>
> You can substitute any size change you want in step 4. For example, to change form normal to large text, step 5 becomes *Ctrl->F8,1,5*.

The Size of Fonts

You might be curious as to how WordPerfect arrives at what may appear to be subjective definitions of words such as fine, small, large, very large, and extra large. As with so many other WordPerfect printing features, these definitions depend upon the printer that you are using as well as the size of the base font.

You saw in Figure 16.7 what small and Extra large sizes look like when the base font is 11 point. What happens if the base font is caged from 11 to 20? Take a look at Figure 16.8 and you will see. Like everything else, it's all relative; the sizes of fonts available on the Size menu are relative to the size of the base font.

Base Font 11

This is small and this is large.

Base Font 20

This is small and this is large.

Figure 16.8 The effect of different base fonts

Appearance - Option #2

The second option on the size menu which deals with the appearance of type reveals the menu shown below.

1 Bold 2 Undrln 3 Dbl Und 4 Italc 5 Outln 6 Shadw 7 Sm Cap 8 Redln 9 Strkout: 0

As with choices in size, the Appearance menu provides you with many options as shown above. You can use these options in the same way that you used those on the size menu.

For example, you can select the italics appearance option through the use of the *Ctrl->F8,2,4* key combination and everything that you enter from that point on will appear in italics. You can also chose to block text and then select this same option.

> Macro Here's a simple macro that changes a block of text to appear in italics.
>
> 1. Ctrl->F10
> 2. ital,<ret>
> 3. changes blocked text to italics,<ret>
> 4. Ctrl->F8,2,4
> 5. Ctrl->F10
>
> You can change the macro to any other appearance option by altering the last digit (4) in step 4. For example, if you want to change it to shadow, then the command would read *Ctrl->F8,4,6*.

Normal - Option #3

This option simply turns off all of the attribute changes that you might have made when you used options #1 and #2. It's a good candidate for an *Alt Key* macro so that you can immediately return to a plain style of type.

Printing in Color - Option #5

If you're so lucky to have a color printer, WordPerfect can easily accommodate your needs to produce text and graphs and images in colors. You can print in black, blue, brown, cyan, green, gray, magenta, orange, red, white and yellow. You can also design your own color by mixing various proportions of red, green and blue.

To print in color, use the *Ctrl->F8,5* key combination which reveals the screen you see in Figure 16.9. Then select the color you would like to print with and you're finished. For example, if you select Red, the reveal code

[Color:Red]

would be placed in the text where the change takes effect. You can return to normal text by selecting the color black.

One thing you cannot do with Print Color that you can do with the attributes of size and appearance is to create a block of text and then select a color. When a block of text is created, you can only change the text's size and appearance and not the color.

Print Color			
Primary Color Mixture	Red	Green	Blue
1 - Black	0%	0%	0%
2 - White	100%	100%	100%
3 - Red	67%	0%	0%
4 - Green	0%	67%	0%
5 - Blue	0%	0%	67%
6 - Yellow	67%	67%	0%
7 - Magenta	67%	0%	67%
8 - Cyan	0%	67%	67%
9 - Orange	67%	25%	0%
A - Gray	50%	50%	50%
N - Brown	67%	33%	0%
O - Other	67%	33%	0%
Current Color	0%	0%	0%

Figure 16.9 Printing in color

Custom Colors

The last choice on the *Print Color* screen shown in Figure 16.9 is *Other*. Selecting this option allows you to design the color of your choice. To design your own color, just enter the various intensities of red, green and blue and exit the menu (using the *F7* key). This "other" color will represent this new combination and can be put into effect whenever it is selected.

You might notice how interesting the color combinations can be. For example, how red, green and blue make white and only red and green make yellow is a mystery that has to do with the additive and subtractive nature of mixing colors.

Using a Laser Printer with WordPerfect

The introduction of the laser printer has revolutionized the use of the personal computer. When you add WordPerfect's powerful word processing features with 5.0's printer capabilities, you get a combination that cannot be beat.

One of the most important features of the laser printer and WordPerfect is the variety of different fonts that can be used and the use of languages such as PostScript. *PostScript* is a special computer language called a *Page Description Language* (or PDL) that helps you to print a wide range of font types, sizes, and styles. There are many PostScript printers available including several Hewlard Packard models and some of the NEC line of printers, plus many others.

Loading Soft Fonts

Although your printer might come with a variety of fonts that are *resident*. You can use other fonts as well. For example, the NEC LC890 contains 34 resident fonts.

These *soft* fonts are produced by several different manufacturers and the selection is so great, that you can probably find a font to fit your specific need.

In general, the procedure that you should follow when loading a new font into your system is as follows:

1. Install the program that helps manage the new fonts. For example, Glyphix (from SWFTE International) uses the WordPerfect Manager to handle the installation.

During the installation procedure you will be asked several things including the location of files, the type of printer you are using and the version of WordPerfect that you will be operating during the use of the fonts.

2. Design the fonts that you are going to use. Programs such as Glyphix ask questions such as the point size, the pitch and the weight of the typeface.

3. Copy the fonts off of the program or font disk onto the directory in your hard drive that you specified to contain fonts.

An Example: BitStream Fontware

However they did it, the WordPerfect people have to be thanked. Included with version 5.0 comes a package called BitStream Fontware (containing six separate disks. In fact, it's an entire installation kit containing several different types of fonts that you can use with WordPerfect. While the Bitstream people do include some instructions for installing and using Bitstream Fontware, here's the step by step procedure for getting started.

Since WordPerfect needs instructions on building these special files, the printer file with the extension *.ALL* must be in the WordPerfect directory.

Setting Up Bitstream Fontware

1. Place Disk #1 titled Bitstream Fontware Installation kit into drive A and enter

a:fontware,<ret>

When the program asks you whether you want to see the menus in more than one color, respond yes or no depending on whether or not you have a color monitor.
2. Select the Set Up Fontware option from the Fontware main menu. You can always return to this menu by pressing the ESC key.
3. For each of the following, you need to tell the Fontware system where you plan on storing the Fontware types faces, WordPerfect, and the printer fonts. Remember to chose directory names that make sense to you and ones that are convenient (not buried in three other levels of sub-directories!)
4. When you are finished, enter *y* and the Fontware system will be installed.
5. The last step in the set up is choosing the model of printer that you plan to chose as well as the character set. Highlight the model and then press the *Enter* key. If your model is not shown on the screen then consult your printer manual or call your dealer. Most printers emulate others, so it's likely that one of the printers listed on the screen will be what you need.

Finally, chose the character set. ASCII is a safe choice since it contains all the characters that you might need.

Adding Fontware Typefaces

After installation, it's time to add the typefaces that you want to use to the directories that were created to store files. To do this, follow these steps.

1. Use the *F3* key from the main menu (use ESC to get there) and insert Disk #1 into drive A. Now press the *Enter* key.
2. Once you see a listing of the available fonts, highlight the ones that you want to use and press the Enter key. When you do this, the typeface is marked by an arrow to its left. Chose all the typefaces you want to use.
3. Now press the *F10* key and the typefaces will be copied to the directory that you identified on your hard disk as the one that will contain the typefaces.

Creating a Font

Once you have chosen the fonts you want to create, follow these steps to "make" the fonts that you will be using.

1. Select the *Make Fonts* option from the main menu.
2. Select a typeface that you want to create and press the *Enter* key.
3. You will now see a recommendation from Fontware as to what size the chosen type should be. You can enter any sizes that you want, but keep in mind that the more sizes you chose, the more memory the typefaces will take and the more time they will take to be created.
4. When you are finished, press the *F10* key and then the *Y* key. Fontware will then generate the fonts.

Using Your New Fonts

Once the fonts are created, you need to select the font you want to use from the list that is generated when you select a printer. It really is this easy and this convenient!

Printing Special Characters

Once you have installed fonts you can use these new ones or some of your resident fonts to create an entirely new set of characters. For example, here are some of the symbols, diacriticals and digraphs that can be created and used within your WordPerfect document.

œ † D ≥ р ç

Advanced Printing 217

Using the Compose Feature

The Compose feature allows you to create special characters. The range of characters that you can create depends up the font that is being used.
For example, here are some of the special characters that can be created:

$$f \quad \dagger \quad Å \quad \div \quad œ \quad ρ \quad °$$

Any special character that is created using the compose feature consists of two separate numbers. The first identifies the character set and the second identifies the character number.
For example, on page 471 of your manual, you can see a listing of characters that correspond to certain set and character numbers. If you use the compose feature with character set 0 and character number 36, a $ symbol will be printed, which will look and be treated no differently from the dollar sign symbol on your keyboard. Or, if you selected character set 4, character number 5, you would see the ¶ symbol for a paragraph.
Follow these steps to create special characters using the Compose feature.

1. Use the *Ctrl->2* key combination to begin the *Compose* operation.
2. Enter the character set, a comma and then the character number you want to print.
3. Press the *Enter* key.

That's it for creating any one of many, many characters. You will probably not be able to print every character from every character set unless you have the hardware and software configuration that supports the various combinations.

Tip You can also use the Ctrl->V key combination to begin the Compose operation. Want to know what any set of characters looks like given a particular font? Retrieve and print the file named CHARMAP.TST and you'll see all 12 sets and how they appear with your printer for the base font that you have selected..

Using Digraphs and Diacriticals

Digraphs (such as Æ) and diacriticals (such as ç) are special characters that are often used in scientific work as well as in foreign languages.

To create a digraph or a diacritical, follow these steps:

1. Press the *Ctrl->2* key combination.
2. Enter the two letters (in the case of a digraph) or the mark and the letter (in the case of a diacritical) and then the Enter key.
   Voila! Done.

Keyboard Definitions

Want to work with your keyboard and perhaps increase your productivity?

Use WordPerfect's keyboard layout/definition option that is accessed through the Set Up *(Shift->F1,6)* option where you are given a choice of keyboard definitions that may be different from the original standard definition that you are now using.

For example, through a redefinition of the keyboard, you can designate F1 to be help rather than F3. Or F7 alone can print, rather than having to use the *Shift->F7* key combination. You can even make WordPerfect's keyboard act like Wordstar's keyboard!

To introduce you to these redefinitions, WordPerfect has already reconfigured three different keyboard definitions; an alternate keyboard, an enhanced keyboard, and a keyboard full of some macros! Let's look at one, the MACRO definition. To redefine the keyboard, follow these steps.

1. Use the *Shift->F1,6* key combination to access the keyboard definition options. If you see nothing on your monitor, it's because you did not tell WordPerfect where to find the files that contain the keyboard definitions. Use the *Shift->F1,7* key combination and enter the path to these files.
2. Highlight the MACROS redefinition and select option #1, Select. Once you press the F7 key, this new definition is in force.
3. Select option #5 - Edit and you will see how the keyboard is defined.
   Here is a listing of macros that have already been created for you with designated keys! In other words, if you did redefine your keyboard, then the *Alt->I* key combination will insert a line and the *Alt->F9* key combination lists the graphics menu on the bottom of your screen.

Designing Your Own Layout

Here are the steps that you should follow to design a keyboard layout of your own. Let's say that you want to have the F1 key be help and the F2 key begin the spell check. These are just examples of reassigning keys to functions. You can do anything you want or need.

1. Get into the keyboard setup menu using the *Shift->F1,6* key combination (see Figure 16.10).
2. Select *Create (option #5)*.
3. Enter the name of the keyboard that you want to use such as *Edit*. Perhaps it would be a specialized one for editing manuscripts or writing letters, etc. Once this is done, you will see the *Keyboard: Edit* screen as

```
Keyboard: Edit

  Name: EDIT

  Key       Description        Macro



  Key: 1 Edit; 2 Delete; 3 Move; 4 Create; Macro: 5 Save; 6 Retrieve: 1
```

Figure 16.10 The key definition screen

```
Key: Edit

     Key      F1

  1 - Description

  2 - Action

     ┌─────────────────────────────────────────┐
     │ {SPELL}                                 │
     │                                         │
     │                                         │
     │                                         │
     └─────────────────────────────────────────┘
```

Figure 16.11 The key edit screen

shown in Figure 16.11.
4. Select option #1 *Edit* and you will be asked to identify the key you want reassign. In Figure 16.13 you can see that the F1 key was selected to become the key used to begin WordPerfect's spell check feature.
5. In this example you would enter the key *F1* and then a description of what the new key does. Once this is done, press the Enter key.
6. Up to now you have just named a key and described its function. You now need to actually define it.
7. Chose option #1 - Description and enter a description of what the new key will do. When you are finished press the Enter key.
8. Chose option #2 - Action, and just as you used the Macro Editor in Chapter 6, here you will also enter the actual keystrokes form the original key definition to define the new key. In other words, use the key combination *Ctrl->F2* and you will see the

{SPELL}

command appear in the box indicating that this is the function of the key named F1.

> ***Macro*** Here's a macro that will return you to the original keyboard. Remember that when you reconfigure a keyboard, you are operating under a different type of key system so don't be surprised if you find some surprises!
>
> 1. Ctrl->F10
> 2. rok,<ret>
> 3. return to original keyboard,<ret>
> 4. Shift->F1,6,6
> 5. Ctrl->F10

You can create as many different and unique keyboards as you might like and reassign as many keys and key combinations as suits your needs. This is a handy and convenient was to customize a keyboard for specific projects, with complete sets of macros that fit exactly what it is you need to do.

Tip *Want to use hundreds of Alt->Key macros! Just reassign keyboards, including macros that do that task and you can create up to 26 Alt->Key macros for each new keyboard definition!*

Tracking, Kerning and Page Orientation

While it is critically important to consider how a document looks, it's equally important to pay attention to the small details of the way that *words* and *letters* look..

There are two concerns that you should have about the way that letters and words appear. The first is *tracking* or the spaces between words and the second is *kerning* or the spaces between pairs of letters.

Tracking

Tracking is the amount of space between characters in a word and the amount of space between words. In WordPerfect terms it is called *word spacing*.

For example, the following set of words needs to have the spacing adjusted.

These words are not spaced properly

To adjust the spacing between words and letters, follow these steps:

1. Place the cursor to where you want to change the setting.
2. Select the word and letter spacing options through the use of the *Shift->F8,4,6,3* key combination.
3. Select a setting for letter spacing from the choices shown below.

Word Spacing 1 Normal; 2 Optimal; 3 Percent of Optimal; 4 Set Pitch: 2

The *Normal* setting will provide spacing that looks best according to the manufacturer of the printer that you are using.

The *Optimal* spacing will provide spacing that looks best according to the WordPerfect people.

You can use option #2, *Percent of Optimal*, to set the word spacing at whatever you might like given the text you are working with. The optimal spacing is 100%. If you change this value to less than 100%, the space between the letters and words is reduced (sometimes called *negative* tracking). If you change the value to more than 100%, the space between the letters and words is increased (sometimes called *positive* tracking). Here are the same words that saw above with the word spacing reduced by 15%.

These words are spaced properly

Finally, the last option, *Set Pitch*, allows you to set the pitch or the number of characters per inch. The conventional settings are 10 character per inch (sometimes called pica) and 12 characters per inch (sometimes called elite). Don't confuse the size of type (expressed in points and picas) with pitch.

Kerning

Kerning is the process through which space between selected letters is increased or decreased. Since letters are not of equal widths, kerning is sometimes necessary so that the spacing appears more attractive than might otherwise be. For example, here is a set of letters before and after kerning has taken place.

Before Kerning: Y a T o   W e
After Kerning: Ya To We

To adjust kerning between adjacent letters follow these steps:

1. Place the cursor between the pair of letters you want to kern.
2. Select the *Shift->F8,4,6,1* key combination.
3. Select option #1 - Kerning and enter "y", turning kerning on.

Unlike tracking, WordPerfect decides what is the best measurement that you need for the spacing between letters. WordPerfect takes into account both the characteristics of the printer as well as the font that you are using. Kerning is especially important when the first letter is a capital and a wide character, such as in some of the examples that you see above.

Page Orientation: Portrait versus Landscape Printing

The default setting for the way in which a document is printed is through the *portrait* orientation where the long side of the paper in the vertical axis.

There comes occasion where you want material designed and printed in a horizontal rather than a vertical fashion, such as in the generation of certificates. This is the *landscape* position. Since the portrait orientation is the default you need not be concerned about setting your printer for this type of output. When you want to print in the landscape orientation, the

Shift->F8,2,8,2

will adjust the paper size and paper type settings so that landscape for standard size (8.5" by 11") is active.

Let's move on now to the way in which WordPerfect can work with many of the other programs (some made by WordPerfect) that are available.

17
WordPerfect and Other Products

Any product that is as popular as WordPerfect is surely to generate a *bunch* of other products that enhance its usefulness. So is the case with WordPerfect. Today there are dozens of software and hardware products on the market that make WordPerfect even more attractive.

So you can get some idea about what these products are and what they can do, this chapter will provide a brief summary and some examples of these packages. We don't cover every one available, but you can surely get some idea of what's out there.

Other WordPerfect Corporation Products

The WordPerfect Corporation not only produces WordPerfect. It also produces a variety of other products.

WordPerfect Library

WordPerfect Library is a program that allows you to easily move between different applications through the use of a *shell*. This shell provides you with a series of choices that you can access using just one command.

For example, let's say that you are hard at work in WordPerfect and need to switch to WordPerfect Corporation's database manager, DataPerfect. After you have installed WordPerfect Library, the *Alt->Shift,d* key combination will place you in DataPerfect without having to first exit WordPerfect and go to DOS and then start DataPerfect.

WordPerfect Library comes with several desk accessories that are briefly described below.

-A *calendar* that contains a memo, appointment, and things to do window all of which can be printed in a user defined format.

-A *notebook* which is a resident scratch pad which saves files as WordPerfect merge files for easy integration into WordPerfect documents.
 -A *file manager* for copying, deleting, moving, and sorting files.
 -A *calculator* that can do trigonometric and financial analysis besides simple computation, and
 -A *macro* and a *program editor* that can be used to create and edit macros and other programs.

In general, WordPerfect Library is like an all around best friend that helps you manage and maintain your files while providing you with excellent tools to make you a more efficient personal computer user.

PlanPerfect

Next on our list is WordPerfect Corporation's spreadsheet, *PlanPerfect*. A spreadsheet like PlanPerfect is an electronic ledger that allows you to record both text and numerical data and manipulate the information as you see fit.

In Figure 17.1 you can see an example that represents part of a spreadsheet that records and computes grades. With PlanPerfect, averages and other statistical measures can be easily computed, students can be sorted on their grades, their names, average grades and so on. PlanPerfect also offers a very sophisticated and easy to use graphics feature so that numerical information can be visually represented in any one of many different formats such as pie, bar, stacked and line graphs.

	A	B	C	D	E	F
1	Grade		Course:		EPR 200	
2			Instructor:		John Poggio	
3			Time:		T-Th 4:15-7:30	
4						
5	--------	--------	----------	--------	--------------	---
6						
7	Last	First	Test 1	Test 2	Average	
8	McKurry	Bill	92	78	85	
9	Wright	John	68	72	70	
10	Rice	Mabel	98	100	99	

Figure 17.1 A PlanPerfect Screen

With little difficulty, graphs designed using PlanPerfect can be integrated into a WordPerfect document.

DataPerfect

Dataperfect, also from the people who bring you WordPerfect, is a database that allows you to collect and store and access information then work with it in a variety of fashions.

For example, Figure 17.2 shows the first record of many that constitute a data base of names and addresses along with other pertinent

```
NAME LIST.DAT

Mr/Mrs/Dr. etc.    First Name        I.Last Name
           Dr.     William           R.Yellon
      Salutation   Dr. Yellon

               Title  President of Delphi Associate
             Company  Mazel Fabrications

Business Phone  (123)456-5345     Home Phone        (123)456-7890

         Address  2123 Sasah Avenue
            City  Williamsburg    ST      NY     Zip    65478-0000
```

Figure 17.2 A DataPerfect screen

information. Using DataPerfect, you can sort on any of these fields, rearrange them to fit a particular format, print out selected ones, and more. As with PlanPerfect, you can design a format that can be easily read into a WordPerfect document. One often used purpose for databases such as DataPerfect is the creation of name and address files (as you see in Figure 17.2) that can then be used as secondary merge file in the creation of form letters.

Repeat Performance

Repeat Performance is a keyboard enhancement program that allows you to speed up the movement of your cursor, up to 1000 characters per second (which is *very* fast). With Repeat Performance you can do several other things such ensure that "cursor skid" is eliminated. Cursor skid is where the cursor keeps moving after the space key, for example, is released. You can also customize the beep of your computer and repeat special characters.

Graphics Programs

Now that WordPerfect handles graphics, it's no surprise that there are vendors appearing with graphics packages that complement WordPerfect.

Most of the image files comes with the .WPG extension that you learned about in Chapter 16 and can be easily retrieved into a graphics box using the *Create* option on the *Definition: Figure* screen.

Publisher's PicturePak

Publisher's Picture Pak (Marketing Graphics Incorporated, 4401 Dominion Boulevard, Suite 220, Glenn Allen, VA 23060) offers a variety of different graphics images for use with WordPerfect. For example, they have images sets in the general areas of finance and administration, executive and management, and sales and marketing.

Each of the images are vector images rather than paint images providing more precision and an elimination of the notorious jaggies! Most of the graphics that were used in the preparations of the images shown in Chapter 15 were *PicturePak* images. As you can see, they are nicely drawn and show up very well using WordPerfect and a laser printer.

Graph In The Box

There may be an easier way to draw graphs, but all you have to do is look this far to see what *Graph In The Box* (New England Software, Greenwich Office Park 3, Greenwich, CT, 06830) can do.

With this RAM resident program all you need do is highlight any block of data and then turn it into one of 11 different types of graphs such as bar, stacked, line, pie and mixed with or without color (depending of course on your systems' capabilities). This is an extremely easy to use program that can graph up to 500 data points and 15 different variables and produces professional looking results.

Fonts and Font Generators

You've already learned about Bitstream Fontware that comes with WordPerfect 5.0. Here are two other packages of fonts and font designers.

Turbofonts

Turbofonts (Image Processing Software, Inc., POB 5016, Madison, WI 53705) provides an extensive selection of specialized symbols for use in business, scientific and foreign language applications including Russian, Hebrew, Greek, European, Arabic, physics, chemistry, engineering and statistics.

While some are similar to those you can generate using the character sets included with WordPerfect, others are unique to Turbofonts and very useful should you have to produce special characters. Turbofonts also comes with a special font editor which allows you to customize fonts to fit your specific needs as well as Graph Graber that allows you to capture graphs and integrate them into WordPerfect.

Glyphix

Another product that offers fonts for use with WordPerfect is *Glyphix* (Swfte, POB 219, Rockland, E 19732) which allows you to select a typeface (such as Olivia, Galaxy, or Orna among others) and then set the point size, weight, pattern, orientation and slant.

Softcraft Fontware

Softcraft, Inc. (SoftCraft, Inc., 16 N. Carroll Street, Suite 500, Madison, WI 53703) offers an extensive package of fonts and other features as part of *Fontware* that you can use to create custom fonts as well as take advantage of the many that are offered as part of the software package. Fonts can be contoured, reversed, shadowed as well as having other special effects added such as basketweave, fillers, and a variety of patterns. Graphics, chart design and development are available as well.

Desk Accessories and Utilities

A desk accessory is a program that makes you a more efficient personal computer user by helping you do everything from organizing your files, restoring lost or accidentally deleted files, and backing up files among hosts of other tasks.

Sidekick

SideKick and *SideKick Plus* (Borland International, 4585 Scotts Valley Road, Scotts Valley, CA 9066) are two very popular versions of the same program that started the resident program fad. Here, you load a program into the memory of your computer and it is always accessible, usually through some simple key combination (much as WordPerfect Library).

SideKick Plus offers a variety of features such as a text editor, text outliner, a telephone number database with an automatic dialer, a time planner, four different calculators, a file manager and even programming aids. As with other resident programs, all of these features are instantly available.

Cruise Control

Ever leave your computer unattended for an extended period of time? Just one of *Cruise Control's* (Revolution SOftware, Inc. 715 Route 10 East, Randolph NJ, 07869) many features is its Auto-Dimmer which automatically dims the monitor screen to damage to your monitor, In addition, this RAM resident program inserts the date and time into a document, increases cursor speed, allows you to repeat any key without holding it down (like the ESC feature of WordPerfect), and allows you to navigate through spreadsheets precisely without any cursor run on.

Mace Utilities

None of us would like to admit it, but we all accidentally delete an important file every now and then. *Mace Utilities* (Paul Mace Software, 400 Williamson Way, Ashland, OR 97520) is a very comprehensive set of DOS utilities that helps you recover lost files as well as do a host of other things. For example, you can even recover a disk that has been accidentally reformatted, unfragment (get rid of empty spaces) a hard disk, and squeeze large files into much smaller spaces.

For many of us, just being able to recover a lost file is worth any price, but this set of utilities comes with many other features that make it invaluable.

Perfect Exchange

Someday all computers will have the same operating systems and all applications will be interchangeable. That's some time away. For now, when you need to convert documents between WordPerfect and other popular word processing packages such as Multimate, Displaywrite, Microsoft Word, Wordstar and Samna among others *Perfect Exchange* (Systems Compatibility Corporation, 401 N. Washburn, Suite 600, Chicago, IL 60611) may be the answer. *Perfect Exchange* also allows for conversion of versions 4.2 as well as 5.0 files.

You may know that WordPerfect offers a Convert utility that can do much of the same, but Perfect Exchange handles a larger variety of specific word processing applications.

Another Thesaurus

Although WordPerfect comes with a terrific speller and thesaurus, there are other products that complement WordPerfect's features quite well. *Word Finder* (Microlytics, Inc., 300 Main Street, East Rochester, NY 14445) is one such program.

With over 220,000 synonyms it can help you find just the correct word to use when none that you can think of fit the bill. It contains an extensive set of key words (15,000) and is very fast.

Seeing All of WordPerfect

You now know that WordPerfect offers many features that make the appearance of text quite attractive. Depending upon your computer system, you may or may not be able to see these features of your screen. With the use of a *Hercules InColor Card* (Hercules Computer Technology 2550 Ninth Street, Berkeley, CA 974410), you get true WYSIWYG (what you see is what you get) capability from bold, to underline, to extra large print.

The Hercules card is a *hardware* modification so that means you have to (horrors!) take apart your computer or have it installed by your dealer. In any case, it really soups up the way that your WordPerfect documents look on your screen and give you a very good idea of what they will look like when printed.

We hope this brief overview of some products that work with and enhance WordPerfect will provide you with the information you need if you chose to add to your library of WordPerfect compatible products. Just remember, that before you buy any product, make sure you have a chance to work with it beforehand and try it out to see if it works on your particular system and if it does what you need.

18
Stylish WordPerfect

Here we go again with another one of those new features that were on many version 4.2 user's wish list; *styles*. In this chapter you'll learn how to prepare and use WordPerfect styles to help cut the time it takes to repeat a document that is full of complex type and formatting codes.

What is a Style?

A style is a combination of text and formatting codes that is stored in a style library under one unique name. It's a file of sorts, that contains all the information you need to format a WordPerfect document in a certain fashion.

For example, the stationery you see in Figure 18.1 was created using a style. The parts of the letter that are part of the style have been bolded. Such a style allows the WordPerfect user to easily repeat a particular format without going through the steps of setting it up each time that format is used.

There are two very good reasons for using styles. First, they save the time and effort that is involved in recreating a particular format and text. Second, they ensure consistency across documents. Say for example that you need to write a letter (like the one shown in Figure 18.1) and then someone else needs to write a similar letter. With a style there is no concern that the appearance of the two letters will not be identical.

This consistency is very important in business settings as well as in your own personal word processing activities. Just think; letters, reports, banners, special forms, invitations, and more can all be done by different people and all look the same (once a style is course agreed upon).

Creating a Style

Let's go through the steps for creating the style for the stationery that you see in Figure 18.1.

```
                    Delphi Associates
                        POB 1465
                   Lawrence, KS 66045

October 1, 1988

Dr. M.A. Rice
1426 Indiana Street
Eudora, CO 12345

Dear Dr. Rice:

Thank you for the invitation tocome and speak to your group about my
recent work in Chaos theory. As it stands now, I am busy for the entire
weekend of your conference and will not be able to attend.

Please accept my apology and my best wishes for continued success.

Sincerely,
```

Figure 18.1 Creating stationery using a style

To begin the style definition process, select the *Alt->F8* key combination and you will see the Styles screen. Here is where the styles that you create will be listed and the various options you can select from to work with styles, are listed across the bottom of the screen.

The first step in the creation of a style is selecting *Create - Option #3* which reveals the screen you see in Figure 18.2.

```
Styles: Edit

    1 - Name
    2 - Type            Paired
    3 - Description
    4 - Codes
    5 - Enter           HRt
```

Figure 18.2 The styles edit screen

Naming a Style

It's time to assign a name to the style that you will be creating. In this case, let's name it heading/bus for a business letter heading. Enter that (or any other name you might want to chose) and press the *F7* key.

Different Types of Styles

WordPerfect allows for two different types of styles; paired or open.

A *paired* style is one that defines a specified amount of text. Paired styles have both opening and closing style codes and the only text that is affected by the style is that which appears between the codes. Once the last paired style code is detected, WordPerfect returns to the original or default text and formatting that was in effect before the first style code was encountered. The best way to remember paired styles is that they have a beginning and an end and should only be used to affect part of a document.

An *open* style is one that has a beginning, but not end! It is turned on and then its design, affects the rest of the document.

Which One When

When to use a paired or open style is not difficult to determine. If you want to use a style that will have an effect on only part of a document, then a paired style is your choice. In other words, you want to work with a style that you can turn on and then turn off.

Since you can block a section of text and then "style" it by selecting the style (and it will automatically turn on and off at the beginning and end of the block) paired styles can be very attractive and easy to use.

If you want to work with one style throughout an entire document, then you want to use an open style, which is turned on once and remains on for the rest of the document.

In the example in Figure 18.1, a paired style is used since it is only affecting the first part of the document.

Describing Styles

After you determine and indicate the type of style you want to use, it is then time to describe it. As with a macro, this description can help you remember what a particular style does.

In our example, the description is

sets business letter heading

and as you can see in Figure 18.3, the Styles screen now contains a style name, its type, and a description.

```
Styles: Edit

    1 - Name           heading/bus
    2 - Type           Paired
    3 - Description    selects business letter heading
    4 - Codes
    5 - Enter          HRt
```

Figure 18.3 Naming and describing a style

Editing a Style

The next step in the creation of a style is to enter the actual codes and text that will be part of the style. When you select *Codes - Option #4* on the *Styles: Edit* screen you'll see in the screen shown in Figure 18.4 which already has all the codes and text inserted.

The stationery heading as it will actually appear is shown in the upper half of the screen and the reveal codes for each entry are shown in the bottom half. You'll notice that you do not see the actual horizontal line that is shown in Figure 18.1 on in the upper half of the screen, but the reveal code is there in the bottom half.

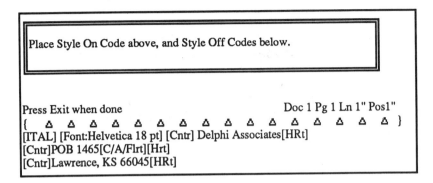

Figure 18.4 The codes edit screen

When you are finished, press the *F7* exit key and this style has been completely defined, except for...

The Enter Key

The Enter (or return key) can take on a particularly helpful role in creating and using styles. This is the last decision you need to make in defining a style and it is *Enter - Option #5* on the *Styles: Edit* screen you see in Figure 18.2.

The Enter key can preform three different functions.

First, it acts just like a hard return. This option is used most often when a style contains several lines which need to be separated by hard returns such as the heading/bus style that is the example in this chapter.

The second option, *Off* is when the Enter key is used to automatically turn the current style off. The one thing this does for you is save the time and effort it takes to go into the Styles menu and manually turn the style off once it is turned on.

Finally, the third option *Off/On*, allows you to turn the style off and then turn it on again, all with the one keystroke.

Tip Want to create a style without really trying? You can block any section of codes and text and then use the Alt->F8,3 key combination to automatically create a paired (which is the default) style. A great way to fool around with different set ups until you like what you see and then create a style. This may be the easiest way of creating a style.

Using a Style

OK, so you've created a style and now it's time to use it.

To use the *heading/bus* style that was just created, you would follow these steps:

1. Place the cursor where you want the style to begin.
2. Use the *Alt->F8* key combination to select the style menu and move the cursor to highlight the style you want to use.
3. Select *Option #1 - On*.

That's all there is to it. The style is in force and your heading is finished. When a style is inserted, you will see the following reveal codes:

> *[Style On: heading/bus][Style Off: heading/bus]*

Other Style Options

You already know how to create and edit and turn styles on an off. Now it's time to turn to some of the other options that you see along the menu in Figure 18.2.

Deleting a Style - Option #5

Deleting a style is as simple as highlighting it and then selection Option #5. WordPerfect will ask you if you are sure that you want this style deleted and thereby confirm your decision. Respond *Y* if you want to and *N* if you do not,

Saving a Style - Option #6

When you create a style it is particular to the document for which it is created. In other words, you could not switch to another file and then use the heading/bus style since it is associated with the file for which it was created.

When you select option #6, WordPerfect asks you to provide a file name within which the style will be saved and WordPerfect will do so

Stylish WordPerfect

for each of the styles that you create. By doing this, WordPerfect is placing the styles into their own file (which is the one that you chose). In this way, you can store all the files that are associated with any one document into one file. While each of the styles that you created are directly linked with the document that was active when they were created, the file of stored styles is not associated with a particular file.

Retrieving Styles - Option # 7

If you do want to retrieve a particular set of styles for use within another document, then select option #7 and indicate the name of the file within which thee styles are stored.

For example, you want to write another letter and want to use some of the styles that you created while writing letter #1 but now need them for writing letter #2. In this case, you would retrieve the file named *letter.sty* and all of the styles that were available for completing the first letter are available for this as well.

Updating - Option #8

The *Updating* option is a shortcut for retrieving the style library.

Sharing Styles - A Style Library

All of this saving and retrieving sounds fine and dandy, but its gets to be a tedious task when you have to recall a file containing a number of styles to use just one.

Once again, the WordPerfect people were really thinking! You can easily store all of the styles that you create in one style library which can be accessed at any time.

To do this, you need to use the *Shift->F1,7,6* key combination which asks you to identify the name of a file where a library of styles is created. Any style that is saved within this library file will automatically be active whenever a new document is started, but this will only be so if you have not yet defined any styles for your particular document and if you press the *Alt->F8* key combination.

How should you use the library? Since it takes some memory to make stored styles active, it may be best only to place styles into the default library that are very general and likely to be used with most of your documents, such as general formatting commands, and so forth.

Rather, why not build a set of files filled with styles that can be associated with certain *types of projects*. For example, how about a *letter.sty* that contains various letter headings, salutations, greetings, and so forth. Or, a set of styles (in one file) used for technical reports that have sub and superscript functions, quotes margins, and even line drawings for the insertion of text.

The WordPerfect Expert 5.0 is finished but you're not. With your mastery of the information contained in this book, you're well on your way to using and enjoying the best designed and most useful word processing package available today. Best wishes and good luck!

Appendix A
Setting Up WordPerfect

WordPerfect is already set for certain defaults. These are the various settings (such as line spacing, page length, justification, and more) that the designers of WordPerfect felt were general enough that everyone could use as a starting point.

On page 191 of the reference section of your manual, you can find the list of what WordPerfect settings are initially in effect. Be sure that you understand what cach of them means before you begin making changes. The best advice, is to use WordPerfect and become familiar with its features, before you begin working with the various default settings.

Using the Setup Option

After a while, you may want to customize WordPerfect to fit your needs. Say for example you work as a freelance writer and you have an editor who wants special margins, triple spacing and no right justification. If this is the how you want WordPerfect to be set up when it first appears, these changes are simple to make.

Tip If you have several different types of formats that you use, set WordPerfect for the most common one, but use a macro (which you learned about in Chapter 6) to set up the others. You can then set up a page format or whatever very quickly.

Changing WordPerfect defaults makes use of the *Shift->F1* key combination, Setup.

Upon doing this, the first screen you will see is shown in Figure A-1 which shows you the eight different areas in which you can change default settings.

```
Setup

1 - Backup
2 - Cursor Speed            Normal
3 - Display
4 - Fast Save (unformatted) No
5 - Initial Settings
6 - Keyboard Layout
7 - Location of Auxiliary Files
8 - Units of Measure
```

Figure A-1. The WordPerfect setup screen

Remember that any changes you make in the setup menu are permanent until you return to the setup menu to change these settings. You can press the F1 function key to return to the DOS level at any time and cancel out any changes that you made.

Backing Up WordPerfect Files

Everyone has their own horror stories to tell about how they lost their text and their hard hours of work. There's the time the squirrel got into the transformer on the telephone pole and the next thing that appeared on the screen was nothing! Or the time that you stretched your legs and knocked out the plug of the computer? Zap! - nothing again. Sounds to silly to be true? Ask any computer user, and you'll hear at least one similar story.

What to do about these unfortunate, but unavoidable mishappenings? Backup your files using WordPerfect's backup option shown in Figure A-2. Here, you can see that you have two choices.

Appendix A - *Setting Up WordPerfect* 243

```
Setup: Backup

Timed backup files are deleted when you exit WordPerfect normally. If you have a
power or machine failure, you will find the backup file in the backup directory
indicated in Setup: Location of Auxiliary Files.

   Backup Directory

   1 - Timed Document Backup        No
       Minutes Between Backups      30


   Original backup will save the original document with a .BK!
extension whenever you replace it during a Save or Exit.

   2 - Original Document Backup     Yes
```

Figure A-2 Backing up WordPerfect files

The first is to have WordPerfect back up your original file every certain number of minutes. For example, if you enter the number 5, WordPerfect will backup you file every five minutes without any further direction from you. The backup option does not create a backup of a file that is saved when WordPerfect is exited.

The second option is to have WordPerfect make a backup of the last saved version of any document. When WordPerfect does this, it assigns extension BK! to the document, so that a file named Joan.ltr, has a backup named Joan.BK!. If you chose both options, you have double insurance. At no time is the expression, "Better safe than sorry" more appropriate!

The Cursor Speed

Cursor speed is the rate at which a key that is held down repeats itself. It is not the rate at which the cursor moves on your monitor screen.

In Figure A-1, you can see how the speed is set 30 characters per second and the alternatives This means that if you hold down any key for one second, it should repeat itself 30 times.

To increase or decrease the speed, enter a number corresponding to the pre-set alternatives that appear when the "2" is selected from the Setup menu. Normal is a repeat of 10 characters per second.

The WordPerfect Display

This option on the Setup menu allows you to customize the way that information is displayed on the monitor screen. You can see in Figure A-3 that you have a variety of choices.

```
Setup: Display

    1 - Automatically Format and Rewrite    Yes

    2 - Colors/Fonts/Attributes

    3 - Display Document Comments           Yes

    4 - Filename on the Status Line         Yes

    5 - Graphics Screen Type                IBM EGA 640x350 16 color

    6 - Hard Return Display Character

    7 - Menu Letter Display                 BOLD

    8 - Side-by-side Columns Display        Yes
```

Figure A-3 WordPerfect display screen

Automatic format means that WordPerfect will automatically reformat and rewrite the entire document as you edit, not just as you scroll through the document.

The second option on the Display menu allows you to decide how you want colors, fonts) such as italics), and attributes (such as bold or underline) displayed on the screen. If you have a monochrome monitor, your choices are limited, but you should still make those selections since you can take advantage of different levels of gray.

Display document comments does just what it says, displays the content of any document comment that has been inserted into the document.

Option #4 determines whether you want to display the name of the file that is current on the status line. If you chose not to, the lower left hand corner of the screen remains blank. For most people, it is a good idea to chose "Yes" for this option since it allows you to keep track of hat the current document and avoid costly mistakes such as accidental erasures.

WordPerfect automatically recognizes the type of screen you have and indicate such on the Display menu. If it does not, you may have to copy the appropriate file drive from the Fonts/Graphics disk that came with your original WordPerfect materials.

When you are typing, WordPerfect automatically inserts a [HRt] code for a hard return. If you want to change that, use setup option #6.

Next, WordPerfect allows you to take advantage of its mnemonic design, where the first letter of many of the words found in menus represents the action that WordPerfect will take. For example, P for Printer on the print menu, or A for Appearance on the Font menu. You can tell WordPerfect to show these first characters in any of the appearance, size, or fonts that are available to you. The default is bold.

Finally, indicating "Yes" for the last option on the Display menu, tells WordPerfect to show columns as they would appear on the printed page.

Fast Saves

If you are interested in saving some of the time that it takes to save a document, then you should select "y" for this setup option. Fast Save, saves a document without formatting it. While this saves you some time, you should know that a document cannot be printed unless it is formatted. If you want to print a fast saved document, you will have to use the Home, Home Down cursor arrow key combination before you save it. It can then be printed.

Changing Initial Settings

This might be the setup menu, shown in Figure A-4, where you invest the most time and energy customizing WordPerfect for your own use.

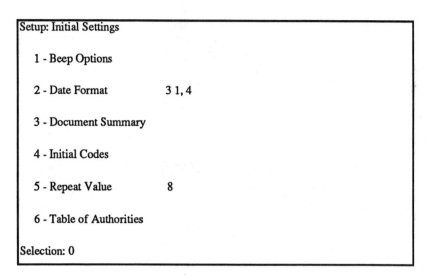

Figure A-4 The initial settings screen

WordPerfect Beeps!

As you work with WordPerfect there will be several occasions where you might make an error or you want to be notified about a particular circumstance that might affect your document. In these cases, you can set WordPerfect to beep you. These auditory cues can be very helpful, especially if you touch type and don't look up at your screen as you are entering text.

First, you can have WordPerfect beep when you try to perform a WordPerfect operation that results in an error message on the status line, such as ERROR: File not found - AAA.

Second, you can have WordPerfect beep whenever the hyphenation option is turned on and when WordPerfect needs you to position the hyphen by pressing the Esc key.

Finally, WordPerfect can be instructed to beep when a search is unsuccessful, so as when you might be trying to find and replace a particular word or phrase but no such text exists (or you have found the last one and WordPerfect continues to search).

Appendix A - Setting Up WordPerfect   247

Setting the Date and Time

Many of the documents that you prepare will have a date associated with them. Certainly letters, reports, and other timely materials will have a date and or a time associated with them, and many will have that information printed n the document itself.

As you can see n Figure A-5, WordPerfect is preset to show the date display the date (using the *Shift->F5* key combination) as Month, Day of Month, and Year, as in May 10, 1988. These settings correspond to the code 3 1,4. You can use the nine single digits and the % sign to configure a date or time as you desire. Military or 24 hour time would be expressed as 7:90, which would show the time as 15:22, which is 3:22 PM on a 12 hour clock.

```
Date Format

    Character  Meaning
        1      Day of the Month
        2      Month (number)
        3      Month (word)
        4      Year (all four digits)
        5      Year (last two digits)
        6      Day of the Week (word)
        7      Hour (24-hour clock)
        8      Hour (12-hour clock)
        9      Minute
        0      am / pm
        %      Used before a number, will:
               Pad numbers less than 10 with a leading zero
               Output only 3 letters for the month or day of the week

    Examples:  3 1, 4     = December 25, 1984
               %6 %3 1, 4 = Tue Dec 25, 1984
               %2/%1/5 (6) = 01/01/85 (Tuesday)
               8:90       = 10:55am
```

Figure A-5 Changing the Date and Time Format

Summarizing a Document

WordPerfect will ask you to make two decisions about the document summaries you may prepare, The first, is whether you want WordPerfect to prompt you to create a summary each time you save or exit a document (and if so, then indicate y, on the document summary setup). Even though this may be a helpful reminder, it may also become tiresome to be reminded each time you save, which presumably is often.

The second decision concerns what is called a Subject Search Text option which automatically enters the text that follows characters that you specify. WordPerfect is set to enter the words that follow the text RE:, which is a abbreviation for the word Regarding, which often precedes the topic of a memo or a report.

Setting Initial Codes

Here's the big one. When option #4 on the Initial Settings menu is selected, you get a split screen. Any of the changes that you make in setting up WordPerfect, will appear in the lower half of the screen using WordPerfect reveal codes. Now is the time to set WordPerfect for changes that correspond to the different combinations of function keys.

For example, you want to change the default margin setting from 10 (from the right hand margin) and 10 (from the left had margin), to 20 and 20. To dot his, follow these steps;

Press the *Shift->F8,1* key combination which will produce the screen shown in Figure A-6. Here you can see the options for formatting a line, page, or document. For this example (resetting a margin) select 1, which produces the line format setup menu shown in Figure A-7. Then it's simply a matter of further selecting option #7 (Margins) on the line format menu and changing the 10 and 10 to 20 and 20. Once this is done, and your press the F7 (Exit) key, you will see a reveal code (such as [L/R Mar:20,20] for the new margin settings entered in lower half of the split screen.

Appendix A - Setting Up WordPerfect

```
Format

    1 - Line
        Hyphenation              Line Spacing
        Justification            Margins Left/Right
        Line Height              Tab Set
        Line Numbering           Widow/Orphan Protection

    2 - Page
        Center Page (top to bottom)   New Page Number
        Force Odd/Even Page           Page Number Position
        Headers and Footers           Paper Size/Type
        Margins Top/Bottom            Suppress

    3 - Document
        Display Pitch            Redline Method
        Initial Codes            Summary

    4 - Other
        Advance                  Overstrike
        Conditional End of Page  Printer Functions
        Decimal Characters       Underline Spaces/Tabs
        Language
```

Figure A-6 The format screen

```
Format: Line

    1 - Hyphenation                     Off

    2 - Hyphenation Zone - Left         10%
                         Right          4%

    3 - Justification                   Yes

    4 - Line Height                     Auto

    5 - Line Numbering                  No

    6 - Line Spacing                    1

    7 - Margins - Left                  10
                  Right                 10

    8 - Tab Set                         0, every 5

    9 - Widow/Orphan Protection         No
```

Figure A-7 The line format screen

You can of course change other things on the line format menu and then continue with changes in the document or the page until you reset whatever you want. Remember, that once you have made all the adjustments and you press the F7 or Exit key, these become permanent settings and will be in effect each time you begin a new WordPerfect session. The only way to change them is by once again entering the setup menus using the *Shift->F1* key combination.

Changing the Repeat Value

Remember when you learned how the use of the Esc key provides a quick and easy way to repeat any WordPerfect operation, such as the printing of asterisks or a macro? If you want the default to me different from 8, enter the new value within Option #5 of the initial settings.

Formatting Tables of Authorities

Some very big words for things like tables of contents and indexes! However, it is this option that allows you to indicate whether you want dot leaders (shown below):

Chapter 1 - Planning The Big Event 43

whether you want to keep underline codes in the text of the table, and whether you want a space between the different authorities that make up the table.

Defining the Keyboard

WordPerfect provides you with a set of 10 single action pre-defined function keys. For example, if you want to underline text, you use the F7 function key. The Keyboard Layout option on the Setup menu allows to redefine the operation that any one key performs.

Using this tool, you can change the function that a key may perform. In fact, WordPerfect provides you with several alternative keyboard layouts, all of which can be further modified, and you can still return to the original whenever you want.

Locating other Files

WordPerfect is smart, but it's not so smart that it knows where you have stored the other important files that it needs to do its work. These auxiliary files need a specific location. In order for WordPerfect to work, you must tell WordPerfect the compete path where files such as the main dictionary, macro files, the thesaurus file, the style file, and others are located. Unless indicated otherwise in this part of the setup menu, it will assume that these files are located in the same directory (or sub directory) where the primary WordPerfect program files can be found.

Perhaps the best practice to create a subdirectory for each type of auxiliary file, within a general WordPerfect directory. That way the files are kept physically together and may be more manageable.

Units of Measure

Finally, this new version of WordPerfect offers a variety of ways to express distance on the screen and on your printed document. As you can see in Figure A-8, you can set up WordPerfect to operate in inches, centimeters, points, and as did WordPerfect 4.2, lines and columns.

```
Setup: Units of Measure

  1 - Display and Entry of Numbers      u
      for Margins, Tabs, etc.

  2 - Status Line Display               u

Legend:

  " = inches
  i = inches
  c = centimeters
  p = points
  u = WordPerfect 4.2 Units (Lines/Columns)
```

Figure A-8 Changing the units of measurement

Why all the alternatives? Depending upon the task at hand, you may need to use different units of measurement. For example, in the publishing world, points (where one inch equals 72 points), rather than inches and centimeters are the unit of choice. A one-half inc letter would be 36 points. Similarly, a one inch margin on the sides would be expressed as 72 points. Some people find that inches works best since that is with which they are most familiar.

When you set the units of measurement. you need to decide for both the display and entry of numbers for margins and the status line display, which type of unit will be used.

That's it for the setting up WordPerfect. As mentioned earlier in this appendix, it's best to leave things as they are when you first begin using WordPerfect until you find out the types of changes that you want to make. Keep in mind that none of these changes are irreversible. It just means that you need to reenter the Setup menus and make whatever changes you might chose.

Appendix B
WordPerfect Reveal Codes

The following is a list of the WordPerfect codes that may appear on the Reveal Codes screen.

[]	Hard Space
[-]	Hyphen
-	Soft Hyphen
/	Cancel Hyphenation
[Adv]	Advance
[Align]	Tab Align
[Block]	Beginning of Block
[Block Pro]	Block Protection
[Bold]	Bold
[Box Num]	Caption in Graphics Box
[C/A/FLRT]	End of Tab Align or Flush Right
[Center Pg]	Center Page Top to Bottom
[Cntr]	Center
[Cndl EOP]	Conditional End of Page
[Col Def]	Column Definition
[Col Off]	End of Text Columns
[Col On]	Beginning of Text Columns
[Comment]	Document Comment
[Color]	Print Color
[Date]	Date/Time Function
[Dbl Und]	Double Underline
[Decml Char]	Decimal Character/Thousands Separator
[Def Mark:Index]	Index Definition
[Def Mark:List]	List Definition
[Def Mark:ToC]	Table of Contents Definition
[End Def]	End of Index, List, or Table of Contents
[End Opt]	Endnote Options
[Endnote]	Endnote

[Endnote Placement]	Endnote Placement
[Ext Large]	Extra Large Print
[Figure]	Figure Box
[Fig Opt]	Figure Box Options
[Fine]	Fine Print
[Flsh Rt]	Flush Right
[Footnote]	Footnote
[Font]	Base Font
[Footer]	Footer
[Force]	Force Odd/Even Page
[Form]	Form (Printer Selection)
[FtnOpt]	Footnote/Endnote Options
[Full Form]	Table of Authorities, Full Form
[HLine]	Horizontal Line
[Header]	Header
[HPg]	Hard Page
[HRt]	Hard Return
[Hyph]	Hyphenation
[HZone]	Hyphenation Zone
[»Indent]	Indent
[»Indent»]	Left\Right Indent
[Index]	Index Entry
[ISRt]	Invisible Soft Return
[Italc]	Italics
[Just]	Right Justification
[Just Lim]	Word/Letter Spacing Justification Limits
[Kern]	Kerning
[L/R Mar]	Left and Right Margins
[Lang]	Language
[Large]	Large Print
[Line Height]	Line Height
[Ln Num]	Line Numbering
[»Mar Rel]	Left Margin Release
[Mark:List]	List Entry
[Mark:ToC]	Table of Contents Entry
[Math Def]	Definition of Math Columns
[Math Off]	End of Math
[Math On]	Beginning of Math
!	Formula Calculation
t	Subtotal Entry
+	Calculate Subtotal

Appendix B - WordPerfect Reveal Codes 257

T	Total Entry
=	Calculate Total
*	Calculate Grand Total
[Note Num]	Footnote/Endnote Reference
[Outln]	Outline (attribute)
[Ovrstk]	Overstrike
[Paper Sz/Typ]	Paper Size and Type
[Par Num]	Paragraph Number
[Par Num Def]	Paragraph Numbering Definition
[Pg Num]	New Page Number
[Pg Num Pos]	Page Number Position
[Ptr Cmnd]	Printer Command
[Redln]	Redline
[Ref]	Reference (Automatic Reference)
[Set End Num]	Set New Endnote Number
[Set Fig Num]	Set New Figure Box Number
[Set Ftn Num]	Set New Footnote Number
[Set Tab Num]	Set New Table Box Number
[Set Txt Num]	Set New Text Box Number
[Set Usr Num]	Set New User-Defined Box Number
[Shadw]	Shadow
[Sm Cap]	Small Capt
[Small]	Small Print
[SPg]	Soft New Page]
[StkOut]	Strikeout
[Style]	Styles
[Subdoc]	Subdocument (Master Documents)
[SubScrpt]	Subscript
[SuprScrpt]	Superscript
[Suppress]	Suppress Page Format
[T/B Mar]	Tob and Bottom Margins
[Tab]	Tab
[Tab Opt]	Table Box Options
[Tab Set]	Tab Set
[Table]	Table Box
[Target]	Target (Auto Reference]
[Text Box]	Text Box
[Txt Opt]	Text Box Options
[Und]	Underlining
[Undrln]	Underline Spaces/Tabs
[Usr Box]	User-Defined Box
[UsrOpt]	User-Defined Box Options

[VLine]   Vertical Line
[Vry Large]   Very Large Print
[W/O]   Widow/Orphan
[Wrd/Ltr Spacing] Word and Letter Spacing

Appendix C
A Macro Library

Editing Macros

ALT->B (MOVE CURSOR TO END OF DOCUMENT)

WHAT ALT->B DOES

Alt->B moves the cursor to the bottom (or the end) of a document.

HOW ALT->B WORKS

Step 1 begins the macro definition.
Step 2 names the macro Alt->B
Step 3 describes the macro.
Step 4 moves the cursor to the bottom of the document.
Step 5 ends the macro definition.

CREATING ALT->B

Step 1) Ctrl->F10
Step 2) Alt->b
Step 3) move cursor to end of document,<ret>
Step 4) Home,Home,Down cursor arrow<ret>
Step 5) Ctrl->F10

ALT->B AT WORK

Alt->B moves the cursor to the bottom of the document.

SPECIAL INSTRUCTIONS AND TIPS!!!

Alt->B should be used for quickly moving to the end of a document. Remember, it will always place the cursor after the last character in the document and not at the end of the screen or the page (unless, of course, the document is that length).

ALT->Q (CHANGE A STRING OF CHARACTERS THROUGHOUT A DOCUMENT)

WHAT ALTQ DOES

Alt->Q pauses for user input to identify the string of characters to be changed and the new string that will replace them.

HOW ALTQ WORKS

Step 1 begins the macro definition.
Step 2 names the macro ALTQ.
Step 3 describes the macro.
Step 4 moves the cursor to the top of the document.
Step 5 begins the search operation without confirmation.
Step 6 pauses for user input for the string to be replaced.
Step 7 defines the string.
Step 8 enters the replacement string.
Step 9 ends the macro definition.

CREATING ALTQ

Step 1) Ctrl->F10
Step 2) Alt->q
Step 3) search and replace a string,<ret>
Step 4) Home,Home,Up cursor arrow
Step 5) Alt->F2,N,<ret>
Step 6) Ctrl->PgUp,1
Step 7) [enter string to search for]
Step 8) F2,[enter replacement string],F2
Step 9) Ctrl->F10

ALTQ AT WORK

ALTQ can search through a document and replace a string automatically. If you want to confirm the change, then change the "N" in Step 5 to "Y" (for confirmation).

Before ALTQ   1111111111
After ALTQ   1 1 1 1 1 1 1 1 1

SPECIAL INSTRUCTIONS AND TIPS!!!

Be careful when you use any kind of global search and replace. Identify the string of characters that you want to change *exactly* before you actually change it. For example, if you want to change the spelling of the word *the* to *the,* don't replace the letter *e* with *h*, since every *e* in the entire document will be changed! Instead, change the string *the*. Also, before you do any kind of global search and replace, save your document so that you have a copy just in case of a disaaaaaaaster!

ALT->T (MOVE THE CURSOR TO THE TOP OF THE DOCUMENT)

WHAT ALT->T DOES

Alt->T moves the cursor to the top of the document.

HOW ALT->T WORKS

Step 1 begins the macro definition.
Step 2 names the macro Alt->T.
Step 3 describes the macro.
Step 4 moves the cursor to the top of the document.
Step 5 ends the macro definition.

CREATING ALT->T

Step 1) Ctrl->F10
Step 2) Alt->t
Step 3) moves cursor to top,<ret>
Step 4) Home,Home,Up cursor arrow
Step 5) Ctrl->F10

ALT->T AT WORK

Alt->T moves the cursor to the top of the document, not to the top of the page.

SPECIAL INSTRUCTIONS AND TIPS!!!

This macro is a good candidate for an Alt Key macro, especially if you need to move to the top of the document.

BLPARA (BLOCK PARAGRAPH)

WHAT BLPARA DOES

BLPARA blocks the paragraph that the cursor is currently on.

HOW BLPARA WORKS

Step 1 begins the macro definition.
Step 2 names the macro BLPARA.
Step 3 describes the macro.
Step 4 begins the search backward function for a tab.
Step 5 begins the block function.
Step 6 searches for a hard return.
Step 7 ends the macro definition.

CREATING BLPARA

Step 1) Ctrl->F10
Step 2) blpara,<ret>
Step 3) block a paragraph,<ret>
Step 4) Shift->F2,Tab,F2
Step 5) Alt->F4
Step 6) F2,<ret>,F2
Step 7) Ctrl->F10

BLPARA AT WORK

Here is paragraph number 1.

HERE IS PARAGRAPH NUMBER 2 IN BOLD.

SPECIAL INSTRUCTIONS AND TIPS!!!

This macro is based on the use of the Tab key (set at a default of 5 spaces) for indenting the first line of a paragraph. If you do not want to use a Tab as a paragraph indent (you might not indent at all), then modify the macro to search backward for the last hard carriage return [HRt], then block to the next one. This is like the macro BLSEN that blocks a sentence. As with that macro, you cannot block the first paragraph of a document (if you do not use the Tab key to indent).

Once you use this macro and the paragraph is blocked, you can perform any of the several types of WordPerfect operations such as save, append to another block (this macro is especially handy for this use), and others.

BLSEN (BLOCK A SENTENCE)

WHAT BLSEN DOES

BLSEN will create a block out of the sentence that the cursor is located on.

HOW BLSEN WORKS

Step 1 begins the macro definition.
Step 2 names the macro BLSEN.
Step 3 describes the macro.
Step 4 searches backwards for the end of the previous sentence.
Step 5 goes to the beginning of the sentence to be blocked.
Step 6 begins the block operation.
Step 7 goes to the end of the sentence to be blocked.
Step 8 ends the macro definition.

CREATING BLSEN

Step 1) Ctrl->F10
Step 2) blsen,<ret>
Step 3) block a sentence,<ret>
Step 4) Shift->F2,.,F2
Step 5) Ctrl->right cursor arrow
Step 6) Alt->F4
Step 7) F2,.,F2

Step 8) Ctrl->F10

BLSEN AT WORK

Once BLSEN is invoked, the sentence in which the cursor is located is blocked from the beginning of the sentence to the period.

SPECIAL INSTRUCTIONS AND TIPS!!!

Since BLSEN looks for the end of the previous sentence to find out where the sentence to be blocked begins, this macro works best when one sentence is being chosen from a group.
   Unlike some of the other macros in this book, BLSEN will block the entire sentence, and not just a selected line. However, be careful about other periods appearing in the sentence. BLSEN will see any period as the end of a sentence, including those in such words as *Dr., Mrs., and Ms., and so on.*

BLW (BLOCK A WORD)

WHAT BLW DOES

BLW will create a block out of the word that the cursor is located on.

HOW BLW WORKS

Step 1 begins the macro definition.
Step 2 names the macro BLW.
Step 3 describes the macro.
Step 4 moves the cursor to the beginning of the word.
Step 5 begins the block operation.
Step 6 moves the cursor to the end of the word.
Step 7 moves the cursor back one space.
Step 8 ends the macro definition.

CREATING BLW

Step 1) Ctrl->F10
Step 2) blw,<ret>
Step 3) block a word,<ret>
Step 4) Ctrl->Left cursor arrow
Step 5) Alt->F4
Step 6) Ctrl->Right cursor arrow
Step 7) Left cursor arrow
Step 8) Ctrl->F10

BLW AT WORK

Once BLW is invoked, the word you select is blocked and remains blocked, even after the macro is finished.

SPECIAL INSTRUCTIONS AND TIPS!!!

Since BLW looks for the end of the previous word to find out where the word to be blocked begins, this macro works best when you are choosing one word from a group.
  Unlike some of the other macros offered in this collection, BLW will block the entire word, not just a selected line.

BTXT (BLOCK TEXT)

WHAT BTXT DOES

BTXT blocks text of any length by pausing for input from the user to set the length of the text to be blocked.

HOW BTXT WORKS

Step 1 begins the macro definition.
Step 2 names the macro BTXT.
Step 3 describes the macro.

Step 4 begins the block operation.
Step 5 pauses for definition of the size of the block.
Step 6 ends the macro definition.

CREATING BTXT

Step 1) Ctrl->F10
Step 2) btxt,<ret>
Step 3) block user defined text,<ret>
Step 4) Alt->F4
Step 5) Ctrl->PgUp,1
Step 6) Ctrl->F10

BTXT AT WORK

This is an example of how **BTXT can be used. Here, part** of the first sentence and part of the second sentence is shown in bold. The bolded type was first blocked using BTXT.

SPECIAL INSTRUCTIONS AND TIPS!!!

To use BTXT, you must place the cursor where you want the block to begin before you invoke the macro. After the macro is invoked, you can use the cursor control keys to define and block as large an area as necessary. You'll notice that when you invoke this macro, the Block On message will appear in the lower left- hand corner of your WordPerfect screen.

You can also block large areas of text using the cursor keys that control screen and page length movements.

This macro is especially useful if you need to block "irregular" sections of text, such as from the middle of one sentence to the middle of another. Once you finish blocking text, you can then bold (F6) or underline (F8).

DIVPARA (DIVIDES PARAGRAPH INTO SENTENCES)

WHAT DIVPARA DOES

DIVPARA divides a paragraph into individual sentences that are then listed.

HOW DIVPARA WORKS

Step 1 begins the macro definition.
Step 2 names the macro DIVPARA.
Step 3 describes the macro.
Step 4 searches for the period at the end of the sentence.
Step 5 moves the cursor to the beginning of the next sentence.
Step 6 breaks the line.
Step 7 repeats the macro.
Step 8 ends the macro definition.

CREATING DIVPARA

Step 1) Ctrl->F10
Step 2) divpara,<ret>
Step 3) divide paragraph into sentences,<ret>
Step 4) F2,.,F2
Step 5) Ctrl->Right cursor arrow
Step 6) <ret>
Step 7) Alt->F10,divpara,<ret>
Step 8) Ctrl->F10

DIVPARA AT WORK

A set of sentences in a paragraph like this:

Sentence 1. Sentence 2. Sentence 3. Sentence 4.

becomes this, after DIVPARA is invoked:

Sentence 1.

Sentence 2.
Sentence 3.
Sentence 4.

SPECIAL INSTRUCTIONS AND TIPS!!!

There are two things to remember about using DIVPARA.
The first is that you need to place the cursor at the beginning of the paragraph that is to be divided into sentences. DIVPARA does not search for this first line, since a first paragraph would not have a [HRt] reveal code to use as a reference point.
  The second is that you need to be in the habit of placing an equal number of spaces between sentences. If you do not do this, the sentences will not appear aligned when separated and listed out from the paragraph.

Formatting Macros

ALT->B (MOVE CURSOR TO END OF DOCUMENT)

WHAT ALT->B DOES

Alt->B moves the cursor to the bottom (or the end) of a document.

HOW ALT->B WORKS

Step 1 begins the macro definition.
Step 2 names the macro Alt->B
Step 3 describes the macro.
Step 4 moves the cursor to the bottom of the document.
Step 5 ends the macro definition.

CREATING ALT->B

Step 1) Ctrl->F10
Step 2) Alt->b
Step 3) move cursor to end of document,<ret>
Step 4) Home,Home,Down cursor arrow<ret>
Step 5) Ctrl->F10

ALT->B AT WORK

Alt->B moves the cursor to the bottom of the document.

SPECIAL INSTRUCTIONS AND TIPS!!!

Alt->B should be used for quickly moving to the end of a document. Remember, it will always place the cursor after the last character in the document and not at the end of the screen or the page (unless, of course, the document is that length).

ALT->Q (CHANGE A STRING OF CHARACTERS THROUGHOUT A DOCUMENT)

WHAT ALTQ DOES

Alt->Q pauses for user input to identify the string of characters to be changed and the new string that will replace them.

HOW ALTQ WORKS

Step 1 begins the macro definition.
Step 2 names the macro ALTQ.
Step 3 describes the macro.
Step 4 moves the cursor to the top of the document.
Step 5 begins the search operation without confirmation.
Step 6 pauses for user input for the string to be replaced.
Step 7 defines the string.

Step 8 enters the replacement string.
Step 9 ends the macro definition.

CREATING ALTQ

Step 1) Ctrl->F10
Step 2) Alt->q
Step 3) search and replace a string,<ret>
Step 4) Home,Home,Up cursor arrow
Step 5) Alt->F2,N,<ret>
Step 6) Ctrl->PgUp,1
Step 7) [enter string to search for]
Step 8) F2,[enter replacement string],F2
Step 9) Ctrl->F10

ALTQ AT WORK

ALTQ can search through a document and replace a string automatically. If you want to confirm the change, then change the "N" in Step 5 to "Y" (for confirmation).

Before ALTQ   1111111111
After ALTQ   1 1 1 1 1 1 1 1 1

SPECIAL INSTRUCTIONS AND TIPS!!!

Be careful when you use any kind of global search and replace. Identify the string of characters that you want to change *exactly* before you actually change it. For example, if you want to change the spelling of the word *the* to *the,* don't replace the letter *e* with *h,* since every *e* in the entire document will be changed! Instead, change the string *the.* Also, before you do any kind of global search and replace, save your document so that you have a copy just in case of a disaaaaaaaster!

ALT->T (MOVE THE CURSOR TO THE TOP OF THE DOCUMENT)

WHAT ALT->T DOES

Alt->T moves the cursor to the top of the document.

HOW ALT->T WORKS

Step 1 begins the macro definition.
Step 2 names the macro Alt->T.
Step 3 describes the macro.
Step 4 moves the cursor to the top of the document.
Step 5 ends the macro definition.

CREATING ALT->T

Step 1) Ctrl->F10
Step 2) Alt->t
Step 3) moves cursor to top,<ret>
Step 4) Home,Home,Up cursor arrow
Step 5) Ctrl->F10

ALT->T AT WORK

Alt->T moves the cursor to the top of the document, not to the top of the page.

SPECIAL INSTRUCTIONS AND TIPS!!!

This macro is a good candidate for an Alt Key macro, especially if you need to move to the top of the document.

BLPARA (BLOCK PARAGRAPH)

WHAT BLPARA DOES

BLPARA blocks the paragraph that the cursor is currently on.

HOW BLPARA WORKS

Step 1 begins the macro definition.
Step 2 names the macro BLPARA.
Step 3 describes the macro.
Step 4 begins the search backward function for a tab.
Step 5 begins the block function.
Step 6 searches for a hard return.
Step 7 ends the macro definition.

CREATING BLPARA

Step 1) Ctrl->F10
Step 2) blpara,<ret>
Step 3) block a paragraph,<ret>
Step 4) Shift->F2,Tab,F2
Step 5) Alt->F4
Step 6) F2,<ret>,F2
Step 7) Ctrl->F10

BLPARA AT WORK

Here is paragraph number 1.

HERE IS PARAGRAPH NUMBER 2 IN BOLD.

SPECIAL INSTRUCTIONS AND TIPS!!!

This macro is based on the use of the Tab key (set at a default of 5 spaces) for indenting the first line of a paragraph. If you do not want to use a Tab as a paragraph indent (you might not indent at all), then modify the macro to search backward for the last hard carriage return [HRt], then block to the next one. This is like the macro BLSEN that blocks a sentence. As with that macro, you cannot block the first paragraph of a document (if you do not use the Tab key to indent).

Once you use this macro and the paragraph is blocked, you can perform any of the several types of WordPerfect operations such as save, append to another block (this macro is especially handy for this use), and others.

BLSEN (BLOCK A SENTENCE)

WHAT BLSEN DOES

BLSEN will create a block out of the sentence that the cursor is located on.

HOW BLSEN WORKS

Step 1 begins the macro definition.
Step 2 names the macro BLSEN.
Step 3 describes the macro.
Step 4 searches backwards for the end of the previous sentence.
Step 5 goes to the beginning of the sentence to be blocked.
Step 6 begins the block operation.
Step 7 goes to the end of the sentence to be blocked.
Step 8 ends the macro definition.

CREATING BLSEN

Step 1) Ctrl->F10
Step 2) blsen,<ret>
Step 3) block a sentence,<ret>
Step 4) Shift->F2,.,F2
Step 5) Ctrl->right cursor arrow
Step 6) Alt->F4
Step 7) F2,.,F2

Step 8) Ctrl->F10

BLSEN AT WORK

Once BLSEN is invoked, the sentence in which the cursor is located is blocked from the beginning of the sentence to the period.

SPECIAL INSTRUCTIONS AND TIPS!!!

Since BLSEN looks for the end of the previous sentence to find out where the sentence to be blocked begins, this macro works best when one sentence is being chosen from a group.
   Unlike some of the other macros in this book, BLSEN will block the entire sentence, and not just a selected line. However, be careful about other periods appearing in the sentence. BLSEN will see any period as the end of a sentence, including those in such words as *Dr., Mrs., and Ms., and so on.*

BLW (BLOCK A WORD)

WHAT BLW DOES

BLW will create a block out of the word that the cursor is located on.

HOW BLW WORKS

Step 1 begins the macro definition.
Step 2 names the macro BLW.
Step 3 describes the macro.
Step 4 moves the cursor to the beginning of the word.
Step 5 begins the block operation.
Step 6 moves the cursor to the end of the word.
Step 7 moves the cursor back one space.
Step 8 ends the macro definition.

CREATING BLW

Step 1) Ctrl->F10
Step 2) blw,<ret>
Step 3) block a word,<ret>
Step 4) Ctrl->Left cursor arrow
Step 5) Alt->F4
Step 6) Ctrl->Right cursor arrow
Step 7) Left cursor arrow
Step 8) Ctrl->F10

BLW AT WORK

Once BLW is invoked, the word you select is blocked and remains blocked, even after the macro is finished.

SPECIAL INSTRUCTIONS AND TIPS!!!

Since BLW looks for the end of the previous word to find out where the word to be blocked begins, this macro works best when you are choosing one word from a group.

Unlike some of the other macros offered in this collection, BLW will block the entire word, not just a selected line.

BTXT (BLOCK TEXT)

WHAT BTXT DOES

BTXT blocks text of any length by pausing for input from the user to set the length of the text to be blocked.

HOW BTXT WORKS

Step 1 begins the macro definition.
Step 2 names the macro BTXT.
Step 3 describes the macro.
Step 4 begins the block operation.
Step 5 pauses for definition of the size of the block.
Step 6 ends the macro definition.

CREATING BTXT

Step 1) Ctrl->F10
Step 2) btxt,<ret>
Step 3) block user defined text,<ret>
Step 4) Alt->F4
Step 5) Ctrl->PgUp,1
Step 6) Ctrl->F10

BTXT AT WORK

This is an example of how **BTXT can be used. Here, part** of the first sentence and part of the second sentence is shown in bold. The bolded type was first blocked using BTXT.

SPECIAL INSTRUCTIONS AND TIPS!!!

To use BTXT, you must place the cursor where you want the block to begin before you invoke the macro. After the macro is invoked, you can use the cursor control keys to define and block as large an area as necessary. You'll notice that when you invoke this macro, the Block On message will appear in the lower left- hand corner of your WordPerfect screen.

  You can also block large areas of text using the cursor keys that control screen and page length movements.

  This macro is especially useful if you need to block "irregular" sections of text, such as from the middle of one sentence to the middle of another. Once you finish blocking text, you can then bold (F6) or underline (F8).

DIVPARA (DIVIDES PARAGRAPH INTO SENTENCES)

WHAT DIVPARA DOES

DIVPARA divides a paragraph into individual sentences that are then listed.

HOW DIVPARA WORKS

Step 1 begins the macro definition.
Step 2 names the macro DIVPARA.
Step 3 describes the macro.
Step 4 searches for the period at the end of the sentence.
Step 5 moves the cursor to the beginning of the next sentence.
Step 6 breaks the line.
Step 7 repeats the macro.
Step 8 ends the macro definition.

CREATING DIVPARA

Step 1) Ctrl->F10
Step 2) divpara,<ret>
Step 3) divide paragraph into sentences,<ret>
Step 4) F2,.,F2
Step 5) Ctrl->Right cursor arrow
Step 6) <ret>
Step 7) Alt->F10,divpara,<ret>
Step 8) Ctrl->F10

DIVPARA AT WORK

A set of sentences in a paragraph like this:

Sentence 1. Sentence 2. Sentence 3. Sentence 4.

becomes this, after DIVPARA is invoked:

Sentence 1.

Sentence 2.
Sentence 3.
Sentence 4.

SPECIAL INSTRUCTIONS AND TIPS!!!

There are two things to remember about using DIVPARA.
The first is that you need to place the cursor at the beginning of the paragraph that is to be divided into sentences. DIVPARA does not search for this first line, since a first paragraph would not have a [HRt] reveal code to use as a reference point.

The second is that you need to be in the habit of placing an equal number of spaces between sentences. If you do not do this, the sentences will not appear aligned when separated and listed out from the paragraph.

RED (REDLINES TEXT)

WHAT RED DOES

RED redlines text to bring it to the attention of the reader.

HOW RED WORKS

Step 1 begins the macro definition.
Step 2 names the macro RED.
Step 3 describes the macro.
Step 4 begins the block operation.
Step 5 pauses for user input (definition of the block).
Step 6 selects the redline option from the mark text menu.
Step 7 ends the macro definition.

CREATING RED

Step 1) Ctrl->F10
Step 2) red,<ret>

Step 3) redlines user defined block,<ret>
Step 4) Alt->F4
Step 5) Ctrl->PgUp,1<ret>
Step 6) Ctrl->F8,2,8
Step 7) Ctrl->F10

RED AT WORK

  When text is redlined
| it has the marker you can
| see in the left-hand margin
| for these three lines.

The reveal code that WordPerfect inserts is:

              [RedLn]

SPECIAL INSTRUCTIONS AND TIPS!!!

Redlining is used to highlight a certain section of text to bring it to the attention of the reader.
   RED redlines text after it has been entered. To redline text before it is entered, use the Alt->F5,3 key combination.

REST (RESET TABS)

WHAT REST DOES

REST resets the tab settings to the default of a tab at every five spaces.

HOW REST WORKS

Step 1 begins the macro definition.
Step 2 names the macro REST.
Step 3 describes the macro.

Step 4 selects the tab option from the line format menu and sets tabs every five spaces beginning with space 5.
Step 5 end the macro definition.

CREATING REST

Step 1) Ctrl->F10
Step 2) rest,<ret>
Step 3) reset tabs,<ret>
Step 4) Shift->F8,1,8,5,5,F7
Step 5) Ctrl->F10

REST AT WORK

REST resets the tab stops at 5, 10, 15, etc.

SPECIAL INSTRUCTIONS AND TIPS!!!

Using the tab key is a convenient way to begin a paragraph as well as construct different "levels" of text, but be sure that you reset the tabs once you change the appearance of text that is indented or tabbed.

RJ (RIGHT JUSTIFICATION ON)

WHAT RJ DOES

RJ turns on right justification.

HOW RJ WORKS

Step 1 begins the macro definition.
Step 2 names the macro RJ.
Step 3 describes the macro.
Step 4 selects the turn justification on option from the print format

menu.
Step 5 ends the macro definition.

CREATING RJ

Step 1) Ctrl->F10
Step 2) rj,<ret>
Step 3) justification on,<ret>
Step 4) Shift->F8,1,3,y,F7
Step 5) Ctrl->F10

RJ AT WORK

RJ turns on right justification as in the following text which has margins set at 10 and 30:

This is an example of right
justification   turned   on
with the columns set at 10
and 30.

The reveal code for right justification on is:

[Just on]

SPECIAL INSTRUCTIONS AND TIPS!!!

When right justification is turned on, the text will be printed justified, but it will not show this way on the monitor. WordPerfect does not show right justification.
   If you do right justify text, there will be extra spaces between words so that the line can be stretched out to meet the right- hand margin. This can be controlled by special printing codes, but without these adjustments, the copy may look awkward.

formatting macros

UBL (UNDERLINE USER DEFINED BLOCK)

WHAT UBL DOES

UBL underlines a user defined block.

HOW UBL WORKS

Step 1 begins the macro definition.
Step 2 names the macro UBL.
Step 3 describes the macro.
Step 4 begins forming a block.
Step 5 pauses so the user can place the cursor at the end of the block.
Step 6 underlines the block.
Step 7 ends the macro definition.

CREATING UBL

Step 1) Ctrl->F10
Step 2) ubl,<ret>
Step 3) underlines block,<ret>
Step 4) Alt->F4
Step 5) Ctrl->PgUp,1<ret>
Step 6) F8
Step 7) Ctrl->F10

UBL AT WORK

Using this macro would cause only this block to be underlined.

SPECIAL INSTRUCTIONS AND TIPS!!!

This is the macro to use when you need to underline a single line such as a title or subheading in a book or a report. Remember, it will underline only the line on which the cursor is placed so you cannot use this to underline anything more than one line. You also have to press the <ret> key after the block as been defined so the underlining will occur.

ULN (UNDERLINE A LINE)

WHAT ULN DOES

ULN underlines the line that the cursor is located on.

HOW ULN WORKS

Step 1 begins the macro definition.
Step 2 names the macro ULN.
Step 3 describes the macro.
Step 4 moves the cursor to the beginning of the line.
Step 5 begins the block operation.
Step 6 moves the cursor to the end of the line.
Step 7 underlines the block.
Step 8 ends the macro definition.

CREATING ULN

Step 1) Ctrl->F10
Step 2) uln,<ret>
Step 3) underlines current line,<ret>
Step 4) Home,Left cursor arrow
Step 5) Alt-F4
Step 6) Home,Right cursor arrow
Step 7) F8
Step 8) Ctrl->F10

ULN AT WORK

You can use ULN to emphasize such things as headings, whether at the first level of an outline or as part of text. Here's an example of each of these:

> Chapter IV
>
> Richard Comes Home

SPECIAL INSTRUCTIONS AND TIPS!!!

As with any other format macro, don't overuse this one. Use it for appropriate emphasis, along with other highlighting tools such as bolding and centering.

UPHEAD (UPPERCASE THE CURRENT HEADING)

WHAT UPHEAD DOES

UPHEAD converts a line or heading from lower to uppercase.

HOW UPHEAD WORKS

Step 1 begins the macro definition.
Step 2 names the macro UPHEAD.
Step 3 describes the macro.
Step 4 moves the cursor to the beginning of the line.
Step 5 begins the block operation.
Step 6 moves the cursor to the end of the line.
Step 7 converts the text to uppercase.
Step 8 ends the macro definition.

CREATING UPHEAD

Step 1) Ctrl->F10
Step 2) uphead,<ret>
Step 3) uppercase line/heading,<ret>
Step 4) Home,left cursor arrow
Step 5) Alt->F4
Step 6) Home,Right cursor arrow
Step 7) Shift->F3,1
Step 8) Ctrl->F10

UPHEAD AT WORK

Here is a heading that was originally entered as lowercase and then converted:

THE EARLY YEARS

SPECIAL INSTRUCTIONS AND TIPS!!!

Use UPHEAD for the titles of sections and the beginnings of other documents. Remember that titles in uppercase communicate special emphasis, so the macro should be used sparingly.

Special Macros for Printing

ADVD (ADVANCE PRINTING DOWN)

WHAT ADVD DOES

ADVD advances the printing of the line down a set amount of space.

HOW ADVD WORKS

Step 1 begins the macro definition.
Step 2 names the macro ADVD.
Step 3 describes the macro.
Step 4 selects the advance printing down.
Step 5 pauses for user definition of distance.
Step 6 ends the macro definition.

CREATING ADVD

Step 1) Ctrl->F10
Step 2) advd,<ret>
Step 3) advances printing down,<ret>
Step 4) Shift->F8,4,1,2
Step 5) Ctrl->PgUp,1,<ret>
Step 6) Ctrl->F10

ADVD AT WORK

ADVD allows you to combine different features of printing on the same line.

SPECIAL INSTRUCTIONS AND TIPS!!!

It may be easier to use this macro if you reset the units of measurements to inches so you can measure how far down the page you need to move. Since accuracy is important, don't print out final copies until you have worked through several drafts.

ADVU (ADVANCE PRINTING UP)

WHAT ADVU DOES

ADVU advances the printing of the line up a set amount of space.

HOW ADVU WORKS

Step 1 begins the macro definition.
Step 2 names the macro ADVU.
Step 3 describes the macro.
Step 4 selects the advance printing up.
Step 5 pauses for user definition of distance.
Step 6 ends the macro definition.

CREATING ADVU

Step 1) Ctrl->F10
Step 2) advu,<ret>
Step 3) advances printing up,<ret>
Step 4) Shift->F8,4,1,1
Step 5) Ctrl->PgUp,1,<ret>
Step 6) Ctrl->F10

ADVU AT WORK

ADVU allows you to combine different features of printing on the same lines.

SPECIAL INSTRUCTIONS AND TIPS!!!

It may be easier to use this macro if you reset the units of measurements to inches so you can measure how far up the page you need to move. Since accuracy is important, don't print out final copies until you have worked through several drafts.

ALT->F (SELECT USER DEFINED FONT)

WHAT ALT->F DOES

Alt->F allows the user to select a new font.

HOW ALT->F WORKS

Step 1 begins the macro definition.
Step 2 names the macro Alt->F.
Step 3 describes the macro.
Step 4 selects the base font from the font menu.
Step 5 allows user to define new font.
Step 6 ends the macro definition.

CREATING ALT->F

Step 1) Ctrl->F10
Step 2) Alt->f
Step 3) select new font,<ret>
Step 4) Ctrl->F8,4
Step 5) Ctrl->PgUp,1,<ret>
Step 6) Ctrl->F10

ALT->F AT WORK

Alt->F allows you to change from Times Roman to Helvetica in a touch of a button.

SPECIAL INSTRUCTIONS AND TIPS!!!

Be sure that when you use Alt->F, you remember to return to the base font (unless you want the change to be permanent).

ATT (SELECT USER DEFINED ATTRIBUTE)

WHAT ATT DOES

ATT allows the user to select an attribute and change it.

HOW ATT WORKS

Step 1 begins the macro definition.
Step 2 names the macro ATT.
Step 3 describes the macro.
Step 4 selects the font menu.
Step 5 pauses for the selection of either size or appearance options form the font menu.
Step 6 ends the macro definition.

CREATING ATT

Step 1) Ctrl->F10
Step 2) att,<ret>
Step 3) selects user defined attributes,<ret>
Step 4) Ctrl->F8
Step 5) Ctrl->PgUp,1,<ret>
Step 6) Ctrl->F10

ATT AT WORK

Using ATT you can change this to this (size) to this (attribute).

CHPS (CHANGES POINT SIZE OF THE CURRENT BASE FONT)

WHAT CHPS DOES

CHPS changes the point size of an already selected base font.

HOW CHPS WORKS

Step 1 begins the macro definition.
Step 2 names the macro CHPS.
Step 3 describes the macro.
Step 4 selects the base font option from the font menu.
Step 5 allows for user input for new pitch.

Step 6 ends the macro definition.

CREATING CHPS

Step 1) Ctrl->F10
Step 2) chps,<ret>
Step 3) changes base font point size,<ret>
Step 4) Ctrl->F8,4,1
Step 5) Ctrl->PgUp,1<ret>
Step 6) Ctrl->F10

CHPS AT WORK

After CHPS, text that looked like this looks like this.

SPECIAL INSTRUCTIONS AND TIPS!!!

If your printer does not support the option to change point size, this macro will not work.

CP (CANCEL ALL PRINT JOBS)

WHAT CP DOES

CP selects the cancel print option from the printer control menu and cancels all current print jobs.

HOW CP WORKS

Step 1 begins the macro definition.
Step 2 names the macro CP.
Step 3 describes the macro.
Step 4 reveals the printing menu and cancels all print jobs.
Step 5 ends the macro definition.

CREATING CP

Step 1) Ctrl->F10
Step 2) cp,<ret>
Step 3) cancels all print jobs,<ret>
Step 4) Shift->F7,4,1,*,y
Step 5) Ctrl->F10

SPECIAL INSTRUCTIONS AND TIPS!!!

CP will cancel all the print jobs that are currently waiting to be printed. When you invoke this macro, all printing activity will stop and any jobs that were waiting to be printed will no longer be in the queue.

DP (SELECTS DRAFT QUALITY PRINTING)

WHAT DP DOES

Selects the draft mode for printing.

HOW DP WORKS

Step 1 begins the macro definition.
Step 2 names the macro DP.
Step 3 describes the macro.
Step 4 selects the draft mode from the printer control menu.
Step 5 ends the macro definition.

CREATING DP

Step 1) Ctrl->F10
Step 2) dp,<ret>
Step 3) selects draft mode for printing,<ret>
Step 4) Shift->F7,t,d
Step 5) Ctrl->F10

DP AT WORK

DP will change from whatever other text mode to draft.

SPECIAL INSTRUCTIONS AND TIPS!!!

Most dot matrix printers will have the capability to print text in draft, medium or high quality. Laser printers do not, so this macro would not be useful if you are printing with a laser printer.

HP (SELECTS HIGH QUALITY PRINTING)

WHAT HP DOES

Selects the high quality mode for printing

HOW HP WORKS

Step 1 begins the macro definition.
Step 2 names the macro HP.
Step 3 describes the macro.
Step 4 selects the high quality from the printer control menu.
Step 5 ends the macro definition.

CREATING HP

Step 1) Ctrl->F10
Step 2) hp,<ret>
Step 3) selects high quality for printing,<ret>
Step 4) Shift->F7,t,h
Step 5) Ctrl->F10

HP AT WORK

HP will change from whatever other text mode to high.

SPECIAL INSTRUCTIONS AND TIPS!!!

Most dot matrix printers will have the capability to print text in draft, medium or high quality. Laser printers do not, so this macro would not be useful if you are printing with a laser printer.

KOFF (TURN KERNING OFF)

WHAT KOFF DOES

Turns off the kern function.

HOW KOFF WORKS

Step 1 begins the macro definition.
Step 2 names the macro KOFF.
Step 3 describes the macro.
Step 4 selects the kerning option and turns it off.
Step 5 ends the macro definition.

CREATING KOFF

Step 1) Ctrl->F10
Step 2) koff,<ret>
Step 3) turns off kerning,<ret>
Step 4) Shift->F8,4,6,1,n
Step 5) Ctrl->F10

KOFF AT WORK

Here is some text that is not kerned. Here is some text that is.

SPECIAL INSTRUCTIONS AND TIPS!!!

Kerning adjusts the spacing between letters so that there are not awkward white spaces when some letters take up more room than others.

KON (TURN KERNING ON)

WHAT KON DOES

Turns on the kern function.

HOW KOFF WORKS

Step 1 begins the macro definition.
Step 2 names the macro KON.
Step 3 describes the macro.
Step 4 selects the kerning option and turns it on.
Step 5 ends the macro definition.

CREATING KON

Step 1) Ctrl->F10
Step 2) kon,<ret>
Step 3) turns on kerning
Step 4) Shift->F8,4,6,1,y
Step 5) Ctrl->F10

SPECIAL INSTRUCTIONS AND TIPS!!!

Kerning adjust the spacing between letter so that there are not awkward white spaces when some letters take up more room than others.

PC (PRINTER CHOICE)

WHAT PC DOES

PC pauses for user input of printer selection.

HOW PC WORKS

Step 1 begins the macro definition.
Step 2 names the macro PC.
Step 3 describes the macro.
Step 4 selects the select printer option.
Step 5 pauses for user selection of printer.
Step 6 ends the macro definition.

CREATING PC

Step 1) Ctrl->F10
Step 2) pc,<ret>
Step 3) printer choice,<ret>
Step 4) Shift->F7,s
Step 5) Ctrl->PgUp,1<ret>
Step 6) Ctrl->F10

PC AT WORK

PC changes to the user specified printer.

SPECIAL INSTRUCTIONS AND TIPS!!!

Once PC is invoked, you need to choose select once you have highlighted the printer you want to select.

PGO (PRINTER GO)

WHAT PGO DOES

PGO sends the printer a go statement to resume printing.

HOW PGO WORKS

Step 1 begins the macro definition.
Step 2 names the macro PGO.
Step 3 describes the macro.
Step 4 selects the printer control option from the printer menu and the "go" option.
Step 5 ends the macro definition.

CREATING PGO

Step 1) Ctrl->F10
Step 2) pgo,<ret>
Step 3) resumes printing,<ret>
Step 4) Shift-F7,4,g
Step 5) Ctrl->F10

PGO AT WORK

PGO will resume the WordPerfect printing function.

SPECIAL INSTRUCTIONS AND TIPS!!!

PGO should be used when you have cancelled or stopped a printing job and then want to resume using the printer or continuing the job that was interrupted. When a printer does not respond to the print command, it is often the case that the go command is needed to resume the printing function.

PMC (PRINT MULTIPLE COPIES)

WHAT PMC DOES

PMC pauses for user input and prints multiple copies of a document.

HOW PMC WORKS

Step 1 begins the macro definition.
Step 2 names the macro PMC.
Step 3 describes the macro.
Step 4 selects the number of copies option from the printer control print menu.
Step 5 pauses for user specification of printer number.
Step 6 ends the macro definition.

CREATING PMC

Step 1) Ctrl->F10
Step 2) pmc,<ret>
Step 3) prints user defined number of copies,<ret>
Step 4) Shift->F7,n
Step 5) Ctrl->PgUp,1<ret>
Step 6) Ctrl->F10

PMC AT WORK

PMC makes a temporary change in the number of copies that are to be printed. If you want more than one copy printed, you will have to use PMC each time, or just repeat the Shift-F7 key combination.

SPECIAL INSTRUCTIONS AND TIPS!!!

When PMC finishes, the printer menu remains on the bottom of the screen so you can make any additional choices necessary. Press the F7 key when you want to escape from that menu.

RUSH (RUSH PRINT JOB)

WHAT RUSH DOES

RUSH places a #1 priority on any job that is waiting to be printed.

HOW RUSH WORKS

Step 1 begins the macro definition.
Step 2 names the macro RUSH.
Step 3 describes the macro.
Step 4 selects the rush option from the printer control menu.
Step 5 pauses for the user to indicate the job number that is to be rushed.
Step 6 ends the macro definition.

CREATING RUSH

Step 1) Ctrl->F10
Step 2) rush,<ret>
Step 3) rushes a selected job,<ret>
Step 4) Shift->F7,4,r
Step 5) Ctrl->PgUp,1<ret>
Step 6) Ctrl->F10

RUSH AT WORK

RUSH will move up what ever print job is in the print queue, which represents the list of jobs that is waiting to be printed.

SPECIAL INSTRUCTIONS AND TIPS!!!

When you want to use RUSH, invoke the macro. You will then be asked to indicate which job you want to rush by entering the number of that job from those listed on the screen. After you indicate which job to rush, you will then be asked if you want to interrupt the job that is currently being printed. If you answer yes, the rushed job will be printed immediately. RUSH assumes that the answer is yes. If you answer no, WordPerfect will first finish the current job and then go on to the rushed one.

SP (STOP PRINTING)

WHAT SP DOES

SP selects the stop printing option from the printer control menu and halts the print job that is currently running. It then asks you to indicate when you want to resume printing.

HOW SP WORKS

Step 1 begins the macro definition.
Step 2 names the macro SP.
Step 3 describes the macro.
Step 4 selects the Stop command from the printer control menu.
Step 5 ends the macro definition.

CREATING SP

Step 1) Ctrl->F10
Step 2) sp,<ret>
Step 3) stops printing,<ret>
Step 4) Shift->F7,4,5
Step 5) Ctrl->F10

SPECIAL INSTRUCTIONS AND TIPS!!!

SP will stop the printing of a file and should only be used when you intend to resume printing the same file. To resume printing after the printer has stopped, enter a G from the keyboard, for "go."
  If you want to cancel the printing job (and all others) use CP.

TRACK (ADJUST SPACING BETWEEN LETTERS AND WORDS)

WHAT TRACK DOES

TRACK adjusts the spacing between letters and words.

HOW TRACK WORKS

Step 1 begins the macro definition.
Step 2 names the macro TRACK.
Step 3 describes the macro.
Step 4 selects the word width option.
Step 5 pauses for user selection of word width.
Step 6 ends the macro definition.

CREATING TRACK

Step 1) Ctrl->F10
Step 2) track,<ret>
Step 3) user definition of word and letter spacing ,<ret>
Step 4) Shift->F8,4,6,3
Step 5) Ctrl->PgUp,1,<ret>
Step 6) Ctrl->F10

TRACK AT WORK

TRACK at work can help turn this set of letters and words into this set of letters and words.

Graphics

DWCR (DRAW A CENTERED RECTANGLE)

WHAT DWCR DOES

DWCR draws a small rectangle centered on the page both vertically and horizontally.

HOW DWCR WORKS

Step 1 begins the macro definition.
Step 2 names the macro DWCR.
Step 3 describes the macro.
Step 4 centers the rectangle vertically on the page (not on the screen!).
Step 5 selects the double line option from the screen menu.
Step 6 draws a down line 3 spaces on the screen.
Step 7 draws a right line 30 spaces on the screen.
Step 8 draws an up line 3 spaces on the screen.
Step 9 draws a left line 30 spaces on the screen.
Step 10 exits.
Step 11 moves to the top of the screen.
Step 12 begins the block function.
Step 13 blocks the screen.
Step 14 centers the screen.
Step 15 ends the macro definition.

CREATING DWCR

Step 1) Ctrl->F10
Step 2) dwcr,<ret>
Step 3 draws a rectangle.
Step 4) Shift->F8,2,1
Step 5) Ctrl->F3,2,2
Step 6) Esc,3,Down cursor arrow
Step 7) Esc,30,Right cursor arrow
Step 8) Esc,3,Up cursor arrow
Step 9) Esc,30,Left cursor arrow
Step 10) F7
Step 11) Home,Home,Up cursor arrow
Step 12) Alt->F4
Step 13) Home,Home,Down cursor arrow

Step 14) Shift->F6,y
Step 15) Ctrl->F10

SPECIAL INSTRUCTION AND TIPS!!!

DWCR makes an impressive header for a title page or for any other short line that you want to emphasize.

Place the text inside of the rectangle after it has been completed. Since WordPerfect treats the lines as text, use the insert mode to enter the text so you won't change the alignment of the rectangle's sides.

DWL (DRAW A HORIZONTAL LINE)

WHAT DWL DOES

DWL draws a centered horizontal line 50 spaces across top of page.

HOW DWL WORKS

Step 1 begins the macro definition.
Step 2 names the macro DWL.
Step 3 describes the macro.
Step 4 centers the line.
Step 5 selects the line draw option from the screen menu.
Step 6 sets repeat at 50.
Step 7 draws the line.
Step 8 ends the macro definition.

CREATING DWL

Step 1) Ctrl->F10
Step 2) dwl,<ret>
Step 3) centers horizontal line,<ret>
Step 4) Shift->F6
Step 5) Ctrl->F3,2,1
Step 6) Esc,50

Step 7) Right cursor arrow
Step 8) Ctrl->F10

DWL AT WORK

Here's a line drawn using DWL.

Title Here!

───────────────────────────────

SPECIAL INSTRUCTIONS AND TIPS!!!

DWL should be used to draw centered horizontal lines separating sections in reports and for other formatting purposes. If you do not want the line centered, modify the macro by removing Step 3 and if you want to change the length of the line (now at 50 character spaces) adjust step 6.

DWLS (DRAW LARGE SQUARE)

WHAT DWLS DOES

DWLS draws a large square beginning in the upper left hand corner of the screen.

WordPerfect Macro Expert 5.0   305

HOW DWLS WORKS

Step 1 begins the macro definition.
Step 2 names the macro DWLS.
Step 3 describes the macro.
Step 4 moves the cursor to the top of the screen.
Step 5 selects the line draw option from the screen menu and line shape.
Step 6 draws a down line 13 spaces on the screen.
Step 7 draws a right line 28 spaces on the screen.
Step 8 draws an up line 13 spaces on the screen.
Step 9 draws a right line 28 spaces on the screen.
Step 10 ends the macro definition.

CREATING DWLS

Step 1) Ctrl->F10
Step 2) dwls,<ret>
Step 3) draws a large square,<ret>
Step 4) Home,Home,Up cursor arrow
Step 5) Ctrl->F3,2,1
Step 6) Esc,13,Down cursor arrow
Step 7) Esc,28,Right cursor arrow
Step 8) Esc,13,Up cursor arrow
Step 9) Esc,28,Left cursor arrow
Step 10) Ctrl->F10

DWLS AT WORK

DWLS will draw a square as shown (on a reduced scale) below:

SPECIAL INSTRUCTION AND TIPS!!!

You can use DWLS with any kind of text. You can either place text inside of the screen border after it is completed, or have WordPerfect draw the screen border after text has been entered.

DWSCB (DRAW A SCREEN BORDER)

WHAT DWSCB DOES

DWSCB draws a border in a pattern around the screen.

HOW DWSCB WORKS

Step 1 begins the macro definition.
Step 2 names the macro DWSCB.
Step 3 describes the macro.
Step 4 moves the cursor to the top of the screen.
Step 5 selects the line draw option from the screen menu.
Step 6 draws a down line 22 spaces on the screen.
Step 7 draws a right line 60 spaces on the screen.
Step 8 draws an up line 22 spaces on the screen.
Step 9 draws a right line 60 spaces on the screen.
Step 10 ends the macro definition.

CREATING DWSCB

Step 1) Ctrl->F10
Step 2) dwscb,<ret>
Step 3) draws a screen border,<ret>
Step 4) Home,Home,Up cursor arrow
Step 5) Ctrl->F3,2,2
Step 6) Esc,22,Down cursor arrow
Step 7) Esc,60,Right cursor arrow
Step 8) Esc,22,Up cursor arrow
Step 9) Esc,60,Left cursor arrow
Step 10) Ctrl->F10

WordPerfect Macro Expert 5.0   307

DWSCB AT WORK

DWSCB will draw a screen border.

SPECIAL INSTRUCTION AND TIPS!!!

You can use DWSCB with any kind of text. You can either place text inside of the screen border after it is competed, or have WordPerfect draw the screen border after text has been entered. The only thing you need to remember is that the border itself takes up a certain number of lines, so you can't place text in the extreme margin settings.

LINES (CREATES LINES)

WHAT LINES DOES

LINES produces horizonal lines with the use of the Esc key.

HOW LINES WORKS

Step 1 begins the macro definition.
Step 2 names the macro LINES.
Step 3 describes the macro.
Step 4 begins the underline operation.
Step 5 repeats 60 times.
Step 6 spaces (60 spaces).
Step 7 ends the underline operation and moves to the next line.
Step 8 ends the macro definition.

CREATING LINES

Step 1) Ctrl->F10
Step 2) lines,<ret>
Step 3) creates a 60 space line,<ret>
Step 4) F8
Step 5) Esc,60
Step 6) space bar
Step 7) F8,<ret>
Step 8) Ctrl->F10

LINES AT WORK

Here's LINES creating two horizontal lines of 60 spaces each:

SPECIAL INSTRUCTIONS AND TIPS!!!

LINES will produce one line 60 spaces long. Remember, you will not see the actual lines on your screen unless your system supports that level of graphics. Instead, if you press the Alt->F3 key combination, you will see the underline reveal codes.

This is a good macro to use in creating forms. Create a form by first using LINES and then entering the standard information that you want on the form such as name, address, etc. The form for recording macros at the end of this book was created using this macro, slightly modified by having two returns, so the lines are double-spaced.

Moving Text

ALT->A (APPEND BLOCK)

WHAT ALT->A DOES

This macro will append (or attach) a block of text to another file that has already been created and saved. This macro will pause and ask you to indicate the file to which you want to append the current text.

HOW ALT->A WORKS

Step 1 begins the macro definition.
Step 2 names the macro.
Step 3 describes the macro.
Step 4 selects the WordPerfect append option.
Step 5 places a pause in the macro for the name of the file to which the blocked text will be appended.
Step 6 ends the macro definition.

CREATING ALT->A

Step 1) Ctrl->F10
Step 2) Alt->A,<ret>
Step 3) appends text,<ret>
Step 4) Ctrl->F4,1,4
Step 5) Ctrl->PgDn,1,<ret>
Step 6) Ctrl->F10

ALT->A AT WORK

This is a simple example of using Alt->A to combine two lists.

File 1 consists of an alphabetized list of names.

Sara
Michael
Lewis
Rachael

File 2 is a new list of names:

John
Doug
Ronda

which is added to File 1 by blocking the list that makes up File 2 and then using Alt->A. SORTL is then used to sort the names and produce the final list:

Doug
John
Lewis
Michael
Rachael
Ronda
Sara

SPECIAL INSTRUCTIONS AND TIPS!!!

This macro is very useful for adding text to already existing text, such as concatenating or linking several files together.

  For example, you might be working on a book and want to place all of the chapters into one "super" file before you generate a table of contents or an index. Alt->A can help you do this by asking you the name of the file you want to add to. It could also be used to place a new reference into the appropriate file (which you would probably want to sort later on).

  Remember that before invoking the macro, you must have already created the file to which the text will be added. Also remember that, whenever you add anything to another file, the addition will go at the end of the file, which may be at the end of the last word in the file or at the beginning of a new page, depending on how you have ended the file to which the text is being appended. For this reason, it's a good idea to end all files with a blank line. That way, when you look at the file with the information added, you can easily see where one ends and the next begins.

MPARA (MOVES PARAGRAPH)

WHAT MPARA DOES

MPARA moves a paragraph to where the cursor is placed.

HOW MPARA WORKS

Step 1 begins the macro definition.
Step 2 names the macro MPARA.
Step 3 describes the macro.
Step 4 selects the cut paragraph option from the move menu.
Step 5 pauses for placement of cursor.
Step 6 retrieves paragraph.
Step 7 ends the macro definition.

CREATING MPARA

Step 1) Ctrl->F10
Step 2) mpara,<ret>
Step 3) moves paragraph,<ret>
Step 4) Ctrl->F4,2,1
Step 5) Ctrl->PgUp,1<ret>
Step 6) <ret>
Step 7) Ctrl->F10

MPARA AT WORK

MPARA changes the ordering of paragraphs as is shown in the following example:

Before MPARA	*After MPARA*
This is paragraph 1.	*This is paragraph 2.*
This is paragraph 2.	*This is paragraph 1.*

SPECIAL INSTRUCTIONS AND TIPS!!!

To use MPARA, place the cursor on the paragraph you want to move, invoke the macro, then move the cursor to where you want the paragraph and press the return key.

When you use MPARA (or any other macro that works with paragraphs), remember that WordPerfect defines a paragraph through the use of a hard carriage return, and not an indent or spacing at the beginning of a paragraph.

MPG (MOVES PAGE)

WHAT MPG DOES

MPG moves a page to the cursor location.

HOW MPG WORKS

Step 1 begins the macro definition.
Step 2 names the macro MPG.
Step 3 describes the macro.
Step 4 selects the cut page option from the move menu.
Step 5 pauses for placement of cursor.
Step 6 retrieves the page.
Step 7 ends the macro definition.

CREATING MPG

Step 1) Ctrl->F10
Step 2) mpg,<ret>
Step 3) moves page to user defined location,<ret>
Step 4) Ctrl->PgUp,1<ret>
Step 5) Ctrl->F4,3,1
Step 6) <ret>
Step 7) Ctrl->F10

MW (MOVE WORD)

WHAT MW DOES

MW moves a word to the location of the cursor.

HOW MW WORKS

Step 1 begins the macro definition.
Step 2 names the macro MW.
Step 3 describes the macro.
Step 4 moves the cursor to the beginning of the word.
Step 5 begins the block operation.
Step 6 blocks the word.
Step 7 selects the cut option from the move menu.
Step 8 pauses for the user to move the cursor to where the word is to be inserted.
Step 9 moves the word.
Step 10 ends the macro definition.

CREATING MW

Step 1) Ctrl->F10
Step 2) mw,<ret>
Step 3) moves word to cursor,<ret>
Step 4) Ctrl->Left cursor arrow
Step 5) Alt->F4
Step 6) Ctrl->Right cursor arrow
Step 7) Ctrl->F4,1,1
Step 8) Ctrl->PgUp,1<ret>
Step 9) <ret>
Step 10) Ctrl->F10

MW AT WORK

MW will move one word from a sentence, list, etc. to a user- selected location. Below, the word "tacks" (which *was* first) is placed last in the following list.

Supplies needed (in order of importance):

nails
wood
joint compound
tacks

SPECIAL INSTRUCTIONS AND TIPS!!!

To use MW, place the cursor anywhere on the word that you want to move (except for the first letter). Then invoke MW, move the cursor to the location where you want the word, and press the return key.

INDEX

align character 38
aligning tabs 39
alt key macros 74
appearance submenu 35
assigning new pages numbers 45
assigning page numbers 45

backing up files, timed 12
base fonts, 207
Bitstream Fontware 214
block on message 28
blocks and sorting 163
blocks, using 28
boilerplates 78
boldfacing text 36
bolding 34
bottom margins, setting 45

calculation formulas 171
canceling a print job 56
center tabs 39, 40
centering page vertically 42
chaining macros 79
changing fonts 50
changing initial settings 48
changing the overflow drive 13
changing the pitch 48
character commands 3
character type through 57
characters, converting 41
choosing paper size 46
clearing tabs 38
clearing the WordPerfect screen 21
column, definition, editing 113
    defining 111
    editing 112
    footnotes 115
    parallel 109
    producing 113
    turning on 114

combining macros 79
combining startup options 14
compose 214
concordance file 128
converting 4.2 macros 70
converting characters 41
copying macros 75, 81
creating a document summary 49
creating a table of contents 118
creating indexes 117
creating lists 117, 124
creating parallel columns 114
creating tables 117
Cruise Control 230
custom colors 213
cutting text 28

DataPerfect 227
date, inserting in merge 98
decimal tabs 39, 40
default settings, return to 14
defining, columns 111
    fields in a merge 95
    macros 20
    newspaper columns 111
    parallel columns 112
    screen size 14
    tables, lists and indexes 118
    of keyboards 218
deleting, characters 24
    paragraphs 24
    reveal codes
    text 24
    words 24
describing a macro 72
diacriticals 217
different tab styles 39
digraphs 214
disk, printing from 54
Doc indicator 15

preview 57
printing 54
summary 49
summary, creating 49
double documentitis 23
double underlining 35
dummy records 99

edit options, move 200
    rotating a graphic 202
    scaling a graphic 201
    inverting an image 202
editing a graphic 198, 199
editing, column definitions 113
    columns 114
    text 23
editor, macro 85
ending a WordPerfect session, macro 22
ending a macro 73
entering a macro 72]
entering text 17
envelopes, printing using merge 106
erasing a WordPerfect disk 11
exiting WordPerfect 22

facing pages, viewing 57
file directory 59
file, finding 66
file management option, ascii files 63
    changing a directory 63
    conditions 65
    copying a file 63
    deleting a file 61
    looking at files 63
    moving and renaming a file 62
    searching for words 64
    printing a file 62
    retrieving a file 61
    wild card searches 66

file management screen 60
file, retrieving on startup 12
finding a file 66
flash, getting rid of 13
font attributes 206
font, changing 50
font options, appearance 211
    base font 207
    changing base fonts 207
    normal 212
    printing in color 212
    size 209
fonts and columns 116
fonts, selecting 205
footer, editing 44
footers 43
footers, page numbers 44
footnotes and columns 115
format document menu 48
format options 33
format page submenu 42
formatting, disks 11
    suppressing 47
    WordPerfect documents 47
    WordPerfect lines 34
formulas, calculation 171
full name macros 75
function keys 5
function keys, key combinations 5

generating tables, lists and indexes 118
Glyphix 229
Goto command 16
Graph In The Box 228
graphic image, editing 199
graphic, rotating 202
graphics, basics 183
graphics box, caption 187
    creating 186
    edit 190

Index

filename 186
horizontal position 188
size 189
type 187
vertical position 188
wrap text 190
graphics, different boxes 184
editing 198
how they work 184
lines 195
graphics options, border style 190
gray shading 194
inside border space 191
numbering methods 192
numbering style 192
offset from paragraph 194
outside border space 192
position of the caption 193
graphics, quality of print 58
graphics, wrapping text around 203

header, editing 44
headers 43
headers, page numbers 44
help, on line 31
toll free support 9
using 9
WordPerfect 31
Hercules InColor Card 232
horizontal lines 195

indenting lines 37
index, creating 127
defining
generating 129
marking text 127
initial settings 48
input files for sorting 156
insert mode, 18
inserting comments in macros 84

inverting an image 202
invoking a macro 75

justifying lines 41

kerning 221
keyboard definition 218
instructions 3
layout 219
keys, sorting 158
keystrokes, using for editing 23

landscape printing 222
laser printers 213
layout, keyboard 219
left tabs 39
line type through 56
lines, formatting 34
indenting 37
justifying 41
list, creating 124
defining
marking text 123
Ln indicator, 15

Mace Utilities 231
macro,
boldface words 36
commands, 82
defining 20
editor 85
enter ^R and ^E codes
moving a paragraph 27
naming 20
of newspaper columns 110
programming language 88
save and exit WordPerfect 22
set spacing 40
starting WordPerfect 13
table of contents level 120
underlines words 35

macros, alt key 74
    chaining 79
    clearing the WordPerfect screen 22
    combining 79
    converting from 4.2 70
    copying 81
    describing 72
    description 6
    ending 73
    entering 72
    full name 74
    inserting comments 84
    introduction 19
    invoking 75
    naming 72
    pause option 83
    placement 75
    renaming 81
    repeating 79
    starting and defining 71
    stopping 76
    temporary 77
    user input 83
    using 69
    when to use 70
managing files 60
managing WordPerfect files 59
margins, resetting 37
margins, setting 37
marking text 117
master document, condensing 180
    creating 176
    definition 176
    editing 178
    expanding 178
    generating tables
    printing 181
math 165
math basics 165
math columns, defining 167

math columns, types 167
math, calculating values 170
    formulas 171
    operators 169
    setting columns 166
    turning on 169
merge codes 97
merge, .sf files 95
    .pf files 95
    and report creation 105
    defining fields 95
    dummy records 99
    inserting date 98
    keyboard entries 97
    macros 99
    messages 100
    primary file 93
    printing documents ^T
    prompts 100
    prompts 100
    secondary file 92
    seeing ^U
merging primary and secondary files 96
moving a graphic 200
moving characters 23
    lines 23
    pages 23
    pages 27
    paragraphs 27
    sentences 27
multiple files, working with 67
multiple lists, working with 126
multiple tabs, setting 38

name search option 66
naming a macro 20, 72
new page numbers 45
new section, outline 147
new text, saving 18
newspaper columns, defining 111

Index

numbering figures and lists 153

old text, saving 21
open styles 235
opening screen, 15
outline, choosing new styles 151
    deleting sections 146
    demoting topics/sections 149
    editing 146
    inserting a new section 147
    moving section 148
    promoting topics/sections 148
    styles 150
    using more than one 150
outlines, simple 144
outlining, use and importance 143
output files for sorting 156
overflow drive 13

page, center vertically 42
page numbers 45
page numbers and footers 44
page orientation 222
pages, formatting 42
pages, moving 27
paired styles 235
paper size, choosing 46
paper size choices 46
paragraphs, inserting new ones 152
    moving 27
    numbering 151
    numbering styles 152
parallel columns 109
    creating 114
    defining 112
password, using 19
Perfect Exchange 231
Pg indicator, 15
pitch, changing 48
placement of macros 75
PlanPerfect 226

portrait printing 222
Pos indicator, 15
previewing a document 57
primary and secondary files, retrieving 101
primary file 93
print menu 51
print menu 52
printer, control 55
printer, selecting 51
PRINTER.TST 55
printing a document 54
printing, canceling a job 56
printing from a disk 54
printing in color 212
programming language, macros 88
prompts and merging 100
Publisher's PicturePak 228

quality of text print 58
quality of graphics print 58

renaming macros 81
Repeat Performance 227
repeating macros 79, 81
replacing text through search 25
replacing with confirmation 26
requirements for using WordPerfect, computer 6
    disk drives 7
    monitor 8
    printer 7
resetting margins 37
resetting tabs 38
retrieving a file on startup 11
retrieving text 18
reveal codes, deleting 30
    searching and replacing 30
    screen 29
right tabs 39, 40
rush job 55

rushing a print job 55

saving "old" text 21
saving a file, password 19
saving new text 18
saving text 18
scaling a graphic 201
screen size, 14
searching and replacing reveal codes 30
searching and replacing text 25
searching backwards 25
       forwards 25
       using wildcards 26
secondary file 92
seeing additional printers 52
selecting a printer 51
selecting font attributes 206
selecting fonts 205
selecting records 161
sentences, moving 27
setting bottom margin 45
setting margins 37
setting multiple tabs 38
setting top margin 45
Sidekick 230
soft fonts, loading 214
Softcraft Fontware 229
sort screen 157
sorting 155
sorting and block 164
sorting, basic 155
sorting, input file 156
sorting options, action 162
       file 156
       keys 158
       order 162
       perform action 158
       select 161
       type 163
       view 158

special characters, printing 216
special forms, merge 103
special merge codes 97
spell check, wild cards 136
spell checker 131
spell, document check 132
spell options 133
spelling option, add word 134
       edit 134
       ignore numbers 135
       look up 134
       skip 134
       skip once 133
       word count 135
spelling, wild cards 136
starting and defining a macro 71
starting WordPerfect, options 12
startup options, combining 14
stopping a macro 76
style, creating 234
style, naming 235
style options, deleting 238
       retrieving 239
       saving 238
       updating 239
       styles 233
styles, describing 236
       editing 236
subdocuments, creating 177
subdocuments, working with 177
subscripts 41
superscripts 41
suppressing formatting 47

table of contents, creating 118
       defining 120, 122
       generating 123
       marking text 119
       planning 118
tabs, aligning 39
       center 39

Index

clearing 38
decimal 39
different styles 39
left 39
resetting 38
right 39
working with 38
temporary macros, using 77
temporary macros 77
text, cutting 28
quality of print 58
retrieving 20
searching forwards 25
searching backwards 25.
undeleting 25
thesaurus 138
thesaurus option, clear column 141
replace word 140
up word 141
view document 140
thesaurus screen 139
times backup of files 12
tips, description 6
top margins, setting 45
tracking 221
Turbofonts 229
type through, line 57
type through, character 57
typeover mode 18

undeleting text 25
underlining 34
underlining, double 35
using blocks 35

variables, assigning values 84
vertical lines 196
vertical lines, vertical position 197
viewing records 158

wild card searches within files 66

wildcard searches 26
word search menu 64
Word Finder 231
WordPerfect library 225
WordPerfect/d, overflow drive 13
WordPerfect (startup) 12
WordPerfect/b, setting timed backup 12
WordPerfect Support Group 9
WordPerfect/x, returning to default settings 14
WordPerfect/nf, no flash option 13
WordPerfect/r, loading WordPerfect into memory 14
WordPerfect, starting 11
WordPerfect/m, starting a macro 13
WordPerfectionist 9
working with multiple files 67
wrap around 17
wrapping text 203